# Discovering Life Skills

## First Edition

*Contributing Writer*
**Annette Gentry Bailey**

**McGraw Hill Glencoe**

New York, New York    Columbus, Ohio    Chicago, Illinois    Peoria, Illinois    Woodland Hills, California

# Teacher Reviewers

Glencoe

The McGraw·Hill Companies

Send all inquiries to:
Glencoe/McGraw-Hill
3008 W. Willow Knolls Drive
Peoria, IL 61614-1083

ISBN 0-07-829847-4

Printed in the United States of America

5 6 7 8 9 071 07 06 05

# Contents in Brief

# Contents

# Unit 2: Charting Your Future ................................122

# A CLOSER LOOK

# How To...

# Explore

# Making Connections

## SAFETY FIRST

## Just For Fun

# Internet ACTIVITIES

# CHECK the Facts

# DID YOU know?

# UNIT 1

# Focusing On You

# Chapter 1

# Discovering Yourself

## You Will Discover . . .

- a positive self-concept.
- how to accept constructive criticism.
- helpful ways to deal with your emotions.
- your value system.
- physical changes that occur during adolescence.

Nicole and Amanda are identical twins. Most people think the girls are exactly alike, but, not even identical twins are exactly alike. Nicole likes to listen to rock music, while Amanda would rather read a mystery. During your teen years you will undergo many physical changes. Your emotions will come into focus and you will begin to discover yourself.

## Key Words

- heredity
- culture
- self-concept
- self-esteem
- constructive criticism
- initiative
- values
- self-actualization
- prioritize
- adolescence

## ➤ Heredity & Environment

No two people act, think, or feel the same way. Everyone comes from a different background and has different experiences. Everything you do, everywhere you go, and everyone you know—especially your family members and friends—have influenced who you are.

Some of the characteristics that make you an individual are a result of heredity. **Heredity** (huh-red-ih-TEE) is the passing on of traits from parents to their children. Some of these traits are physical—your eye color, your facial features, and your body build. Heredity also plays a part in determining your intelligence.

You have other qualities that make you a unique individual. These traits are a result of your environment. Some of your interests and abilities are acquired, or learned from the people and things in your environment. Perhaps your sister taught you how to skate. Maybe a friend sparked your interest in technology. See Fig. 1-1.

**Fig. 1-1 Many of these factors influence who you are.**

Heredity

Family

Environment

Experiences

Roles

Culture

# Making Connections

**Science.** You have probably heard people say things like "Mike has his grandfather's nose," or "Juanita looks just like her mother." These are inherited traits.

### Get Involved!

Interview a family member. Ask the family member to identify at least two traits that he or she inherited. Do you have any of these same traits?

## Family Roles

Your family has one of the strongest influences on the person you become. Are you the oldest, the youngest, or in the middle? What activities do you do with family members? These questions suggest some of the ways you are influenced by your family.

The roles you have determine how you relate to other people and how you act in various situations. You have many roles. At home you may be a daughter or a son, a brother or a sister. At school you may be a student, a best friend, and a team member. In the community you may be a volunteer or a member of a Scout troop. Your role varies, depending on the people with whom you interact and the situations involved. See Fig. 1-2.

You learn your roles by talking to and watching people who are important to you. Role models are people who help you see what is expected of you in certain situations. Role models can be parents, older siblings, relatives, teachers, coaches, or religious leaders. Who are some of your role models?

Fig. 1-2 **You may be a role model for someone younger.** How can you make sure the example you set is a positive one?

## Internet ACTIVITIES

## Culture

Your culture also influences who you are. **Culture** refers to the ways of thinking, acting, dressing, and speaking shared by a group of people. Cultures may be based on ethnic group, geographic location, or social class. Culture often determines certain traditions people follow. You may not even think about your culture until you meet someone who speaks another language, or celebrates different holidays from yours.

## ➤ A Unique Person

Although you share some common qualities with other teens, you are an individual. What qualities do you have that make you different from your friends? Whether you are shy, outgoing, funny, or serious—you are unique.

## Personality Traits

Your personality shows in the way you look, the way you communicate, and the way you act. It is the part of you that you reveal to other people. Your personality continues to change as you have new experiences and meet new people. You become a more interesting person when you develop your skills and talents, learn to do new things, and participate in school and community activities.

Everyone's personality is different. Take a look at your personality traits to see how other people relate to you. How dependable are you? Can people count on you to be true to your word? Are you easy to get along with? Can you be trusted? Personality traits such as dependability, cooperation, and honesty help determine the type of relationships you will have with other people. When friends and family members know they can count on you to follow through, you will be trusted to do more on your own. By learning more about yourself you will appreciate yourself and other people more.

## ➤ A Positive Self-Concept

Your success in life depends on developing a positive **self-concept**, or mental picture of yourself. Self-concept includes your views about your personality traits and about what activities you perform well. Your self-concept is also influenced by the people around you. It gives you the confidence to try new things. If you have a positive self-concept, you are willing to make new friends, go to new places, and try new things. See Fig. 1-3.

Your self-concept does not always stay the same. It may change as the situation you are in changes. When you help a neighbor, for example, you feel really proud of yourself. On the other hand, if you have an argument with a friend, you may not feel as good about yourself. Even people with a strong self-concept get discouraged when something does not work out as they planned.

It is possible to improve your self-concept. Try to do something each day to help build the qualities you want to improve. Being recognized for an achievement will give your

Fig. 1-3 A mirror shows your physical image. Close your eyes and ask, "How do I see myself?" The answer is called your self-concept.

self-concept a boost. In what other situations might your self-concept improve? See Fig. 1-4.

Here are some qualities that will help you build a positive self-concept.

- **Honesty.** Telling the truth and being sincere are ways to show your honesty.
- **Thoughtfulness.** Think about how your actions affect other people. Help others without being asked. Remember to say "please" and "thank you."
- **Cheerfulness.** Being cheerful means being happy, friendly, and seeing the bright side of life.
- **Responsibility.** Being responsible means doing your homework, your chores, and being home on time. It also means accepting the consequences of your actions.
- **Self-control.** Thinking before you act and setting limits are ways to practice self-control. This includes using your knowledge of right and wrong to guide your actions.

Fig. 1-4 When your achievements are recognized, your self-concept improves. What other situations might improve your self-concept?

## Building Self-Esteem

When you have a positive self-concept, you like yourself. In turn, you will develop **self-esteem**, or the ability to respect yourself. Respecting yourself helps you to use your own judgment, resist peer pressure, and achieve your goals. Learn to recognize the things you do well. Be realistic about your expectations, and realize that no one does everything well. Give yourself credit for your successes instead of dwelling on your mistakes.

How do you feel when someone criticizes you? Do you become defensive? **Constructive criticism** is someone's evaluation of you that helps you grow and improve yourself. For example, if your music teacher suggests a different song to fit your voice, you could improve your performance by following that advice. Learning to accept constructive criticism is a good way to improve your self-esteem.

# Explore

## Responsible Choices

### State the Task

- React to the following situations.

**Situation A**

A student is being bullied in the hallway of your school. You don't know him very well, but he looks afraid. You know that he gets picked on all of the time. What will you do? Why?

**Situation B**

Your best friend has been very sad lately. You discovered she has been cutting her forearms and thighs on purpose. You're afraid she's really hurting herself. What will you do? Why?

### Develop a Plan

1. Think of a situation in your own life.
2. Discuss that situation with an adult you trust.
3. Determine the best course of action.

### Implement the Plan

1. Consider several different actions you could take.
2. Choose the best answer for your situation.

### Evaluate the Result

1. Why did you choose the action you did?
2. What did you learn from this activity?

## DID YOU know?

**Self-destructive behavior.** Sometimes a person can feel so much pain and fear he or she will become self-destructive. These types of behaviors can consist of alcohol or drug abuse, eating disorders, cutting, burning, or head banging. If you know someone who is exhibiting self-destructive behavior, encourage the person to ask for help from a trusted adult. No one should feel so helpless that he hurts himself.

## ➤ Showing Responsibility

Each day you make many choices. You are responsible for your own behavior and actions. You can show responsibility by making wise choices. For example, you can take care of your health by choosing to eat healthful foods, to exercise, and to get enough rest. At school you can choose to complete your schoolwork on time and to try to do your best. The more you show responsibility, the more freedom and trust you will be given in the future. Here are a few ways you can show responsibility.

- **Obey rules.** Families, schools, and communities have rules that help maintain order and keep people safe. You act responsibly when you follow the rules.
- **Help others.** Responsible people look out for their families, friends, and neighbors—not just for themselves. If you see someone in trouble, try to help.
- **Keep your promises.** If you told a friend that you would help him study for a test, you have an obligation to keep that promise. In this way, you will show friends and others that they can count on you.
- **Carry out tasks.** If it is your job to clear the table, do it without being told. When you see other tasks that need to be done, take the initiative (IHN-ish-uh-tiv). **Initiative** is taking action without being asked.

### Learning Responsibility

Not everyone has the same responsibilities, and your responsibilities will change over time. As a teen, you will be expected to assume more complex jobs, such as preparing dinner. Helping others will make you feel good about yourself. See Fig. 1-5.

Learning responsibility can be hard, but it has many rewards. You will feel good about yourself, and other people will respect you and start treating you like an adult. Follow these guidelines for success.

- **Expectations.** Find out what is expected of you. Listen carefully. Ask questions if you don't understand.
- **Adult role models.** Look to good adult role models. Ask them to help you learn the right thing to do.

- **New tasks.** Take on new tasks gradually. You will avoid stress if you don't take on too much at once.
- **Learn patience.** Be patient with yourself. If you forget to do something or do it wrong, learn from your mistake and try harder the next time.

Certain characteristics go along with being responsible. Do you have any of these characteristics? Responsible people:

- are reliable.
- keep their word.
- show respect for other people and their property.
- are trustworthy.
- admit their mistakes and don't blame others.

## ➤ Your Value System

The way you satisfy your needs and wants is based on your values. **Values** are your ideas about right and wrong and about what is important in life. Most people share some common values, such as a good family life, trust, freedom, and health. Other values are individual, such as being a good student and playing a sport well.

### Needs

You have the same basic needs that all people have. Physical needs are basic to your survival and well-being. They include food, clothing, and shelter. You also have emotional needs such as feeling safe and secure. These needs also include a sense of belonging and the need to be loved and accepted by other people. When your emotional needs are met, you feel good about yourself.

**DID YOU know?**

**Strengths and Abilities.** Personal strengths and abilities have a direct impact on the choices you make in life. For example, a person of courage is more likely to take risks. Likewise, someone who is artistic will likely pursue the arts in his or her career or as a lifelong hobby. What are your personal strengths and abilities?

As psychologist Abraham Maslow outlines in Fig. 1-6, you also need self-actualization (ACT-yool-ih-ZAY-shuhn). **Self-actualization** means to realize your full potential. When you strive to reach your full potential, you use your skills, talents, and abilities to become all you can be.

## Wants

Wants are different from needs. Wants are things that you would like to have, but are not necessary for survival. You may want the latest DVD, but you can live without it.

Sometimes people confuse wants and needs. Have you ever wanted something so much that you convinced yourself that you really needed it? Perhaps you felt that you could not live without a new outfit. Did you really need it, or was it something you simply wanted to have?

## Values

Like most young people, you probably grew up sharing your family's values related to tradition, culture, religion, education, and marriage. Perhaps your family placed a value on how birthdays and holidays are celebrated. A good family life is a common value shared by most people.

**Fig. 1-6 Maslow's Hierarchy of Human Needs. Beginning at the bottom, each level of needs must be met before the next level can be reached.**

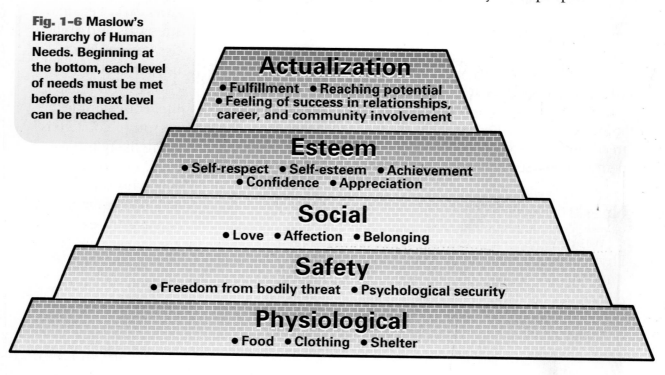

Actualization
• Fulfillment  • Reaching potential
• Feeling of success in relationships, career, and community involvement

Esteem
• Self-respect  • Self-esteem  • Achievement
• Confidence  • Appreciation

Social
• Love  • Affection  • Belonging

Safety
• Freedom from bodily threat  • Psychological security

Physiological
• Food  • Clothing  • Shelter

People have different values because their interests and experiences vary and because they come from diverse backgrounds. The way you **prioritize**, or rank, your values may also be different from the way others rank their values. For example, some people put a high priority on exercising regularly. You should respect other people's values, even though their values are different from yours. Other people should also respect your values. See Fig. 1-7.

Knowing what you value will help you make good decisions. As you develop your value system, you may notice that some of your values are in conflict with each other. For example, you may spend the afternoon finishing a math assignment because you value good grades. What if your friends are going to the movies that same afternoon? You will have to decide which value is more important—completing your math homework or being with your friends. What you value says a lot about you.

**Fig. 1-7 Everyone has values. What are your values?**

## ➤ Emotional Changes

An important part of your personality is related to your emotions. By understanding your emotions and why they change, you will better understand yourself.

You have many emotions. You may feel pleased and excited when you do something well. At other times you may feel sad or frustrated when you have a disagreement with a friend. When was the last time you experienced anger or joy?

Adolescent Development.
**Teens experience social, emotional, physical, intellectual, and moral changes during adolescence.**

**Fig. 1-8 Two people can have different emotions about the same news. Why is it important to understand your emotions?**

One of the difficult things about emotions is that you may experience more than one at the same time. You may feel both excited and scared about being in the school play. You may feel proud that a college accepted your sister, yet sad that she will be going away. Having two different emotions at the same time makes it hard to sort out your feelings.

**Adolescence** (AD-uhl-EHS-ens) is the period of great growth and change between childhood and adulthood. During adolescence you will be adjusting to many physical and emotional changes. For example, your emotions will seem stronger and harder to control. This is because your body is developing and changing. Your feelings may be hurt more easily. You may also feel ignored or become irritated easily. Sometimes you will feel happy and want to be with your friends. At other times you may want to be alone and not talk to anyone. See Fig. 1-8.

Adjusting to new emotions can be challenging. When your moods are constantly changing, it may seem as if you lack control over your life. Instead, you can learn to handle your emotions.

## Dealing With Your Emotions

Even though these new and changing emotions are difficult to understand, you should not let them rule your life. For example, everyone feels angry at times. However, it is the way you handle your emotions that is most important. Try these healthy ways to deal with your emotions.

- Admit how you feel and why you feel that way.
- Talk about your feelings with a family member, friend, teacher, or counselor.
- Write down your feelings in a journal.

- Work off your feelings by doing something physical, such as pounding a pillow or taking a walk.
- If you are angry with another person, wait until you have cooled off before speaking to him or her. Tell the person how you feel and what you need or want.

## Physical Changes

You must also learn to adjust to physical changes in height, weight, and body shape during adolescence. You may have noticed that you or your friends seem to grow inches overnight. Sometimes the different parts of your body don't all grow at the same rate. It can be frustrating when your body is constantly changing and growing. Just when you get used to it one way, it changes again. These rapid changes can make you feel awkward and clumsy.

Every teen does not change and grow at the same rate. Some teens grow and change very quickly; others do so more slowly. These changes can make you feel embarrassed or out of place. Try not to worry—your classmates are all growing and changing too. See Fig. 1-9.

Fig. 1-9 Everyone grows and changes at different rates. What can you do to adjust to these physical changes?

## Personal Grooming

How many ads have you seen about grooming aids for teens? These advertisements may lead you to believe that it takes time, money, and certain products to look good. The fact is that you can look your best by following a basic grooming routine every day. Take care of your skin, hair, hands, feet, nails, hair, and teeth. Make sure your clothing is neat and clean. Although there are physical features that you can't change, such as your height, you can still look your best.

# A CLOSER LOOK

## ...at Grooming Habits

Good grooming habits will help you make a positive impression, enhance your self-esteem, and help you stay healthy.

### Skin Care

Wash your face every morning and evening with a mild soap. Bathe every day. Use deodorant or antiperspirant daily.

### Hair Care

Wash your hair regularly. Brush or comb your hair every day.

## Hand Care

Wash your hands often to remove dirt and to prevent the spread of germs. Keep your fingernails trimmed.

## Foot Care

Wash your feet to prevent odor. Keep your toenails trimmed.

## Dental Care

Brush all tooth surfaces and your tongue at least twice a day. Floss daily.

## Clothing Care

Choose clean clothing and change each day. Wash your clothing regularly.

## Your Skin

During the teen years, the oil glands in your skin begin to work harder. The extra oil can clog your pores and cause skin problems such as acne. Teens who have severe acne may need to consult a dermatologist, a doctor who treats skin disorders. To best care for your skin:

- Get enough rest and exercise.
- Drink six to eight glasses of water each day.
- Bathe every day and wash your face and neck with mild soap and water at least twice a day.
- Use deodorant or antiperspirant daily.
- Use over-the-counter medications if blemishes are a problem. Do not pick at or squeeze pimples.
- Choose grooming products that will not irritate your skin. Look for products that are labeled "mild" or "hypoallergenic."
- Protect your skin from the sun. Use a sunscreen with a sun protection factor (SPF) of at least 15. Reapply the sunscreen if you go swimming.

## Your Hair

For many teens, hair is a means of self-expression. Regardless of the hairstyle you prefer, your hair is most attractive when it is clean and healthy. Here's how to care for your hair:

- Wash and brush or comb your hair regularly.
- Choose a shampoo made for your type of hair.
- Shampoo your hair gently, using your fingertips to work the lather through your hair. Rinse thoroughly.
- When using a conditioner after shampooing, follow the directions on the bottle.
- Use the lowest temperature when blow drying, curling, or straightening your hair.

## Your Hands & Feet

Good grooming includes taking care of your hands and feet, including nails. To best care for feet and hands:

- Wash your hands, feet, and nails with soap and water to remove dirt, dead skin, and germs.

- After washing, be sure to dry your feet thoroughly.
- Do not wear wet socks or shoes. This practice can promote growth of bacteria.
- Moisturize your hands and feet with lotion. Powder your feet to control odor.
- Trim and file your fingernails to shape them. Trim your toenails straight across.

## Your Teeth

Your teeth affect not only your appearance but also your health. Your teeth help you chew food and shape your mouth and your smile. Taking care of your teeth will help prevent cavities and gum disease. The best way to avoid these problems is to keep your teeth clean. Follow these tips for healthy teeth:

- Choose a brush with soft bristles, and use a toothpaste that contains fluoride.
- To brush, use gentle up-and-down strokes to clean between the teeth and massage your gums.
- Floss your teeth once a day. Ask your dentist to show you the proper technique.
- Keep sweets to a minimum, especially between meals, and eat a balanced diet with nutritious foods.
- Get regular dental checkups.

## Your Clothing

Clothing is another form of self-expression. Clothing choices should be based on function, style, and durability. Here are some basic tips on clothing care:

- Clothing should be clean and changed daily.
- Treat stains as soon as you take off the garment.
- Fix any rips or tears as soon as possible.
- Choose the appropriate clothing for each occasion.
- Mix and match separate pieces for new combinations.

## ➤ First Impressions

People form an opinion about you the first time they meet you. This instant opinion is called a first impression. It is based on the way you look, talk, and act. First impressions are important because they help people decide whether they want to know you better. What type of first impression do you make when you are considerate of others? In contrast, what do people think if you use poor table manners?

First impressions are not always accurate. When people have a chance to get to know you better, they may change their opinion. Sometimes, however, the first impression is the only chance you have to make a good impression. See Fig. 1-10.

**Fig. 1-10 Practicing good grooming will help you make a positive first impression.** What other habits will help you make a good first impression?

# How To...

## Manicure Nails

### State the Task

- To give a manicure.

### Develop a Plan

1. Gather the necessary supplies.
2. Partner with someone to give and receive a manicure.
3. Discuss the steps involved in giving a manicure.

### Implement the Plan

1. Begin by removing any nail polish with the nail polish remover.
2. Wash hands with a mild hand soap and warm water.
3. Moisturize hands with hand cream.
4. Apply cuticle cream, if available.
5. Gently push back cuticles with a cuticle stick. If the cuticle does not move, continue to soften it with cuticle cream or hand cream.
6. Trim any hangnails without digging too deeply.
7. Clip nails.
8. Shape and file nails using the emery board.
9. Use the nail buffer to buff and shine the nails. Gently rub the buffer back and forth across each nail.
10. Wash hands and nails with a mild soap. Dry them completely.

### Supplies

- Nail polish remover (optional)
- Cotton balls
- Hand cream
- Cuticle cream (optional)
- Cuticle stick
- Cuticle scissors
- Nail clippers
- Emery board
- Nail buffer
- Nail brush

### Evaluate the Result

1. Were you able to push your cuticles back?
2. Were your nails filed evenly?

# Career CHOICES

## Psychiatrist

Diagnoses and treats patients with mental, emotional, and behavioral disorders. Also determines the nature and extent of the patient's treatment program using a variety of methods and medications.

## Dentist

Diagnoses and treats diseases, injuries, and malformations of teeth, gums, and related oral structures. Cleans, fills, extracts, and replaces teeth. Provides education in oral and dental hygiene.

## Makeup Artist

Applies makeup to performers or models to enhance or alter their appearance. Confers with photographer or stage and motion picture supervisors to determine what makeup is to be used.

## Cosmetologist

Provides beauty services for customers. Shampoos and styles hair. Applies bleach, dye, or tint to color hair. Styles hair by cutting, trimming, and tapering. Suggests styles and current trends, or listens to customer's instructions.

## Psychologist

Provides individual and group counseling services. Assists individuals in achieving personal, social, educational, and vocational adjustment. Collects data through interviews and observational techniques.

**A cosmetologist uses these tools to alter a customer's appearance. Consider interviewing your cosmetologist about his or her career choice.**

### AT School

Select three of the careers listed. Research the education, training, and work experience required for each career. Compare the results to select a career to investigate further.

### IN THE Workplace

When you get a job you'll be an employee. Make a list of at least five expectations your employer will have of his or her employees.

## Chapter Summary

- A positive self-concept is important for success in life.
- Learning to accept constructive criticism will help you improve your skills.
- You develop your own set of values based on what you believe is right or wrong.
- Handling your emotions in a positive manner can help you have control over your life.
- Emotional and physical changes are a part of adolescence.

## Words You Learned

1. Why is heredity important to you?
2. What is self-concept?
3. Define the term culture.
4. What might cause low self-esteem?
5. Give an example of constructive criticism.

6. Describe how you could show initiative.
7. What are values?
8. What is self-actualization?
9. Explain what it means to prioritize.
10. Why is adolescence considered a mixture of childhood and adulthood?

## Check Your Facts

1. Describe how you express your personality.
2. Explain what might happen to your self-concept if you don't deal with your emotions in a healthy way.
3. Explain the difference between needs and wants.
4. Explain how emotional changes affect teens.
5. Name the seven areas of personal grooming.

## Apply Your Learning

1. Name several of your role models and explain why they are positive role models for you.
2. Name the qualities you have that help promote a positive self-concept.
3. Explain how your values may conflict with one another.
4. Explain three healthy ways to control your emotions.
5. **You are unique.** What types of interests and abilities make you unique? Decorate the outside of a paper lunch bag with pictures and words that describe what others already know about you. Then, place pictures or items inside the bag that symbolize what you want others to learn about you.

# Chapter 2

# Your Family

## You Will Discover . . .

- the importance of families.
- several types of family structures.
- how to strengthen family relationships.
- ways to get along with family members.
- the changes that occur throughout the family life cycle.
- ways to adjust to changes that affect families.

## Key Words

- traditions
- siblings
- empathy
- responsibly

What comes to mind when you think of family? Can you create a description of a family? Is it being together for a holiday? Is it the group of people living next door? Perhaps you think of a large family with lots of children. There are many kinds of families.

## ➤ Family Structures

Try to describe each person in your family and his or her relationship to you. This description will identify the type of your family's structure. It will probably match one of the family types described in Fig. 2-1.

Regardless of the structure, a healthy family life is a source of pleasure and growth for its members. Healthy families consist of people who care about each other and work together as a team. Family members work together to:

- provide food, clothing, and a place to live.
- create a loving environment.
- encourage independence.
- teach values and life skills.
- give friendship, guidance, and support.

## Your Unique Family

The people who make up your family have different skills, talents, and personalities. For example, your father may be an artist. Your sister may play on the soccer team. Your brother may play in a band and have an outgoing personality. The skills, talents, and personalities of its members make each family unique.

**Fig. 2-1 This chart lists some common family types.**

## Family Types

**Nuclear Family.** Includes two parents and one or more children.

**Single-parent Family.** One parent and one or more children.

**Blended Family.** Formed when two people marry and at least one has children from a previous marriage.

**Extended Family.** One or two parents and children as well as other relatives, such as grandparents or aunts and uncles.

Families also have different ways of expressing themselves and their emotions. You have probably noticed that some show their love for each other more openly than others. They may show affection by hugging one another and saying, "I love you." This does not mean that families who don't hug feel less love. They just express it in different ways.

It is not surprising that families have different ways of expressing themselves. Families have various **traditions**, or customs and beliefs handed down from one generation to another. These traditions might influence how they celebrate holidays, the foods they like, and their religious beliefs. Even people in different parts of this country have their own customs. It is important to realize that customs can be different without being wrong. By sharing ideas with a variety of people, you can learn more about them. At the same time, they will learn more about you.

## ➤ Family Relationships

Families can become closer when family members spend time together. By becoming involved in each other's daily lives and participating in similar activities, hobbies, and interests, family members strengthen their ties with each other. See Fig. 2-2.

Think about the activities you like to share with your mother, father, and **siblings** (brothers and sisters). Perhaps you like to go hiking with your parents or shopping with your sister. Even sharing daily events, such as talking about what happened at school or going to the beach together, can help strengthen family relationships. Other ways to enrich family life include:

- sharing games or hobbies.
- attending religious services.
- planning special celebrations. See Fig. 2-3 on page 46.
- discussing books, movies, and current events.

**Fig. 2-2 Spending time together brings family members closer.**

**Fig. 2-3** The traditions you practice as a family strengthen your values and relationships. What traditions are practiced by your family?

Family members do things with and for each other. When her mother had a baby, Maya helped out by making dinner each night. Maya's actions increased the bonds of the family unit. Strong family relationships are especially helpful during difficult times. For example, when a family member becomes ill, it is helpful when the rest of the family pitches in and is supportive.

## Getting Along With People

Within your family, you practice the skills of consideration, cooperation, reliability, and understanding. These skills help you get along with family members and also prepare you for relationships with people at school, at work, and in the community.

- **Consideration.** Think about other people and their feelings. Treat people the same way you would like to be treated.
- **Cooperation.** Pitch in and do your share of work. Keep your room clean and help out around the house.
- **Reliability.** Do you do what you say you will do? People like to know they can depend on you. Prove to them that you will keep your word.
- **Understanding.** Try to understand how other people feel. Respect others' viewpoint and feelings. Show **empathy** (EHM-pah-THEE), or the ability to put yourself in another person's place. Respect that person's viewpoint and feelings.

**DID YOU know?**

**Family Relationships.** Characteristics of positive family relationships are easy to spot. Does your family have these positive characteristics?

- Support one another.
- Laugh and play together.
- Share responsibilities.
- Trust one another.
- Respect one another.

# Internet ACTIVITIES

1. **Search the Internet for information on your family background. See how far back you can trace your roots.**

   **Key Search Words:**
   - **genealogy**
   - **family history**

2. **Search the Internet for information on specific holidays your family celebrates. Share your research results with the rest of your family.**

   **Key Search Words:**
   - **holidays**
   - **celebrations**

## Your Parents

As you move toward independence, it helps to understand that parents are people, too. Parents have strengths and weaknesses. They, too, are working toward goals. Perhaps they are going back to school or saving for a family vacation. Sometimes parents face trouble at work, financial difficulties, or health problems. Just like you, they have good days and bad days. It helps to recognize your parents' point of view. If you give your parents love and understanding, family life will go more smoothly.

Communicating with your parents is especially important during your teen years. Talk openly to them about your problems, thoughts, and concerns. This can help both you and your parents understand one another's feelings. Remember, they want to be supportive, but they can't read your mind. See Fig. 2-4 on page 48.

## Your Siblings

You may enjoy many activities with your brothers and sisters. However, you also may have difficulty getting along with them. Here are some suggestions:

- Avoid teasing them. Speak kindly. Compliment them.
- Share your belongings with them, and ask permission before you use or borrow their belongings.
- Do your share of the chores.

### DID YOU know?

**Rights of Family Members.** Each member of a family has the right to expect support, empathy, trust, and respect from other family members. Supportive families make sure each member's rights are provided and their expectations met. When these basic needs are not met, relationships tear apart and anger takes control. It is important to support each family member's emotional needs.

# Communicating With Parents

Choose a time when you can be alone and when your parent is not busy or upset.

Try to understand your parents' position.

Make it a habit to talk with your parents every day, not just when you have a problem.

Keep your emotions in control. Do not raise your voice or lose your temper.

Begin the conversation with positive comments about what happened during the day.

Fig. 2-4 Follow these tips for communicating with your parents.

## Older Relatives

Grandparents and great-grandparents are part of your extended family. They may live with you, nearby, or far away. You can benefit by interacting regularly with your older relatives. Perhaps your grandparents enjoy taking you out to movies, sporting events, or fishing.

Young and old can enjoy shared activities such as board games, gardening, cooking, or stamp collecting. Older relatives can share family stories and traditions, providing a sense of family history. Some take on a parenting role by caring for grandchildren while parents work.

When grandparents live far away, letters, phone calls, and email can maintain a long distance relationship. How do you like to stay in touch with your grandparents?

## Sharing Space

Whether you are sharing a bedroom, a bathroom, or the kitchen, you must work with other family members to keep the space organized and clean. Sharing space will be easier if you remember the following guidelines:

- **Respect other people's privacy.** If someone's door is closed, knock and wait for a response before entering. Keep your music or television turned low, or use headphones if another person wants to sleep or study. Never read another person's mail or look through others' belongings without their permission.
- **Be considerate of others.** Show your consideration by not leaving your belongings in someone else's way. When you have finished using the kitchen or the bathroom, be sure to leave it at least as clean as you found it.
- **Cooperate with family members.** Is there a "morning rush hour" at your house? This can happen when several family members are trying to get ready for work or school at the same time. The morning will go more smoothly if everyone agrees on a schedule.

## ➤ Family Responsibilities

Being part of a family means being responsible for yourself and also showing responsibility to your family. Acting **responsibly** means being reliable. You can show your family that you are responsible by doing the chores that are expected of you without complaining. See Fig. 2-5.

Acting responsibly at home also includes following the rules and showing respect for other people's feelings. It also means calling home to let someone know if you are going to be late and cleaning up after yourself.

Acting responsibly outside of your home means showing respect to your teachers and coaches, staying away from drugs, and doing what you know is right. As you get older and earn greater amounts of freedom, you will also need to act responsibly at work.

**Fig. 2-5 Doing your chores without being told demonstrates responsibility.**

# Explore

## Family Responsibilities

### State the Task

• Create a schedule of responsibilities for family members.

### Develop a Plan

1. List all of the responsibilities that need to be accomplished. List household chores, pet care, and any care of young children.
2. Discuss each person's schedule of activities outside of the home so you'll know when everyone is available.
3. List each day of the week and write down each family members' extracurricular activities.
4. Divide the responsibilities. Write down responsibilities for each day of the week, working around extracurricular activities.

### Implement the Plan

1. Post the schedule on the refrigerator, in the family room, or in the laundry area.
2. Check the schedule every day to see what your personal responsibilities are. Follow through and complete each task you are assigned.
3. Mark off the tasks as you complete them and encourage other family members to do so as well.

### Evaluate the Result

1. How did each family member react to the new schedule?
2. Were there any family members who didn't complete their responsibilities?
3. Would you make any changes to the schedule?
4. What have you learned about responsibility from your schedule?

Plan a meeting at least once a month with your entire family so that you can discuss schedules and special dates. Let your parents know what items you need for upcoming school projects. Also take this time to discuss television rules or discipline and reward systems. Fill out a calendar with special dates and post it where everyone is sure to see it. Make the meeting fun by popping a bowl of popcorn for snacking.

# ➤ Changing Family Roles

Change is a normal part of life. Think of how you have changed over the years. Think of how your life has changed. Some life changes are the result of things you do, or don't do. For example, if you need to make up a class but do not go to summer school, you probably will not be promoted to the next grade.

Other changes you cannot control. If your family moves to a new house, you may have to go to a different school. An accident can put you in the hospital. Whether you want to or not, you will experience life changes. See Fig. 2-6.

As each individual grows and changes, the rest of the family adapts and changes. Your roles change as family members grow and change. If your older sister gets married, you may find that you have more chores to do at home. You may also find that you have more time to spend with your parents. Sometimes the changes are planned or expected. Other times they come as a surprise. New family members may be born or adopted. Older brothers or sisters may move out of the home, or back home again. A grandparent may move in with your family. The following chart describes the four stages of the family life cycle.

Fig. 2-6 Moving to a different city means changes for everyone in the family.

| The Family Life Cycle | |
|---|---|
| **Beginning Stage** | Newly married couples without children. |
| **Parenting Stage** | Children are born and parents care for their needs. |
| **Launching Stage** | Teens become independent and leave home. |
| **Senior Stage** | Parents adjust to being a couple again and enjoy more leisure activities or change careers. |

# A CLOSER LOOK

## ...at Relaxing Family Activities

**You can do your part to help your family relax with fun activities in or around your home. Plan a fun evening and use one or more of the following ideas, or come up with your own ideas.**

### Now You're Cooking
Make a family favorite like pizza or get creative and try something new. Cooking is a fun way to get everyone together and talking.

### Candid Collage
Gather up all the family photos that are stashed away. Ask all members in your family to choose their favorites to make a photo collage.

## You've Got Game

Games and puzzles are a great way to unwind. Gather your favorites, or design a new game with personal appeal.

## On the Hunt

Create a scavenger hunt for your family by hiding objects around the house and passing out clues as to where they are hidden. Mix in special treats along with standard objects to keep everyone guessing.

## A Great Escape

If everyone in your family has been longing to get away, plan a theme night. Turn your kitchen and family area into your travel destination. For example, have a camp-out in your living room with sleeping bags.

## Divorce

When changes are the result of separation or divorce, families must learn to accept them, even when the changes are painful. You may not only have to deal with one parent moving out, but you may also have to deal with a parent going to work for the first time. You may have to take on more responsibilities. You may feel more alone. Tell your parent how you are feeling. He or she is probably worried about the changes, too. You can reassure each other.

When Justin's father remarried, his stepmother brought her two young children to live with Justin and his father. Now Justin has found himself in a new role—as an older brother and sometimes as a babysitter. See Fig. 2-7. What roles do you have within your family?

## Remarriage

After a divorce, one or both parents may remarry. This causes more changes. New stepbrothers or stepsisters may join the family. You are blending a new family and need to share games, space, and parents. You may also have to get used to a visitation schedule, going from one parent to the other at designated times. This may be difficult, but it will allow you to spend time with each of your parents.

Fig. 2-7 As family roles change, you may find yourself with different responsibilities. How has your family role changed?

## Disabilities

You may have a sibling or parent with a disability. It could be a permanent or temporary physical, mental, or emotional condition. Your family member may act out in a way that draws attention to your family. Feeling angry, embarrassed, or scared are natural reactions. Understand that your family member can't control his or her condition. It is up to you to be supportive and loving. Look for ways to be helpful. See Fig. 2-8.

Fig. 2-8 Talking with disabled family members about what they need for support is always helpful.

## Job Loss

Some changes are the result of the economy. A parent's job may be lost and the family will have less money to spend. When a parent loses a job, you may fear what will happen to your family. Your routine will be upset and you should discuss your feelings. If money is an issue, do your part to help. Your parents will appreciate your efforts.

## Serious Illness

When a family member is seriously ill, it can be very stressful for the whole family. Perhaps your brother or sister has cancer, or your mother has diabetes, or your father has heart disease. Constant trips to the doctor, reactions to medications, and pain management are common. You may wonder why it is happening and whether your family member will get better. Confide your fears in someone you trust—a parent, grandparent, teacher, or another responsible adult. Find out what you can do to help. Perhaps choosing quiet activities when the ill person is sleeping, taking on extra chores, or reading to the person could be your contribution.

## Death

One of the most difficult changes for a family to deal with is the death of one of its members. People find it hard to accept that a part of the family is gone. They sometimes feel guilty about what they did not say or do when the person was alive. These reactions are normal. Everyone in the family can support and comfort one another. Some families seek professional counseling to help them deal with the loss of a family member.

## ➤ Adjusting to Change

Not all changes are sad. Getting your own bedroom and making a new friend are examples of happy changes. No matter what changes occur in your life you will have to adjust to them. Here are some positive ways to accept change:

- **Plan ahead.** If you know about a change in advance, prepare for it even if you do not want it to happen. For example, if you are transferring to a new school, find out about the school before your first day.
- **Talk.** Discuss your feelings. Your family and friends can be a great source of strength and encouragement. Teachers, counselors, coaches, religious leaders, and family service workers can also help you understand and handle the change.
- **Look for the positive.** Remember that changes are part of life and they will help you grow. It does not help to keep thinking about what is wrong or different. What can you learn from the experience?
- **Be supportive.** When your family faces changes, you can help just by being there. If your brother is nervous about a new job, point out his strengths.

# How To...

## Plan a Family Evening at Home

### State the Task

- Plan an evening of family activities.

### Develop a Plan

1. Choose activities that appeal to your family. If time allows, choose more than one. Some suggestions are: cooking together, playing a board game, creating your family tree, planting a garden, or tape-recording family stories.

2. Decide how much time each activity will take and plan activities that can be done between dinner and bedtime. It will take more than one evening to complete some activities.

3. Gather the supplies you will need ahead of time: dinner ingredients, games, books, or craft supplies. By planning ahead, you can ask your parents to shop when it is convenient for them.

4. Make sure all family members are available on the evening you choose so no one feels left out.

### Implement the Plan

1. On the evening you choose for your family activities, finish your homework before the activity begins.

2. Relax and enjoy the moment. If you planned too many activities for one evening, don't rush through them. You can always save something for another time.

### Evaluate the Result

1. Did all family members participate in the evening? Why or why not?

2. Did the evening turn out as you had planned?

3. What would you do differently next time?

# Career CHOICES

## Family Counselor

Provides individual and family counseling services to adults and children. Analyzes information about clients to determine counseling needs. Counsels clients about personal and interpersonal problems.

## Family Practitioner

Examines patients, orders tests, and diagnoses condition of patient. Prescribes treatments and medications. Advises patients about diet, hygiene, and methods for prevention of disease.

## Portrait Photographer

Photographs people using still cameras and other photographic equipment. Arranges setting to produce desired effect. Poses subject to take candid photos.

## Recreation Aide

Assists with recreation activities at community center or other recreation facility. Arranges exercise equipment in designated areas for scheduled group activities. Posts activity schedules and registration requirements. Monitors sports events to ensure orderly conduct.

## Elementary School Teacher

Teaches elementary school students. Writes lesson plans according to curriculum guidelines. Administers and scores tests. Assigns activities and corrects papers. Discusses pupils' academic achievements with parents.

### AT School

Select three of the careers listed. Research the education, training, and work experience required for each career. Compare the results to select a career to investigate further.

### IN THE Workplace

Many companies began as family businesses. Ford Motor Company is one example. Brainstorm a list of other famous companies that began as family businesses.

**Family practitioners study for many years before treating patients. Consider job shadowing someone in a medical career. Ask the person about his or her career choices.**

# Chapter 2 Review & Activities

## Chapter Summary

- There are nuclear, single-parent, blended, and extended family structures.
- Family members do things with and for each other.
- Successful family relationships help prepare you for positive relationships at school, at work, and in the community.
- Changes occur in family roles throughout the life cycle.
- Adjust to change by being positive.

## Words You Learned

1. Define traditions.
2. What are siblings?
3. What is empathy?
4. How do people act responsibly?

## Check Your Facts

1. What needs do family members meet?
2. How are family relationships strengthened?
3. How can learning to get along with family members now improve your relationships in the future?
4. List three things siblings can do to get along.
5. How can you show responsibility to your family?
6. Name two of your family roles.
7. What are three examples of changes that can occur within the family?

## Apply Your Learning

1. Name three ways family members support one another.
2. What three guidelines should you remember when sharing space with family members?
3. List four ways that you can adjust to change.
4. **Gift Certificates.** Sometimes the best present isn't something that costs a lot of money. You can make a customized gift certificate that says, "This certificate entitles [name] to [one car wash] or [three games of checkers]." You can use these gift certificates to say thank you, happy birthday, or to tell a family member that he or she is appreciated.

# Chapter 3

# Your Friendships

## You Will Discover . . .

- the qualities of friendship.
- why friendships may change.
- the positive and negative influences of peer pressure.
- ways to handle peer pressure.
- how to be assertive.

## Key Words

- acquaintance
- peers
- expectations
- peer pressure
- addiction
- abstinence
- assertive

Who are your friends? Are they people you can talk to about your secrets and goals? Are they other teens who also like to go to the movies? Are they your teammates or the people in your science club? Can you really define your friends in such simple terms? You probably can't. Friends may be all those things, but they are also much more.

## ➤ What Is a Friend?

A friend is someone you like and who likes you. It is someone you can talk to. A friend is a person who shares similar interests and goals. For instance, you may enjoy going to the mall with your friends. Perhaps you study with your friend. You and your friend may have the same career goal of becoming a lawyer or a firefighter. The important quality you have in common is that you care about one another's lives.

### How Do Friendships Begin?

Friendships begin and develop when people meet and like each other. You do not automatically have a friend just because you meet someone. Some people are only acquaintances. An **acquaintance** (uh-QUOHNT-ence) is a person you greet or meet fairly often, but with whom you do not have a close relationship. It may be a classmate, a neighbor, or the librarian at school.

Friendships usually develop from the acquaintances that you have. They are formed with people you are interested in knowing better. They grow into true and lasting friendships as you learn more about one another. See Fig. 3-1.

**Fig. 3-1 As you get to know others, friendships often develop. How did you meet most of your friends?**

## Give & Take

Good friendships are based on a give-and-take relationship. No two people are alike in what they give to you as a friend or in the benefits they receive from you. Some people may just be casual friends. You may enjoy their company at school or rollerblade with them in the park. Others may become close friends whom you know very well and in whom you confide. Almost all friends learn from each other. They have something to offer one another. Some of the ways that friends share and contribute to each other's lives are by:

- sharing good times.
- demonstrating a feeling of acceptance.
- depending on each other to listen when one person needs to talk about a problem.
- offering help when it is needed.

## Making New Friends

Beginning a new friendship is not always easy, but you can be successful if you make the effort. Everyone has to make new friends at times. Old friends may move away, or friendships may change as you grow and develop new interests. For example, you may want a new buddy to go swimming with or to find a person who shares your love of crafts. Making new friends is a skill that you can learn.

As you go through life, you will have many opportunities to develop new friendships. Some may begin easily. Others take more effort, and you may need to keep trying. However, not all friendships will work out. The person with whom you hoped to be friends may be too busy or have different interests. With experience, you will recognize which friendships are worth pursuing.

You live in a society that is filled with lots of different people—old, young, ethnically diverse, and with varying points of view. Differences make people interesting. Establishing a relationship with someone different from you broadens your perspective. Diversity can enrich your life. It will also prepare you for the work world, where understanding all kinds of people is essential.

**DID YOU know?**

**Friendship Day is August 5th.** Plan on spending the day with a good friend doing something extra special, or plan your own "friendship day."

# Explore

## Places to Meet New Friends

> ### Supplies
> - Local newspapers
> - Access to Internet
> - Local park-district schedule
> - Chamber of Commerce newsletter

### State the Task

- Find places that you could meet new friends.

### Develop a Plan

1. Search through newspapers, newsletters, community bulletin boards, or park-district schedules for events.
2. Call your public library and ask about reading groups or special events.
3. Check the Internet for local television station and Chamber of Commerce Web sites that may list community events.
4. Consider joining a club such as FCCLA (Family, Career and Community Leaders of America), Boy or Girl Scouts, or 4-H, to name a few.
5. List several of the events or clubs on a sheet of paper.
6. Explain why you chose the event or club.
7. Make a separate list of all free events you can find listed in your community. Explain why these would be good places to meet other kids.

### Implement the Plan

1. Check the times of the events and make sure they are appropriate for your age. If they aren't listed, a telephone call should do the trick.
2. Find out what kind of adult supervision is available.

### Evaluate the Result

1. Discuss the reasons you chose your events or clubs. Explain exactly what part of the event or club sounded interesting to you and why you thought others would participate.
2. Explain what you intend to get out of the event or club.
3. Explain what qualities you are looking for in a friend.

Once you have compiled a list of places to meet new friends, check with your teacher to see if you can post it in your school's newsletter or on the community bulletin board.

# ➤ What Makes a Friend?

When friendships are formed, they are based on caring, sharing, and good communication. These qualities, along with trust and reliability, help to strengthen friendships. They show others that you want to be a good friend. However, in order to have friends, you cannot be on the receiving end all the time. You have to be willing to contribute something. Listening to your friend and offering your help when it is needed are signs of friendship. For instance, have you ever helped a friend practice for baseball tryouts or finish chores so that you both could go to the movies? Doing your part when working with others and praising your friends when they do well are also ways to show that you are a good friend.

As you develop new interests, you will want to make new friends who share those interests. What interests do you have in common with your friends? See Fig. 3-2.

Fig. 3-2 **When your friend shares the same interests, it is fun to spend time together.** What interests do you share with your friends?

## Being Part of a Group

During adolescence, most teens seek approval from their peers. **Peers** are people the same age as you. Your peers' acceptance and recognition help you develop a sense of belonging. Being accepted by your peers strengthens your self-esteem.

Most teens strive to become part of a peer group. Peer groups are groups of people the same age. Your peer group helps to fill your need for companionship and support. Within the group, you will practice skills that can be used in other groups throughout your life.

1. Does your friend remind you of an important figure in history? Perhaps he or she is interested in nursing like Florence Nightingale, or loves computers like Bill Gates. Search the Internet for information on a historical figure and write a one-page report on his or her life accomplishments. Share it with your friend.

**Key Search Words:**

- historical figures
- "type in a famous person's name"

2. When the weather doesn't permit outdoor fun, find something to do inside the house. Search the Internet for crafts you can make and share with your friends.

**Key Search Words:**

- friendship crafts
- rainy-day crafts

## ➤ Changes in Friendships

Your friendships will probably change over the years. Some of your friends may move away or transfer to different schools. Some of your friends may have new responsibilities after school. Friendships can also change when you and your friends discover new interests and activities.

The important point to remember about changes in friendships is that you can grow and learn from them. You may not have chosen the changes, but you can use them to understand more about yourself and others.

### Differences in Expectations

Has there ever been a time when a friend let you down? Some changes in friendships are due to changing expectations. **Expectations** are a person's ideas of what should be or should happen.

**Fig. 3-3** Problems arise when your expectations don't match those of your friends. Changes in friendships are common during the teen years.

A common expectation in friendships is to have and to be a best friend. Best friends expect to be able to confide in and trust each other and share common interests. Changes in friendships may occur when someone who was your best friend develops different interests and no longer shares as much with you. Changes in best friends are common as you learn what to expect from your friends and what your friends expect from you.

Expectations in friendships between boys and girls also change often during the teen years. Sometimes a boy and girl who have been friends develop a boyfriend-girlfriend relationship. This usually means that they have special caring feelings for one another. Problems also may arise when one friend expects more from the relationship than the other friend wants to give. See Fig. 3-3.

## ➤ Peers & Decision Making

Everyone wants to be accepted and liked by his or her peers. In many situations, the desire to belong to a peer group is a positive influence. There are times, however, when peers can be a negative influence in your life. Learning to recognize the differences between these types of influences will help you decide whether to go along with the group or act as an individual.

DID YOU **know?**

**Jealousy is an emotion.** Jealousy occurs when you don't want to share something or someone with another person. It also results when someone else has something that you want. People often feel jealous when they are insecure about themselves or their relationship with someone else. When you feel jealous of a friend's accomplishments, do something for yourself.

## The Influence of Peers

Having good friends and being part of a peer group can be a satisfying experience. Their attitudes toward school, sports, or after-school activities can encourage you to do your best. The support and confidence peers give you can help your self-confidence. At times, your peers may expect you to join in their actions and activities. **Peer pressure** is the influence you feel to go along with the behavior of your peers.

## Positive Peer Pressure

The acceptance of your peers helps you feel good about yourself. A peer group can give you a sense of belonging and encourage positive behavior. See Fig. 3-4. Suppose that you were competing in a tennis match. Wouldn't you feel good knowing that your friends were cheering you on? You would feel confident and want to do your best. This type of peer pressure is a positive force.

Fig. 3-4 Spending time with your peers can have a positive influence on you. How does spending time with your peers make you feel about yourself?

## Negative Peer Pressure

Peer pressure can also be a negative force. Some groups make outsiders feel uncomfortable, unpopular, or unwanted. If one member of a group is critical or has a bad attitude, it may influence the entire group. It may be difficult for you to go against the wishes of your peers—for instance, to be friendly to someone the group has excluded.

Another negative kind of peer pressure is feeling pushed to participate in activities that go against your values. Maybe you have been faced with making a choice about skipping school, smoking, drinking alcohol, joining a gang, or doing something else that you know is dangerous or illegal.

## ➤ Handling Peer Pressure

Eventually, you will be faced with decisions about following the group or following your own conscience. When this happens, you need to ask yourself: Are the wishes of a few people more important than doing what I believe is right? If I did something only because of peer pressure, would I regret it later?

Here are some ways to deal with negative peer pressure.

- **Think ahead.** Decide in advance what you will do if certain situations arise. You might even practice what you will say and do.
- **Practice refusal skills.** Use refusal skills if your friends suggest you do something that is wrong or against your values. See Fig. 3-5.

**Fig. 3-5 Refusal skills help you stay true to your values.**

## Refusal Skills

- ◆ State exactly how you feel, directly and honestly.
- ◆ Do not apologize for your decisions—or for your values.
- ◆ Use direct eye contact to show that you mean what you say.
- ◆ Use a firm yet friendly tone of voice.
- ◆ Use the other person's name.
- ◆ Suggest an option that is more acceptable to you.
- ◆ Avoid compromise, which can be a slow way to saying yes.

Inhalants—also known as sniffing or huffing—starve your body of oxygen and make your heart beat more rapidly and at an irregular pace. This can cause severe damage to your heart muscle.

- **Suggest other activities.** Think of things to do that are fun, healthy, safe, and legal. Let your friends know that you would like to be with them, but not if it means doing something wrong, unsafe, or illegal.
- **Choose your friends carefully.** Develop friendships with peers who share your values and interests.
- **Talk to parents and counselors.** Let them know if you're having problems. They can give you the support and encouragement you need to resist giving in.

## Avoiding Harmful Substances

Everyone wants to be liked and accepted, but some people feel that gaining popularity is essential. Some teens think that they can become popular by smoking cigarettes, using alcohol or other drugs, or sniffing substances. They may do these things to impress friends or because their friends have dared them to take part. It is important to learn to use refusal skills when you feel pressured to engage in activities that you believe, or know, are wrong.

If you have ever thought about trying alcohol or other drugs, think again about the reasons why. Carefully consider the long-term effects of such a decision. Using alcohol and other drugs does not make a person popular, build self-confidence, or solve problems. What alcohol and other drugs do is trap a person into a cycle of self-abuse. These harmful substances slow down your ability to act and think normally, and they weaken your ability to make sound decisions. If you are faced with negative peer pressure, it is best to say "NO" and walk away.

Many people who try tobacco, alcohol, or other drugs soon find themselves addicted. **Addiction** is a person's physical or mental need for a drug or other substance. Many people die each year from alcohol and drug abuse. See Fig. 3-6.

## Avoiding High-Risk Behavior

Negative peer pressure can cause more than regrets. Accepting a ride from someone who has been drinking alcohol can result in injury or death from a serious accident. Sexual involvement can result in pregnancy. It can also have harmful, even life-threatening, results in the form of AIDS and other sexually transmitted diseases (STDs).

Responsible people avoid such risks, knowing that a healthy future is at stake. Refusing to participate in unsafe behaviors or activities is called **abstinence** (AB-stuh-nuhnts). To abstain means to say "NO" to sexual activity before marriage. It also means saying "NO" to the use of tobacco, alcohol, and other drugs. Abstinence is the only sure way to protect yourself against the potentially dangerous consequences of high-risk behaviors. By saying "NO" to behaviors that go against your values, you will feel better about yourself and have more self-respect.

**Fig. 3-6 Always think about the consequences before choosing to participate in any high-risk behavior. The price is never worth it.**

## Say "NO" to Negative Peer Pressure

Abstinence is the only sure way to be safe. Here are some ways to say no to peer pressure:

- This goes against my values.
- I don't want to get hooked on alcohol or drugs.
- I don't smoke.
- I value my life too much to do that.
- I am not into that—go away.
- I'm not ready. I want to wait until I'm married.
- I don't want to get AIDS or an STD.

# A CLOSER LOOK

## ...at Saying "NO"

You will be faced with many choices and situations—some will involve choosing the way you will behave toward others and some will involve reacting to how others behave toward you. Some situations will make you feel uncomfortable or put you in danger. Remember to "Say NO" in these situations.

☑ **Say "NO" to Tobacco, Alcohol, and Drugs**
True friends won't ask their friends to do things they don't want to do. You know what is right and wrong. Do not offer tobacco, alcohol, or drugs to anyone. Refuse any offers of these things from others. Stand up to peer pressure. "Say No."

☑ **Say "NO" to Bullying**
Never try to bully anyone, and do not allow yourself to be bullied, either. Bullies should not be allowed to hassle anyone. Get an adult to intervene if you are being bullied or if you see someone else being bullied.

☑ **Say "NO" to Shoplifting**
The penalties are never worth the price of stolen items. Shoplifters may think they won't get caught, but a clerk or hidden camera is always watching. The shame of shoplifting can ruin your life for a long time.

☑ **Say "NO" to Guns**
You know that guns are not toys and are dangerous. Never try to bring a gun to school. If someone asks to show you a gun at school, just walk away. Report the situation immediately to an adult.

☑ **Say "NO" to Strangers**
Never take anything from a stranger. Never go anywhere with a stranger. A person's looks can be deceiving. You won't know if their intentions are bad or good.

## ➤ Asserting Yourself

You will be better prepared to handle negative peer pressure if you learn how to use refusal skills and to act assertively. Being **assertive** means standing up for yourself in firm but positive ways.

Assertiveness means speaking in a confident manner, not giving in to others when you feel something is wrong, and standing up for what you believe. Assertive teens don't wait for someone else to decide what the group is going to do. They are the ones who suggest going skating, renting a video, or playing a computer game. Learning to be assertive will make you feel more in control of your life.

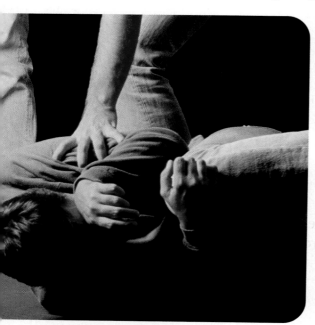

Fig. 3-7 Bullying is a coward's technique. Report bullying to a responsible adult.

### Handling a Bully

A bully is a person who physically or verbally abuses someone and intends to cause injury or discomfort with those actions. You may wonder why people become bullies. Many reasons exist, including the need for attention, feelings of low self-esteem, abuse in their own lives, or even peer pressure. See Fig. 3-7.

You can do your part to prevent bullying by following these tips:

- Tell your parents, a teacher, counselor, or another trusted adult if someone is bullying you or another person.
- Do not get angry and strike back.
- Either respond firmly or walk away.
- Stick up for another person who is being bullied.
- Stay away from bullies and the places they hang out.

# How To...

## Walk Away

### State the Task

- Recognize and walk away from negative situations.

### Develop a Plan

1. **Recognize the symptoms.** When you feel your heartbeat begin to race, your palms sweat, or the hairs on the back of your neck stand up, you're probably in an uncomfortable situation. Walk away when you are:

   - listening to gossip.
   - with a friend who is accepting drugs.
   - shoplifting.
   - joining a gang.
   - being asked to do something that you know is wrong.

   You have the power to walk away from these negative situations.

2. **Recognize why.** At times you will find yourself in negative situations. You should never stay in a negative situation. Learn to trust your instincts. It is okay to walk away.

### Implement the Plan

1. Think of a negative situation. List why you think the situation is negative.

2. Explain how you would walk away from the situation.
3. Explain why you chose to walk away.

### Evaluate the Result

1. Share your list with a few classmates. What was the most common negative situation listed in your group?
2. Choose one negative situation listed by someone in your group. How could this situation be avoided altogether?

**Adrenaline Surge. When faced with a threatening situation, your brain automatically triggers your adrenal glands to release more adrenaline (uh-DREH-nuh-luhn). This will increase your heart, pulse, and respiration rates, which in turn causes you to want to get away from the threat. The "fight-or-flight response" is your body's physical and mental response to a threat.**

# areer CHOICES

## Police Officer

Patrols assigned area. Controls disturbances of the peace, and arrests violators. Notes suspicious persons and establishments and reports to superior officer. Reports hazards. Breaks up unruly crowds at public gatherings. Directs and reroutes traffic around fires or other disruptions.

## Postal Clerk

Sells postage stamps, postal cards, and stamped envelopes. Registers and insures mail and computes mailing costs of letters and parcels. Weighs parcels and letters on scale and computes mailing cost based on weight and destination.

## Nurse Practitioner

Performs physical examinations and preventive health care within prescribed guidelines and instructions of an attending physician. Helps assess patient's clinical problems and health care needs. Discusses case with physician to prepare comprehensive patient care plan.

## Firefighter

Responds to fire alarms and other emergency calls. Uses ladders to gain access to upper levels of buildings or to rescue individuals from burning structures. Administers first aid and artificial respiration to injured persons and those overcome by smoke.

### AT School

Select three of the careers listed. Research the education, training, and work experience required for each career. Compare the results to select a career to investigate further.

### IN THE Workplace

List five other careers that help people in your community. Explain how people in these careers help others.

**Firefighters risk their lives for others every day. Their career choice includes keeping people safe. Are you interested in a similar career? Do some research to find out.**

# Chapter 3 Review & Activities

## Chapter Summary

- A friend is someone who shares your interests and goals.
- Friendships often change over time.
- Peer pressure can be either positive or negative.
- Deal with negative peer pressure by saying "NO" and walking away.
- Abstinence will protect you from the dangerous consequences of high-risk behaviors.

## Words You Learned

1. What is an acquaintance?
2. Define peers.
3. What are expectations?
4. What is the difference between positive and negative peer pressure?
5. Define addiction.

6. Why is abstinence the only sure way to protect yourself?
7. What does it mean to be assertive?

## Check Your Facts

1. What is the difference between an acquaintance and a friend?
2. Name four ways in which friends share and contribute to one another's lives.
3. Which qualities are the most important in a friendship?
4. Why can friendships change?
5. Name four ways to handle negative peer pressure.
6. Name two harmful substances.
7. Name three ways to say "NO" to peer pressure.
8. What can you do to prevent bullying behavior?

## Apply Your Learning

1. Why is it important to be yourself, no matter who your friends are?
2. Describe a situation in which you received positive peer pressure. How did this experience make you feel?
3. Describe a situation in which you received negative peer pressure. What was your response?
4. **Friendship T-Shirts.** You and your friend will need clean T-shirts, fabric markers, and cardboard. Slip cardboard inside each T-shirt. Use fabric markers to decorate each shirt with drawings and words that describe your friend. Trade shirts when you're both finished.

# Chapter *4*

# Communicating With Others

## You Will Discover . . .

- how to better communicate with others.
- the importance of being an effective listener.
- the importance of asking questions.
- reasons why conflicts occur.
- how to resolve conflicts.

**C**ommunication is the process of sending and receiving messages about ideas, feelings, and information. You began life communicating your needs to your parents. Then you learned to communicate for fun with your friends. Recognizing why communication is important, and how to do it properly, will help you better relate to others. This will also help you resolve conflicts.

## Key Words

- communication
- body language
- perceptions
- feedback
- gossip
- conflict
- prejudice
- compromise
- negotiation
- peer mediation

## ➤ Verbal Communication

Messages are sent with and without words. Verbal communication can be spoken or written. Whenever you use words to communicate, carefully select the right words to express yourself. Say what you think and feel, but always be polite.

Effective verbal communication guidelines include the following:

• **Speak for yourself.** Use "I" statements. Share your own experiences and feelings. Don't assume that other people know what you think, how you feel, or what you want. You have to tell them.

**Fig. 4-1** Listening is just as important as speaking. Are you a good listener?

• **Avoid speaking for others.** Don't assume that you know what other people think, how they feel, or what they want. Ask them. Let them speak for themselves.

• **Be clear and direct.** Tone of voice reveals your feelings. You send mixed messages if your tone does not match the words you are using.

• **Be aware of your listener.** Check to see that your listener understands what you are saying.

• **Ask questions.** Ask "who," "what," "when," "where," and "how" questions. These questions help others share their thoughts and feelings. See Fig. 4-1.

## ➤ Nonverbal Communication

Nonverbal communication is sent without using words. When you use nonverbal communication, you show how you feel about yourself and others. Here are three ways this is done.

• **Body language.** You communicate a lot through **body language**, or gestures and body movements. Sometimes you use body language as a substitute for words.

- **Physical appearance.** Your posture often signals your interest level. Your appearance conveys your self-image.
- **Personal space.** Your personal space is an invisible bubble that surrounds you. You use the space around you to communicate how you want to relate to others.

## ➤ Listening Is Key

The ability to listen is just as important as the ability to express yourself. Listening is not the same as hearing. When you hear, you are aware of the words being said. When you listen, you try to understand the message. If you are a poor listener, you are probably a poor communicator. You can improve your listening skills by using the following guidelines.

- Give your full attention to the speaker. Do not interrupt.
- Concentrate on what the speaker is saying, not on what you will say next.
- Listen for the overall meaning, not just the details.
- Remember to notice nonverbal cues.
- Avoid making quick judgments.
- Resist distractions.
- Give feedback to indicate you have understood.

### Patterns of Communication

Communication is only effective when you can exchange ideas or information. How well you listen affects your **perceptions**, or how you select, organize, and interpret information. As this occurs, relationships are built among people. Each person's interpretation of the message can prevent successful communication. Likewise, where we grew up, our educational background, and our cultural heritage affect how we communicate. Therefore, it is very important to learn how these factors affect the way verbal and nonverbal messages are sent and received. Do not expect everyone to use your communication style. The *Closer Look at Body Language* on pages 82-83 describes common communication patterns. Can you think of exceptions to these examples?

Effective Communication. **To be an effective communicator, remember to:**
- speak clearly.
- use appropriate language.
- use correct grammar and spelling.
- be a good listener.
- avoid giving mixed messages.
- use an appropriate tone of voice.

**DID YOU know?**

**Active Listening.** An active listener will restate what the speaker says to make sure he or she understands the message.

# A CLOSER L👓K

## ...at Body Language

Watch people when they aren't speaking and you will see they are still communicating. This type of communication is known as body language.

### LEANING FORWARD

When a person leans forward while having a conversation, it means the person is interested and responsive to what you are saying.

### HANDS ON HIPS

Placing hands on hips means a person is ready to get involved in the discussion.

## STARING DOWN

A person looking at the ground could be lying to you, guilty about something, disinterested, or simply showing a defeated attitude.

## SPACING OUT

A person staring into space is either bored or is contemplating an issue or idea. A blank stare might indicate boredom, while a slight smile could indicate an idea.

## BLUSHING

When a person's face reddens, it means the person is nervous, angry, or embarrassed about something. The person may also look away or down at the ground.

## ➤ Conversation

Conversation is the sharing of ideas, thoughts, and feelings. It is a two-way street. You must be willing to express yourself as well as to listen to others.

For a conversation to be interesting, it is important for each person to have a chance to talk. Keep conversations lively by including others.

You can draw others into conversation by finding out what their interests are. Most people like to talk about their own experiences and current events. It is important to give feedback during a conversation. **Feedback** is the response given to a message sent.

### Asking Questions

Asking good questions helps you find out about other people's interests. Consider the following example. Rena asks, "Do you like baseball?" Eric answers, "Yes." End of conversation. It has nowhere to go.

Suppose Rena had asked, "What did you think of the game today?" If Eric is interested in baseball, he will have something definite to say. This conversation is off to a good start.

Avoid asking "why" questions. A question such as, "Why did you change your mind?" forces the other person to explain or defend his or her actions. You also should avoid leading questions. For instance, the question "Don't you think that...?" is really a statement of what you think. It is designed to get the other person to agree with you.

### Avoiding Gossip

Do you know people who gossip? **Gossip** is talking about other people and their personal lives. It can destroy friendships and ruin reputations. Gossip can also lead to confrontations. By avoiding gossip you can show that you are a mature and responsible person. See Fig. 4-2.

Fig. 4–2 Gossip always harms someone. What should you do when a friend wants to gossip?

# Explore

## Creating a School Newsletter

### State the Task

• Create a school newsletter.

### Develop a Plan

1. Brainstorm topic ideas with your classmates. Some suggestions are sporting events; science, math, or speech events; your school's recycling program; a teacher's favorite recipe; and a list of upcoming events in your school.
2. Assign each person a topic to cover.
3. The reporting team should then research or attend the events you've decided to cover.

### Implement the Plan

1. Write down the information answering "who, what, when, where, how, and why." Think up a title for each article. Remember that the information should be short, to the point, and written in a conversational style.
2. Use a computer to input each article in a two-column format. Insert clip art, if desired. If clip art is not available, use colored pencils or markers to draw pictures to accompany each article.

3. Create a title for the front of your newsletter.
4. Print your newsletter, using both the front and back of each sheet.
5. Distribute the finished newsletter to your classmates.

### Evaluate the Result

1. What types of information did you include in your newsletter?
2. What was the reaction of other students when they read your newsletter?
3. What would you change about the process?

---

## Townsville Junior High News

**Townsville Tigers Win!**
Congratulations to the Townsville boy's track team for their win against Brownsville Thursday night! The parent club also had a great night. They sold popcorn at the meet and raised over $200 for the upcoming sports banquet.

**Welcome New Teachers**
Townsville Junior High welcomes Mrs. Canfield (8th grade science), Mr. Adamson (7th grade math), and Mr. Smith (physical education).

**Library Happenings**

• **On review.** Read a book and write a review. Your one page review should cover important points in the story without giving away the book's ending. Include the title and author of the book. Reviews will be on display at the library's front entrance.

• **Computer know-how.** Join the new computer club. Club members will share tips and shortcuts and learn to use new software. Limited Internet access will be allowed with parental permission.

• **Math blast.** Mr. Adamson will be available to tutor students in any grade in need of extra math help. Sign up at the library help desk.

**Office Staff Honors**
It's time to let all of the secretaries and administrative assistants now much you appreciate their hard work. Write them special notes and place them in one of the boxes in the main office or library. The deadline is May 10.

**Yearbook Savings**
Yearbooks will be on sale for only $15 during all lunch periods. After May 1 the price will go up to $20.00.

**Flag Team Auditions**
Townsville 8th graders who are going to Central High School next year may try out for the High School Cadette Flag team. Sign up to receive an information packet in the main office by Friday, May 12. Tryouts will be held May 26 in the high school gym. If you have questions please call Ms. Wright at 555-2838.

**Save Those Labels**
We need the help of several student volunteers to sort, count, and band our soup can labels. Please contact Miss Jones if you would like to help. Please keep saving the labels from Campbell's soup cans, V8 Splash fruit drinks, and Pepperidge Farms goldfish crackers (the FULL label, not just the UPC code). You may put your labels in the appropriate container in the school office. The more labels we save, the more items we can get for our school.

**Recycling Drive**
The Student Council will again hold a recycling drive the week of May 1st. Bring your bundled newspapers, plastic containers and aluminum cans to the recycling area in the cafeteria. Thanks to all who participated last month.

The Townsville Junior High Newsletter is published monthly by the Townsville publishing class. Editor: Chandler Bailey; Co-editor: Beth Curry, Proofreaders: Kyle Meyer and Kert Glenner. Copies are free in the cafeteria.

## ➤ Facing Conflict

Do you get along with everyone all of the time? If you are like most people, your answer is probably no. In fact, you might even find that lately you are getting into more arguments than you did when you were younger. That's because you are developing opinions of your own. Learning how to handle and communicate your opinions in a positive way is an important part of becoming an adult.

A **conflict** is any disagreement, struggle, or fight. Conflicts can occur just about anywhere, and everyone experiences them at one time or another. See Fig. 4-3. You have probably had disagreements with both friends and family members.

### Causes of Conflict

Think about the last time that you had a disagreement. Can you remember the cause? Maybe you felt that someone wasn't respecting your feelings. Perhaps you and the other person wanted two different things. Then again, maybe you wanted the same thing. On page 87 are some reasons why conflicts occur.

Fig. 4-3 Conflicts come in all sizes. Too much conflict can destroy a friendship. How can you avoid conflict?

- **Misunderstandings.** Conflicts often occur when people don't communicate effectively. Sometimes one person doesn't take the time to listen closely to what the other person is saying.
- **Differing opinions.** Culture can shape your opinions. You may also have your own opinions about a wide range of topics. If someone put down your favorite football team, for example, you might feel a need to defend your team.
- **Gossip and teasing.** When people gossip about or tease someone, it may start a conflict. For instance, if a group of teens started teasing your best friend about his braces, your friend would probably feel hurt and angry. You might feel angry, too.
- **Jealousy.** When one person envies something that someone else has, a conflict may occur. If you and a friend both tried out for the lead in the school play and your friend got the part, you might become jealous.
- **Prejudice.** Some conflicts are caused by **prejudice** (PRE-juh-dis), an opinion about people that is formed without facts or knowledge about those people. Prejudice causes people to judge others without taking the time to get to know them. Prejudice often leads to conflicts.

Fig. 4-4 Sometimes you need to be alone while thinking about a situation. By examining your behavior you may be able to prevent conflict.

## ➤ Preventing Conflict

You can prevent some conflicts by heading off problems before they start. The best way to do this is to pay attention to your own behavior. How do you treat others? Why do you say or do certain things? By exploring your actions, you may find that there are some qualities you can improve in yourself. For example, you might work on accepting other people as they are, even if they are different from you, and try looking at situations from their point of view. See Fig. 4-4.

**Conflict Resolution. The following techniques will help you resolve conflicts.**

- **Use effective communication skills.**
- **Control your anger.**
- **Listen to the other person.**
- **Negotiate a solution.**
- **Compromise to reach agreement.**

Learning to control your anger is another important way to prevent conflicts. Controlling anger is not always easy. When you feel yourself getting angry, try one or more of the following.

- Take a deep breath and count to ten.
- Go for a walk or a bike ride.
- Take a few minutes to have a "talk" with yourself. Remind yourself of the reasons why you don't want to act angry.
- Think about why you are feeling angry. Talk about your anger with a trusted adult.

## ➤ Resolving Conflict

If you do find yourself in a conflict, how do you handle it? You may have the urge to turn and run—or to leap in and fight. These are emotional reactions and they are natural. They will not solve your problems, however.

Conflict resolution means that you and the other person work out your differences in a way that satisfies both of you. You and the other person must work as a team. Try these basic guidelines to resolve conflicts.

- **Open communication lines.** The first step in conflict resolution is to open the lines of communication. Choose a neutral location that is quiet. You and the other person must both be willing to listen to each other and to explain your point of view.
- **State your viewpoint.** You should explain how you feel and how you see the problem. When you are talking, try not to start sentences with the word "you." The other person might feel attacked and stop listening. Start sentences with the word "I" instead. Express your point of view as clearly as possible. Try to stay calm, and avoid using an angry tone of voice.
- **Listen carefully.** When you are talking, you want the other person to listen. You should do the same. Don't interrupt. If you have questions, save them until the other person has finished. It is helpful if you sum up the other person's point of view to make sure that you understand it.

**88    Unit 1** Focusing on You

# Internet ACTIVITIES

1. **Search the Internet for information on the language of another culture and find out how "hello" is said in that language. Share the message with your classmates.**

   **Key Search Words:**
   - **language**
   - **communication**

2. **Find out more about the steps in the negotiation process by searching the Internet. Make a list of the steps you think are most important and why.**

   **Key Search Words:**
   - **negotiation**
   - **bargain**

- **Watch your body language.** The way you look at a person, the way you stand, and the way you move your body all communicate your feelings to others. You want your body language to show the same feelings as your words.

   Even if you are not involved in a conflict yourself, you can help other people solve conflicts with communication. Instead of taking sides, try to get the people involved to talk to each other. Giving friends this kind of support will help them see that they don't have to fight to impress anyone.

## Compromise

Resolving a conflict often means reaching a compromise. A **compromise** (KAHM-pruh-myz) is an agreement in which each person gives up something in order to reach a solution that satisfies everyone.

Negotiation is one of the best ways to compromise. **Negotiation** (ni-GOH-shee-AY-shuhn) is the process of talking about a conflict and deciding how to reach a compromise. This requires a lot of give-and-take, in which both sides give up some demands.

For negotiation to work, both sides must be willing to stop asking for certain things or at least change their demands. For instance, Rachel gets angry when her younger brother, Mark, borrows her CDs without asking. Mark, however, cannot always ask because Rachel is at basketball practice when he has time to listen to them. Perhaps Rachel could agree to let him borrow certain CDs when she is not home. In return, Mark could let her borrow his handheld electronic game without asking when she wants to play it after he has gone to bed.

- **Follow up.** When you are negotiating you must also make sure that you can follow through with your promises. If you agree to behave differently, you must actually do so. Otherwise, your agreement is worthless. For example, if you have agreed to stop teasing a friend about her haircut and she has agreed to stop teasing you about your clothes, you must both keep your word.

- **Get help.** Sometimes compromises can best be reached with the help of a third person who is not involved in the conflict. This person may be a parent, teacher, school counselor, or other trusted adult. Sometimes this third person is a peer. **Peer mediation** is a process by which peers help other students find a solution to a conflict before it becomes more serious. See Fig. 4-5.

Fig. 4–5 A peer mediator helps others resolve conflicts. **What personal qualities would a peer mediator need?**

## ➤ Avoiding Conflict

Let's say that you have made every effort to head off problems before they spark conflict. You have tried to resolve problems through communication, negotiation, and compromise. Still, a conflict is growing to a dangerous point. You are at school and a classmate is bullying you. What do you do? Sometimes the best response is to walk away. In such situations it is helpful to seek out and talk to an adult at school or at home. You can't solve every problem alone. What is important is that you do your best to behave in a way that reflects your values.

# How To...

## Conduct Peer Mediation

### State the Task

- Practice the steps in peer mediation.

### Develop a Plan

1. Make a set of rules for the process. Write them down.
2. Assign two students for the dispute and another to be the mediator.
3. Each student will tell his or her side of the story or complaint. If necessary, the mediator can meet with each person separately.
4. Create and discuss possible solutions.
5. Once a solution is reached, both students should sign a "contract" stating that they agree to the solution.

### Implement the Plan

1. Each student should tell his or her side of the story. Each student will listen quietly until the other is finished.
2. The mediator will discuss the stories with both students and ask any questions necessary.
3. The mediator should paraphrase the stories back to make sure he or she recognizes the issues.
4. Each side offers several solutions to the conflict.
5. The peer mediator chooses the best solution.
6. Both students sign a contract of agreement to the solution.

### Evaluate the Result

1. What problems did you encounter in this exercise?
2. Were you able to work out a solution to which both students agreed?
3. Would you make any changes to the process? Why or why not?
4. Do you think peer mediation could be a positive way to solve conflicts in your school? Why or why not?
5. Would you ever want to serve as a peer mediator in your school? Why or why not?

# Career CHOICES

## Speech Pathologist

Evaluates speech and language skills as related to educational, medical, social, and psychological factors. Plans, directs, or conducts treatment programs. Provides language development therapy. Administers and interprets specialized hearing and speech tests.

## Newscaster

Broadcasts news items of local, national, and international significance. Prepares or assists in preparation of script. Presents news over radio or television. May specialize in political, economic, or sports broadcasting.

## Advertising Sales Representative

Sells classified and display advertising space for print publications. Prepares list of potential customers. Obtains information concerning past and current advertising. Visits advertisers to point out advantages of placing ad space. Exhibits layouts for sales presentations.

## Actor

Plays roles in dramatic productions, commercials, or other media. Interprets or presents characterization to audience. Rehearses part and cues as directed. Interprets role by speech, gestures, and body movements to entertain or inform audience. May write or adapt own material.

## Public Relations Specialist

Plans and conducts programs designed to create and maintain a favorable public image for employers or clients. Prepares and distributes fact sheets, news releases, photographs, scripts, videos, CDs or DVDs to media representatives.

### AT School

Select three of the careers listed. Research the education, training, and work experience required for each career. Compare the results to select a career to investigate further.

### IN THE Workplace

Communication in the workplace continues to change. Make a list of all the ways people communicate in the workplace.

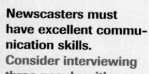

**Newscasters must have excellent communication skills.** Consider interviewing three people with careers in the field of mass communication.

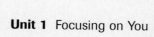

# Chapter 4 Review & Activities

## Chapter Summary

- Practice good communication skills by sending clear, direct messages.
- Listen carefully to understand the message being sent.
- Asking questions helps you find out about other people's interests.
- Conflicts can occur among friends, family members, and strangers.
- Resolving a conflict means working out differences through compromise.

## Words You Learned

1. Define communication.
2. How is body language a communication tool?
3. How does listening affect your perceptions?
4. Why is feedback important in a conversation?

5. Explain why gossip is dangerous.
6. What can cause conflict?
7. Define prejudice.
8. Why is it important to compromise?
9. What takes place during negotiation?
10. What is peer mediation?

## Check Your Facts

1. Name three forms of nonverbal communication.
2. Which of the listening skills do you think you do well? Which do you need to work on? Explain your answers.
3. What is the difference between compromise and negotiation?
4. Describe four basic ways to resolve a conflict.

## Apply Your Learning

1. Why is it important to listen when others are speaking?
2. Describe a situation in which you read another person's body language. What was the person saying to you nonverbally? How did you know that?
3. Describe a situation in which you experienced a conflict. How did you resolve it?
4. **Conversation or a letter?** Team up with another student. Have a conversation about your favorite sports star or musical group. Then write a letter on the same topic. Compare your conversation to the letter. Which did you like better—the conversation or writing and reading a letter? Explain why.

# Chapter 5

# Citizenship & Leadership

## You Will Discover . . .

- ways to be a good citizen.
- ways to build and demonstrate leadership skills.
- how team members work together to achieve goals.

## Key Words

- volunteer
- citizen
- citizenship
- leadership
- leader
- teamwork
- apathetic

Every Saturday Selena volunteers to pick up groceries for her elderly neighbor. Have you ever volunteered? A **volunteer** is a person who donates time and energy, without pay, to help others. Being a volunteer has many benefits. It makes you feel good about yourself. Volunteers also gain valuable experience and a sense of accomplishment. Being a volunteer makes you a contributor to your community.

## DID YOU know?

**Tutoring.** A fun volunteer activity is tutoring. Younger students always enjoy having some-one older to admire. You both will grow from a tutoring relationship.

## ➤ Citizenship

A **citizen** is a member of a community such as a city, state, or country. As a citizen you are entitled to certain rights, such as the right to vote. In return, you have responsibilities to your community, such as obeying the law.

The way you handle your responsibilities as a citizen is called **citizenship**. One of those responsibilities is to contribute to the community. Volunteering is a good way to demonstrate your citizenship skills. Why does being a volunteer make you feel good? You will discover that what you have given of yourself helps another person. This gives you a sense of accomplishment that is very satisfying. See Fig. 5-1.

There are many ways you can volunteer your talents and skills. For example, you can hand out magazines and newspapers to people in a hospital or nursing home. Another way you can volunteer is by teaching computer skills to a neighbor.

**Fig. 5-1 Volunteering will improve your self-esteem. What types of volunteer activities do you enjoy?**

# Explore

## Volunteer Opportunities

**Supplies**

- Newspapers
- Telephone directory
- Computer

### State the Task

- Participate in volunteer opportunities in your community.

### Develop a Plan

1. Make a list of volunteer activities that interest you. For example, if you love animals, a local animal shelter might be of interest. If you don't like the sight of blood, don't volunteer at a hospital.
2. Search through newspapers, the telephone directory, and the Internet for local volunteering opportunities. Call your public library and ask about various organizations that meet there. In addition to animal shelters and hospitals, consider a food pantry, nursing home, retirement community, park district, baseball stadium, or golf course, to name a few.
3. List several organizations that use volunteers on a sheet of paper.
4. Explain why you chose each organization and what you can contribute as a volunteer.

### Implement the Plan

1. Find out what type of help each organization needs from its volunteers. For example, the animal shelter might want you to play with the kittens, but you want to walk the dogs. Would you still want to volunteer your time there?
2. Make a list of what you find out and compare it with your values.
3. List the times each organization needs volunteers. Are you available? Do you have transportation?
4. Volunteer your time with at least one organization, if possible. Keep a journal of your experiences.

### Evaluate the Result

1. List the reasons you chose a specific volunteer opportunity.
2. Explain what you gained from the volunteer experience.
3. Would you volunteer with the same organization again? Why or why not?

In addition, you can show your citizenship skills by:

- taking a moment to pick up litter and put it in the proper place.
- returning lost items to the lost-and-found department or to the rightful owner.
- caring for pets when neighbors go out of town.

Whether you demonstrate your citizenship skills alone or in a group, being a good citizen gives you a sense of belonging. You also are able to develop skills that could possibly lead you into a career. What other ways can you think of to show your citizenship skills?

## Making Connections

**Social Studies.** Many immigrants become citizens of the United States. Immigrants are people who come from one country to live in another.

### Get Involved!

Research the requirements to become a citizen of the United States. Prepare a presentation to share with the class.

## ➤ Leadership

**Leadership** is the direction, or guidance, that helps a group accomplish its goals. Every group needs a **leader**, a person with the ability to guide and motivate others. Leaders can be found in front of the team, showing the way, or they may be in the background, encouraging others. Leaders must use good communication skills and know how to work with people. See Fig. 5-2.

Sometimes leaders are chosen or elected. For example, the captain of your hockey team and the mayor of your

increase renewable energy use in the United States

Fig. 5-2 A leader motivates others to accomplish goals. School and community organizations offer many leadership opportunities.

community were probably elected. At other times the job of a leader is not a formal one. For example, when you organize a birthday party for a friend or get your siblings to help rake the leaves without being asked, you are being a leader.

You can become a good leader by following these tips:

- **Motivate others by setting a good example.** Be the first person to jump in and work on a project.
- **Encourage others with positive words.** You can always find something nice to say.
- **Know when to share responsibilities.** Don't try to do every job yourself. Share the work, and the fun, with others.
- **Have a positive attitude about every task.** Even the jobs that aren't considered fun are important. A positive attitude can make the difference in how well a job gets done.
- **Get all of the facts before making a decision.** You should never make a snap decision. Investigate the details first.

## ➤ Teamwork

A group such as a family, a school, or a community needs all of its members to work together. When people use **teamwork**, everyone works together to reach a goal. Without the cooperation and support of all members, a team cannot operate effectively. See Fig. 5-3. For example, you demonstrate teamwork when you:

- participate in a school fundraiser.
- play on a sports team.
- join the student council.
- pitch in to help your family with yard work.
- take part in a walk-a-thon.

**Fig. 5-3 Teamwork requires that everyone be involved.** Which person below is not demonstrating teamwork? How does this picture differ from the one on the next page?

**Serve as part of the team, not the boss.** Get everyone involved. Ask for and listen to everyone's opinion. Let group members help set goals and make decisions.

When you interact with other people you will find they have many different personalities, opinions, and ways of doing things. Here are a few tips:

- Be respectful of others.
- Be tolerant of different opinions and ideas. Everyone does not think the same. Keep an open mind.
- Be considerate of other people's feelings.
- Don't say everything that is on your mind, even when you think you're right.
- Take every opportunity to compliment others.
- Don't let an **apathetic** (AP-uh-THEH-tik) person, or someone who lacks interest, distract you from your task. Invite the person to get involved. Stay positive and keep your energy focused on the goal.

**Encourage team spirit.** Be enthusiastic and positive. Use effective communication skills.

**Show appreciation.** Thank people who help the group reach its goal. Tell people that you appreciate their efforts.

# How To...

## Elect a Classroom Council

### State the Task

- Establish a Classroom Council.

### Develop a Plan

1. Students are nominated by their classmates. Those interested in running for election should inform their teachers and classmates. The Council will consist of three officers and three members at-large. Nominees may run for the positions of: President, Vice President, Secretary/Treasurer, or Class Representative.
2. A date is set for the election. Ballots listing each candidate's name can be created on the computer. A voting area should be set up in the classroom. Use a secure box to hold the ballots until they can be counted.
3. Nominees will be allowed to make a two-minute campaign presentation to their classmates. Campaign posters may be displayed on the day of the election.

### Implement the Plan

1. Each student is allowed one vote. Student volunteers should monitor the voting area. These same volunteers count the ballots and announce the election results.
2. Once elected, the Classroom Council should meet to discuss projects and activities. Suggestions might be to take responsibility for a school hallway or to organize a clothing drive.
3. Students who were not elected to the Classroom Council also participate in the meetings.
4. The Council should conduct all business using parliamentary procedure. Once all discussion is heard, the Council votes on the project or activity. The majority rules.

### Evaluate the Result

1. How did your classmates react to electing a Classroom Council?
2. Would you change any part of the process? Why or why not?

## ➤ Good Manners

Your home is where you first learn to respect yourself. Your parents probably taught you at an early age to share your toys and say "please" and "thank you." That's just the beginning of good manners. Here are some other tips to use at home, at school, and in your community.

- When you bump into someone, say "Excuse me."
- Don't cut in line. Wait your turn.
- If you knock something over, pick it up. Don't leave the mess for someone else to clean up. See Fig. 5-4.
- Apologize when you make a mistake.
- Don't disrupt someone when he or she is speaking. Wait until the person is finished speaking.
- Open doors for people when you reach the entryway first.
- Always be courteous when playing sports, whether you win or lose.
- Practice good table manners. This shows respect for others.

**Fig. 5-4** Always clean up after yourself. Using good manners is appropriate in every situation.

## Internet ACTIVITIES

1. **Search the Internet for information on a person you consider to be a leader. Write a list of that person's leadership qualities. Create a list of guidelines that teens could use to develop leadership skills.**

   Key Search Words:
   - **famous leaders**
   - **historical leaders**

2. **Good manners should be used by everyone. Search the Internet for information on manners and etiquette. Share your findings with your classmates.**

   Key Search Words:
   - **manners**
   - **etiquette**

# A CLOSER LOOK

## ...at Citizenship Skills

**You can learn and practice**

**good citizenship skills when**

**you follow these guidelines:**

### Do Your Share

Offer to pitch in and help. Look for ways that you can lend a hand to family members, neighbors, teachers, and friends. Volunteer to help at school or in your community. Get involved in a community-sponsored event, such as a park clean-up or recycling campaign.

### Show Respect for Others

Treat others as you would like to be treated. For example, wait your turn instead of trying to get to the front of a line. Give others in your family a chance to use the telephone. Speak respectfully to adults—including parents, grandparents, teachers, and police officers. Remember to show respect for everyone, not just people you know well or especially like.

### Help Other Students

Make new students feel comfortable, and introduce them to other people. If someone holds different values from yours, be open and accepting. When you disagree with someone, give that person a fair chance to explain his or her opinion.

### Take Care of Shared Property

Be as careful with library books or park equipment as you would be with your own possessions. Then the next person will be able to use and enjoy them too. The same is also true for recreation areas, school buildings, and streets and sidewalks.

# Career CHOICES

### State Legislator

Helps establish laws and policies in accordance with the state constitution and by-laws. Addresses concerns of citizens. Reviews reports and financial statements to determine progress and status. Gives speeches and travels his or her state to meet with citizens.

### Park Naturalist

Plans, develops, and conducts programs to inform public of historical, natural, or scientific features of parks. Works with park staff to determine program schedule. Surveys park conditions. Presents lectures, constructs visitor displays, and guides field trips in the park.

### Hospital Housekeeper

Cleans hospital patient rooms, bathrooms, laboratories, offices, halls, and other areas. Washes bed linens and remakes beds. Replaces soiled drapes and cubicle curtains. Keeps utility and storage rooms in clean and orderly condition.

### Election Clerk

Compiles and verifies voter lists from official registration records. Requests voter identification at polling place. Distributes ballots to voters and answers questions concerning voting procedures. Counts valid ballots and prepares official reports of election results.

### Umpire

Officiates at sporting events. Observes actions of participants to make sure that rules are not broken. Decides the outcome of close plays according to established regulations. Makes sure all plays are fair.

**AT School**

Select three of the careers listed. Research the education, training, and work experience required for each career. Compare the results to select a career to investigate further.

**IN THE Workplace**

People in community service positions practice good citizenship skills. What type of volunteer work could you do now that might lead you into a community service career?

**A park naturalist loves the outdoors and cares about plants, animals, and people.** Consider the wide variety of community service careers by job shadowing someone in that field.

# Chapter 5 Review & Activities

## Chapter Summary

- Doing volunteer work is a good way to demonstrate your citizenship skills.
- Leaders motivate people.
- A group of people can work as a team to achieve a goal.
- Manners should be used at home, at school, and in your community.

## Words You Learned

1. How does a volunteer differ from an employee?
2. What is a citizen?
3. Define citizenship.
4. What is leadership?
5. What makes a person a good leader?
6. How do you show teamwork when you participate in a team sport?
7. Describe a person who is apathetic.

## Check Your Facts

1. What are some benefits of being a volunteer?
2. Name two ways that you can practice your citizenship skills.
3. List five ways to build leadership skills.
4. How does teamwork help everyone accomplish goals?
5. List three things to keep in mind when working with others.
6. Where do you first learn manners?

## Apply Your Learning

1. Name some volunteers who are working to make life better for the people in your community. Share articles that describe their activities.
2. Describe the responsibilities citizens have to their communities.
3. Describe a community group for which you could volunteer. How could you make a difference?
4. **Reading Roundup.** Team up with a kindergartener, a neighbor, or younger sibling and read a book together. Write a children's story and draw pictures to go with it. Bind the "book" together with yarn or ribbon. Read your story to a young friend and discuss the characters. Give the book to your young friend to enjoy again later.

# Chapter 6

# Managing Your Life

## You Will Discover . . .

- the importance of making short-term and long-term goals.
- how to set realistic goals.
- the difference between routine and major decisions.
- how to make responsible decisions.

## Key Words

- goal
- long-term goals
- short-term goals
- trade-off
- decisions
- alternatives
- consequences

Can you list the things that are important to you? Having things to strive for gives purpose and direction to life. Just as in sports, scoring life goals takes strategy and skill. Others can help you achieve your goals. If you know what is important to you, it is easier to set goals and make decisions that will help you reach them.

## ➤ Goal Setting

Goals are essential for success in life. A **goal** is something you want to achieve. Your goal may be becoming the class treasurer, learning how to fly a plane, or earning a college degree. A goal serves as a guide for what you do and gives you something to work toward. Personal goals help you do your best and achieve the things you want in life. See Fig 6-1.

### Long-Term & Short-Term Goals

Even though you may not often think about setting goals, you do it all the time. Some of your goals may take a long time to reach—months or even years. These are called **long-term goals**. Your long-term goals may include owning a car, going to college, or saving enough money to buy a new computer.

**Short-term goals** can be reached quickly, perhaps in a few days or weeks. Your short-term goals might include completing a science project or passing a math test.

Sometimes short-term goals can help you achieve a long-term goal. Setting short-term goals, such as completing a CPR course, can prepare you for your long-term goal of becoming an emergency medical technician. What are your short-term goals? What are your long-term goals? See Fig. 6-2.

### Setting Realistic Goals

When you set goals, you need to make sure that they are realistic. If your goals are too hard to reach, you may become discouraged and give up. If they are too easy, you may lose interest in them. Realistic goals are both reachable and challenging.

**Fig. 6-1 Reaching your goal is a rewarding experience.** What are some of your goals?

**Success.** People who set specific goals and make a clear plan to reach them are more likely to succeed than those who do not have a plan.

**CHECK the Facts**

The way you set your goals has a lot to do with your success. Your goals should be:

- **Specific.** You will have something to work toward.
- **Challenging.** You will stay interested.
- **Organized.** You know which goal to work on first, second, and so on.
- **Realistic.** You can reach your goals.
- **Evolving.** You can change your plans if you need to.

Goal setting requires planning. By identifying a long-term goal and making a list of what must be done to reach it, you establish a plan. Each step you take toward that long-term goal could become a short-term goal. Creating a plan that includes short-term goals as well as long-term goals will provide you with the needed direction to be a success. A written plan really helps you see progress.

Fig. 6-2 Completing a science fair project was Melissa's short-term goal. Her long-term goal is to become a botanist.

Internet
ACTIVITIES

1. **Search the Internet for information on how to achieve goals. Write down some tips to share with your classmates.**

Key Search Words:
- goal setting
- achievement

2. **Search the Internet for information on three types of careers that interest you. Make a list of goals you would have to reach before entering these careers.**

Key Search Words:
- careers
- career goals

**Fig. 6–3 Achieving a goal deserves a reward. Would this "A" make you feel rewarded?**

## Achieving Your Goals

Achieving your goals is not something that just happens. You have to plan how you will reach each goal. Writing down the goal is a good first step. This will help you get a clear picture of what you want to accomplish.

You also need to determine what resources will be required to reach your goal. Your resources include your time, money, energy, knowledge, and skills. Your family and friends are also resources that are available to you. Using your resources wisely helps you achieve goals. See Fig. 6-3.

You may need to plan more than one way to reach your goal in case your first plan doesn't work. For example, suppose that you want to take up a new sport. If you find that you don't like team sports, you could try an individual sport such as swimming, jogging, or biking.

## Attitude Counts

A positive attitude goes a long way toward helping you achieve your goals. Your attitude is the way you feel about something. A positive attitude helps you do your best even if the task is something you do not enjoy. It helps you tackle a difficult job rather than put it off. It also helps you be flexible when things don't go exactly as you had planned. A positive attitude will help you be successful in whatever you try to accomplish.

## Setting Priorities

Some of your goals will be more important to you than others. You may even find that two or more goals are in conflict with each other. When this happens, you need to set priorities for your goals. This will let you concentrate on the goals that are most important to you.

Setting priorities for your goals may involve making trade-offs. A **trade-off** is something that you give up in order to get something more important. For example, if being on the debate team is very important to you, you may need to put off trying out for the band.

# How To...

## Create a Goal-Setting Worksheet

### State the Task

- Outline your short-term and long-term goals.

### Develop a Plan

1. Divide a sheet of paper into two columns.
2. Answer the following questions on the left column of the sheet:
   - What are your goals for this year?
   - What are your goals for the next five years?
   - What are your goals for the next ten years?
3. In the right column across from each goal, list what you hope to receive when you accomplish the goal. For example, you may receive praise, self-esteem, a good grade, or family commitment.

### Implement the Plan

1. On a separate sheet of paper, list what steps you need to take to accomplish your goals for this year.
2. Make a list of the activities you will do during the next month that relate to your goals for this year.
3. How will you feel when you accomplish each of the steps relating to your goals? List the rewards.

### Evaluate the Result

1. What did you learn from this exercise?
2. Will you change any of your goals? Explain your answer.
3. How can you continue this process to help you reach your future goals?

**Goals. Remember these tips about setting goals:**

- **Set realistic goals.**
- **Set challenging goals.**
- **Set realistic limits for achieving goals.**
- **Revise your goals as needed.**

## Successful Experiences

As you experience success in reaching your goals, you will begin to feel good about yourself. Having successful experiences will help you grow and develop during your teen years. You will want to set new goals and to try new things. This will add to your sense of personal worth. See Fig. 6-4.

There may be times when you do not achieve all the goals you set for yourself. If you fail to reach a goal, try to figure out what went wrong. Was your goal realistic? Did you have a clear picture of what you wanted to accomplish? Did you use your resources wisely and plan alternative ways to reach your goal? Did you have a positive attitude? Did you set priorities? Knowing what went wrong will help you improve your chances for success the next time.

**Fig. 6-4** Experiencing success as a teen will help you achieve success throughout life. Why is this true?

## ➤ Decision Making

You will make many **decisions**, or choices, in your life. Each day you have the choice of what to eat for lunch, what to do with your free time, and how hard to study. In fact, life is made up of all kinds of decisions.

You will find that being successful in life depends a lot on your ability to make wise decisions. Learning to make good decisions now will help you make more difficult decisions as you get older. The ability to make decisions gives you a sense of independence.

Decisions are made in several different ways.

- **Planned decisions.** You weigh all the facts before making a choice.
- **Default decisions.** You let someone else, or the circumstances, make the decision.
- **Impulse decisions.** You take the first alternative available.

- **Emotional decisions.** You choose the alternative that "feels right," without thinking it through.
- **Resistance decisions.** You choose the alternative that will result in the least amount of conflict.

Sometimes you make decisions by responding to something that has happened, such as deciding to start an exercise routine after doing poorly in gym class. You also make decisions that cause something to happen, such as deciding to be honest so that your family can trust you. Even if you decide not to decide, such as not responding to an invitation to a party, you have made a decision. Failing to make a decision is like deciding to leave the outcome to chance.

Fig. 6-5 Buying groceries involves making decisions. Make a list of all the decisions you have made today.

The decisions you make now will affect the choices you have in the future. For example, deciding now to explore different careers will make you aware of your **alternatives**, or choices, and will give you more to choose from later on. What other ways can you think of in which the decisions you make now will affect your future choices? See Fig. 6-5.

## Making Responsible Decisions

Learning to make responsible decisions will give you a sense of control over your life. Instead of accepting whatever happens to you, you can help control how things happen. See Fig 6-6.

Here are some suggestions to help you make responsible decisions.

- **Use good timing.** Make your decisions at the right time. Avoid making quick decisions. Give yourself time to consider all the facts. On the other hand, don't put off a decision too long. If you do, you may find that some of your options are no longer available.

| Decision-Making Process |
|---|
| 1. Identify the decision to be made or the problem to be solved. |
| 2. List all the possible alternatives. |
| 3. Choose the best alternative. |
| 4. Act on the decision. |
| 5. Evaluate the decision. |

**Fig. 6-6** The decision-making process is a good guide to use when faced with complex situations.

**DID YOU know?**

**Priorities.** The personal priorities that you set have a direct impact on the decisions you make. For example, going to college is Ida's priority. She has a summer job that pays well. When Ida's friends invited her to spend a week at the beach she declined. Her priority of saving money for college helped her make that decision. What are your personal priorities? How do they influence your decisions?

- **Consider the consequences.** Think about how your decision will affect your life now and in the future. **Consequences** (CAHN-suh-kwen-sez) are the results of your choice. How will your decision affect you, your family members, or friends?
- **Be willing to take risks.** Any time you make a decision, there is a risk involved. There is always a chance that you will make a mistake. You must have the courage to act on your decisions despite the risk.
- **Seek advice when you need it.** Advice from family members and friends can help you make decisions. Sometimes they have had to make similar decisions. Listen to others and use their advice if it is helpful.
- **Accept responsibility for your decisions.** Making your own decisions means accepting responsibility for the choices you make. You cannot make excuses or blame others when you make a poor decision. Accepting responsibility for your decisions and the consequences of those decisions is a sign of maturity.

# Explore

## Decision Making

### State the Task

- Use the decision-making process to make a decision.

### Develop a Plan

1. Think of a situation or a problem you are facing. Write it down.
2. Identify the decision you must make. Be clear about the real question facing you before you look for the best answer.
3. List the possible alternatives. Usually more than one is available to you.
4. Think about the advantages and disadvantages of each alternative. Ask yourself, "What would happen if I...?" Consider your needs, wants, and goals. Thinking through all the possibilities will help you make a better decision.
5. Choose the best alternative. Use your values as guidelines to make your decision. You will not be happy with a decision that goes against your values.

### Implement the Plan

1. Make a decision and act on it. A decision is not a real decision until you take action.
2. After you have made a decision, you must take responsibility and follow through.

### Evaluate the Result

1. Was your decision the best one? Analyzing the outcome will help you make decisions in the future.
2. Are you satisfied with the results? Explain your answer.
3. Was there a better alternative than the one you chose? If so, write down why you may make a different decision in the future.

Resources. **It is important to make the best use of all resources available when making decisions. Here are a few resources to consider:**

- **Information**
- **Advice from others**
- **Past experiences**
- **Time**
- **Energy**
- **Money**

# A CLOSER LOOK

## ...at Decisions

You'll have to make many types of decisions throughout your life. Some will be easy, routine decisions. Others will be major, life-altering choices. Think carefully before making decisions.

### Everyday Decisions

Some decisions are choices that you make every day. They usually do not require a lot of time or thought. Deciding what clothes to wear is a routine decision. It is important to you at the time, but it really does not change your life very much.

## Decisions with Long-Term Effects

Decisions that have long-term effects on your life are major decisions. Some of the major decisions you will make as a teen are what courses you choose to take in high school and whether to get a part-time job.

## Decisions That Become Habits

Some routine decisions become habits. These are decisions that you repeat without thinking about it. For example, you probably do your homework everyday.

## Life-Changing Decisions

Some major decisions, such as whether or not to go to college, can be life changing. They require much time and thought and may be difficult to make. They are decisions that will impact you throughout your life.

# Career CHOICES

## Coach

Prepares players and athletes for games and athletic competitions. Coaches players individually or in groups by showing them what to do. Oversees practice sessions. Instructs players in areas where they need help. Determines strategy during game, independently or with other coaches.

## Airline Pilot

Flies airplanes that transport passengers, mail, or freight. Makes decision as to how to operate in certain weather conditions and follows schedule. Con-trols airplane according to flight plan and government regulations. Logs information, such as time in flight, altitude, and fuel consumed.

## Air-Traffic Controller

Controls air traffic according to established procedures. Prevents collisions and minimizes delays arising from too much traffic. Answers radio calls from arriving and departing aircraft. Issues landing and take-off instructions and information. Alerts airport emergency crew and other designated personnel when needed.

**Airline pilots have a stressful job. They must stay alert at all times.** Consider how well you might be suited for this career.

## Scientist

Prepares samples and performs laboratory tests. Creates reports and research papers. Makes formal presentations of research findings. Works with private and public institutions, corporations, and organizations.

### AT School

Select three of the careers listed. Research the education, training, and work experience required for each career. Compare the results to select a career to investigate further.

### IN THE Workplace

Make a list of jobs that require decision making that could save someone's life.

## Chapter Summary

- Short-term goals can be reached more quickly than long-term goals, which may take months or even years.
- Realistic goals are goals you can reach.
- Make responsible decisions by considering the consequences of each alternative and accepting responsibility for your decisions.

## Words You Learned

1. What are goals?
2. What can you do now to work toward a long-term goal?
3. Describe one of your short-term goals.
4. What is a trade-off?
5. Describe two decisions you made last week.

6. Define alternatives.
7. How are consequences different from decisions?

## Check Your Facts

1. Why is it important to set realistic goals?
2. How can short-term goals contribute to long-term goals?
3. Why is it necessary to set priorities for your goals?
4. Give an example of a decision you might make now that could affect you in the future.
5. Why do people sometimes make decisions by default?
6. What are four tips for making responsible decisions?

## Apply Your Learning

1. Describe the steps in the decision-making process.
2. Describe a long-term goal. What steps can you take to reach that goal?
3. **Mystery lunch.** Sometimes decision making can be fun. Get together with several of your friends and plan a mystery lunch. Have each person write down a type of sandwich and fruit he or she likes on a small piece of paper. Fold the papers up, drop them in a box or hat, and mix them up. Ask each person to draw one of the slips of paper. After guessing whose lunch it is, each person agrees to prepare a mystery lunch the next day.

# UNIT 2

# Charting Your Future

# Chapter 7

# Exploring Careers

## You Will Discover . . .

◆ considerations for choosing a career.
◆ why you should plan your career path.
◆ how to research careers.
◆ reasons why people work.

## Key Words

◆ aptitudes
◆ networking
◆ entrepreneur

"What do you want to be when you grow up?" You have probably heard that question before. Have you really thought about your answer? Perhaps you are interested in becoming a gourmet chef or an astronaut. You have many choices. Whether you choose to be a full-time homemaker or a musician, it is not too soon to start thinking about the career you might want to pursue.

## ➤ Exploring Your Options

It is a good idea to start exploring career opportunities now. That way you will be better prepared to make a career choice. When you think about your options, consider your strengths, interests, abilities, values, and goals. Decisions based on these factors will lead you to work you enjoy. By asking other people how they got started in a career, you might get ideas for your own life.

### Career Planning

It is a good idea to begin planning a career path. Thinking ahead will give you time to learn some of the specific skills that will help you get a job. It will also help you determine what kind of education and training you will need for the career you choose. For example, if you enjoy math or science in school, you may choose a career in accounting or medicine. See Fig. 7-1. To make a career plan, follow these steps.

Fig. 7-1 If you enjoy science, there are many careers you can explore.

1. List all the careers that interest you.
2. Gather occupational and labor market information about each career.
3. Compare what you know about yourself to the information you gathered about each career.
4. Choose a career that best matches what you know about yourself and create a career plan.
5. Review your career plan often and modify it as needed.

When considering a career, you should also think about your values and goals. What is important to you? What do you want to do with your life? Do you want to help other people? Consider a career in health services. Do you like to build things? Look into construction or architecture. Knowing your values and goals will help you focus on an area that suits the sort of person you are.

If you can't decide, there are special tests that can help you discover your aptitudes. **Aptitudes** are natural abilities or talents. An aptitude test predicts a person's ability to learn certain skills. A test of this kind can help reveal your strengths. However, it may not take into consideration your interests. For example, the field of family and consumer sciences includes a wide variety of career options. The chart below shows eight career clusters within Family and Consumer Sciences and the career fields that they include. Can you name a career that fits each of the eight career clusters?

## Family & Consumer Sciences

### Child Development, Education & Services Careers

- Business & Management
- Arts & Communication
- Human Services & Education

### Consumer & Resource Management Careers

- Human Services & Education
- Natural Resources
- Business & Management

### Family Studies Careers

- Health & Medical
- Business & Management
- Human Services & Education

### Hospitality Careers

- Arts & Communication
- Business & Management
- Human Services & Education

### Nutrition & Wellness Careers

- Natural Resources
- Health & Medical
- Human Services & Education

### Food Science & Technology Careers

- Health & Medical
- Natural Resources
- Human Services & Education

### Textiles & Apparel Careers

- Engineering & Industrial
- Arts & Communication
- Natural Resources

### Environmental Design Careers

- Arts & Communication
- Engineering & Industrial
- Human Services & Education

# A CLOSER LOOK

## ...at Researching Jobs

**When you know what to expect from a job, it will be easier to decide which one really interests you. Here are some points you will want to research.**

### Educational Requirements

What education is required for the job? You may need a college degree or proper certification in the field.

### Job Responsibilities

What responsibilities or duties are performed on the job? Your workday may include different tasks or require you to perfect certain tasks.

## Salary Potential

What is the average income of entry-level workers in this position? Your job performance will directly impact your income level.

## Promotion Opportunities

What opportunities for promotion exist? You may have to travel or move to a different location. Additional training may be required.

## Working Conditions

What are the working conditions? You may be required to attend safety orientation or training on the job.

## Future of Field

Will there be a need for more workers in this field in the future? You will likely have to upgrade your education or training to stay employed.

## ➤ Researching Careers

Talk over career possibilities with your parents, family members, school counselors, and teachers. They can offer you advice and answer questions. Choose a few careers that interest you and do some basic research. See Fig. 7-2.

When researching a career, you need to gather the following information:

- Education and training requirements.
- Job responsibilities.
- Working conditions.
- Salary potential.
- Promotion opportunities.
- Job outlook.

### Networking

If you've ever followed up on a job tip you received from a family member or friend, you have practiced networking. **Networking** means making use of personal connections to achieve your goals. When you seek job information from people you know, you have a good chance of going into the job application process informed and confident. Networking is the most direct way of finding a job. In addition to networking with your family members and relatives, you can also network with:

- friends and classmates.
- teachers and mentors.
- employers and coworkers.
- school organizations such as FCCLA.
- community organizations.

When you network, be courteous. Don't pressure people for information. If you are given a job lead, follow up in a responsible manner. It is important to follow up when someone passes on information that can help you. Your behavior reflects not only on you, but on the person who recommended you.

**Fig. 7-2 Many skilled workers learn their trade in formal apprenticeship programs.**

## Professional Organizations

Another source of job postings is professional organizations. These organizations are made up of people already employed in a field. You must pay a membership fee to join professional organizations. The services they offer include employment listings, job placement services, scholarships, and network opportunities.

## The Internet

You can also learn about careers through the Internet. Ask your librarian to recommend some Web sites.

Thousands of employment resources are available on the Internet. You can:

- Search *The Occupational Outlook Handbook* or the *Dictionary of Occupational Titles*.
- Read job postings and job descriptions.
- Post a résumé.
- Check out professional organizations.
- Register with on-line employment agencies.

**FCCLA.** Family, Career and Community Leaders of America is a national organization of middle and high school students enrolled in family and consumer sciences courses. FCCLA activities provide opportunities for leadership development. Students can also participate in STAR events. Check the Internet for more information.

1. **Search the Internet for careers that are likely to be in demand in the future. Make a list of careers that interest you. Share your list with your classmates.**

   Key Search Words:
   - **employment projections**
   - **occupational outlook**

2. **Search the Internet for different types of career assessments. Make a list of your key traits to see what career opportunities might fit you.**

   Key Search Words:
   - **career assessments**
   - **personality tests**

# How To...

## Figure Education & Training Costs

**State the Task**

- Figure the costs of higher education and training.

**Develop a Plan**

1. Find out approximately how much money you will need for education and training after high school. Your options include: loans, scholarships, grants, military aid, and holding a job.

2. Grant and scholarship applications always have deadlines. Find out what kind of paperwork you will need to complete. Make a list. If you do not meet the deadlines, you will not be eligible for aid.

**Implement the Plan**

1. Search for the names of grants and scholarships in the career guidance office at school, on the Internet, and at your local library and bookstores. Many schools and communities have special scholarships set up to honor past students or important people from their community. Make a list of the opportunities available.

2. Find out what you have to do to win or earn a grant or scholarship. There are athletic scholarships, academic scholarships, and others that might require you to show financial need to qualify. It is very important that you follow the directions exactly when submitting your application.

3. Make a list of what you would need to do to apply for one local grant or scholarship and one national grant or scholarship. Compare the differences.

4. Find out with whom you would follow up about the status of your application.

**Evaluate the Result**

1. For what types of grants and scholarships are you eligible?

2. Was there any part of the process that you found difficult? If so, what was it and why?

## ➤ Preparing for Work

Without a high school education your job opportunities will be limited. Your school counselor will have a lot of information. There are many ways to continue your education and training after high school. See Fig. 7-3. You may choose to:

- **attend college.** Community colleges, four-year colleges, and universities offer degrees in a wide variety of fields.
- **enroll at a career and technical center.** A technical training program will train you for specific occupations, such as computer programming, automotive technology, or the culinary arts.

**Fig. 7-3 Education and training continue beyond high school. What plans do you have after high school graduation?**

- **get a job.** Some companies use on-the-job training. Others will help you go to school while you're working. Many offer formal apprenticeship programs that require both coursework and work experience.
- **join a branch of the military.** You can get training in specified fields and save money for college. You may even decide to choose a military career.

## Working Part-Time

Before you look for a full-time job, you will probably have part-time jobs. You can get valuable experience by babysitting or delivering newspapers and by working in restaurants, businesses, and stores. See Fig. 7-4.

Part-time employment is part of your preparation for full-time employment. Part-time work helps you:

- learn to get along with your supervisors and coworkers.
- find out how you like a certain type of work.
- gain work experience that will be helpful when you apply for a full-time job.
- become aware of job requirements and other qualities that you need to acquire for full-time work.

**Fig. 7-4 Part-time jobs provide valuable work experience. What types of part-time jobs have you held?**

# Explore

## Your Career Interests

### State the Task

- Identify careers related to your personal interests.

### Develop a Plan

1. Make a list of all of the activities you enjoy.
2. Identify your interests and the careers they might match.
3. Research five careers that interest you by looking on the Internet and by talking to people who already have jobs in those fields.

### Implement the Plan

1. Compare your list of interests to five careers that interest you. Consider researching some of the careers listed on this page.
2. Make a list of the careers you want to research further.
3. Make a list of the type of education or job training you will need for each career.

### Evaluate the Result

1. Make a list of goals that you will need to meet in order to get the career you want.
2. Which career on your list did you find surprising? Why?
3. Make a file for your potential careers. Add to the file as you discover new careers of interest.

**Career Fields to Investigate**

- Arts & Communication
- Business & Management
- Child Development, Education & Services
- Consumer & Resource Management
- Engineering & Industrial
- Environmental Design
- Family & Consumer Sciences Education
- Family Studies & Human Services
- Health & Medical
- Hospitality
- Human Services
- Natural Resources
- Nutrition & Wellness
- Food Science & Technology
- Textiles & Apparel

## Using Technology at Work

At work, you can use technology as effectively as you use any other resource. Depending on your job, this may mean knowing how to operate anything from an electronic ordering system to an aerospace production line. No matter what your job, here are some tips to keep in mind:

- **Don't expect technology to do your job.** Technology can assist you enormously, but it can't think or solve problems. Commit yourself to learning the technology that applies to your job.
- **Apply your computer skills.** You know how to work standard computer software, so you can adapt your knowledge and skills to a variety of uses. Remember to use technology only for business purposes. Personal e-mail, Web-surfing, on-line chatting, and computer games are inappropriate uses of your employer's resources.

## Entrepreneurship

For some people, the way to begin a career or to advance is to strike out on their own. An **entrepreneur** (AHN-truh-pruh-noor) is a person who starts and runs his or her own business. Running your own business has many advantages. You are your own boss. You get credit for all of your successes. Of course, when you are an entrepreneur you are also responsible for every part of the business. If the business does not do well, you lose money. Do you know anyone who is an entrepreneur? If you were an entrepreneur, what type of business would you have?

**Just For Fun**

Lawn mowing, babysitting, and dog walking are common teen businesses. Starting a business is fun when you do it as a team. Be inventive! Create a flyer or business card for a teen business. As a team, write down your business plan and a work schedule. Decide what each team member will do within the business. Share your business idea with your classmates.

## ➤ The World of Work

You will have several jobs during your lifetime. One of the first steps in finding a job that satisfies you is to consider your interests. Do you have special skills that could be useful in a particular type of work? Would you volunteer or work part-time to strengthen those skills?

People work for many reasons. The main reason is to earn a living, but there are many other benefits. People take pride in their work and get a feeling of accomplishment from a job well done. Work is also a way to meet people and make friends.

Most people choose jobs based on their interests and skills. Some people enjoy physical tasks, such as installing machinery. Others prefer artistic work, such as taking photographs or designing homes. Still others want jobs in which they can help people, such as responding to medical emergencies, or caring for young children.

Most people spend 40 or more years in the workforce. Wouldn't you rather spend that time doing something you enjoy? See Fig. 7-5.

# areer CHOICES

## Employment Relations Liaison

Establishes and maintains relationships with employers. Promotes employment programs and services. Contacts employers new to area and arranges to visit company representative responsible for hiring workers. Helps resolve problems in local employment office and employer complaints. Helps employers recruit qualified applicants.

## School Career Counselor

Collects career information. Assists students and teachers with materials. Orders, catalogs, and maintains files relating to careers, technical schools, colleges, scholarships, and armed forces programs. Scores self-administered interest and aptitude tests.

## Employment Interviewer

Interviews job applicants. Reviews employment applications. Evaluates work history, education and training, job skills, and other qualifications. Describes job duties and responsibilities, benefits, company policies, and other information with applicants.

## Military Recruiter

Informs individuals of opportunities, incentives, benefits, and advantages of military careers. Interviews people to determine their suitability for placement into specific military occupations.

**Some careers require you to carry your "office" with you. How would you like to pursue a career that includes travel, but also requires you to do paperwork on the road?**

## Job Analyst

Prepares occupational information to help with the personnel, administration, and management functions of organizations. Studies current occupational data. Interviews workers and supervisors to determine job and worker requirements. Examines data and training requirements of jobs and workers. Develops job descriptions, job specifications, and career paths.

### AT School

Select three of the careers listed. Research the education, training, and work experience required for each career. Compare the results to select a career to investigate further.

### IN THE Workplace

Look through the local want ads and make a list of jobs that match your career interests.

## Chapter Summary

- When considering a career, think about your strengths, interests, abilities, values, and goals.
- Planning ahead will give you time to learn some of the specific skills that will help you get the job you want.
- Research a career by finding out all you can about it from various sources.
- People work to earn a living, to get a feeling of accomplishment from a job well done, and to meet people.

## Words You Learned

1. What are aptitudes?
2. Why is networking a great way to research careers?
3. Why would someone become an entrepreneur?

## Check Your Facts

1. Why might aptitude tests give you an incomplete picture of career options?
2. What is the most direct way to find a job?
3. How can organizations such as FCCLA help you choose a career?
4. How can you use the Internet to research careers?
5. Where can you find resources about education and training beyond high school?
6. How can part-time work help you prepare for full-time employment?
7. What is the benefit of using technology at work?

## Apply Your Learning

1. Name three reasons people choose a particular career.
2. Name three points you can research about careers.
3. Describe a career that you think is perfect for you. Write a short essay to explain why.
4. **Career Network.** Gather information about a career that interests you. Find out the education required for jobs in that field, responsibilities or duties to be expected, working conditions, and the employment outlook. Create a file for the career. Exchange information with other students who are researching careers.

# Chapter 8

# Employability Skills

## You Will Discover . . .

- how basic skills like reading, writing, math, science, speaking, listening, and technology contribute to success in life.
- why technology is essential in the workplace.
- how to apply for a job.
- how to prepare for a job interview.
- how you can advance on the job.

## Key Words

- comprehension
- references
- flexibility
- team
- work ethic
- work record
- promotion
- terminate

Getting a job requires employability skills. Marla learned about these skills when she looked for an after-school job. She had to gather the required forms, learn how to find the kind of job she wanted, then apply for the job. Marla had good basic skills and liked working in a team. She got a part-time job at a garden center.

## ➤ Developing Basic Skills

The most important key to your success is developing basic skills in reading, writing, math, science, speaking, listening, and technology. These skills help you function in life and at work. For example, you will need reading and writing skills to fill out a job application and to create a résumé. To understand the information on your paycheck and to budget your money, you will need math skills. Science skills will help you understand how technology affects people and their environment. Listening and speaking skills are necessary to communicate with people at home, school, and work. Technology skills help you do things efficiently.

Using your basic skills every day is the best way to develop them. How can you apply your basic skills every day? See Fig. 8-1.

### Reading Skills

Reading provides a foundation for the other basic skills. Without reading skills, you could not write, read directions, understand and solve math problems, or use a computer.

Building your vocabulary is one way to develop your reading skills. You can use a dictionary to learn to pronounce words correctly and find out what they mean. You must also learn how to follow written directions. The main goal of reading is **comprehension**, or understanding what you read. With practice, you can improve your comprehension. One reading comprehension technique is called SQ3R.

**Fig. 8-1 You use basic employability skills every day.**

- **Survey.** Skim the headings and summaries to get an idea of what will be covered.
- **Question.** Ask questions about what you are reading.
- **Read.** Read to answer the questions.
- **Recite.** After reading, recite what you read in your own words.
- **Review.** Go back over your reading to make sure all the questions were answered. Ask yourself what you learned.

## Writing Skills

Writing is a way to express your ideas. Developing writing skills will help you feel good about yourself and make a positive impression on others. The ability to express yourself clearly in writing will improve your chances for getting and keeping a job.

You can improve your writing skills by taking time to organize your thoughts. Think about the purpose of what you are going to write. Perhaps you are writing a letter to a prospective employer. How can you convince the employer to call you in for an interview? Outline the major points you want to make. Write a rough draft, and reread it to see if it can be improved. Proofread, or check for errors in your grammar. Use a dictionary to be sure that you used the right words and spell them correctly. Check to be sure that your work is neat and accurate. Ask a parent or guardian to also proofread your letter. You want to make a good first impression with your letter.

## Math & Science Skills

You use math and science skills every day in ways you may not realize. For example, you use math and science when you compare prices, prepare a meal, or remove stains from your clothes. See Fig. 8-2.

**Fig. 8-2** You use basic math skills each time you shop.

Some of the math skills you must develop are addition, subtraction, multiplication, and division. You also need to master fractions, decimals, and percentages. These math skills will help you figure your weekly earnings. Correct use of a calculator is another essential math skill. Developing good math skills now will open the door to many opportunities later.

You use science skills every day. Knowing how chemical and physical reactions occur is useful in many practical situations. For example, what happens when food is cooked or frozen? Science skills will also help you develop an appreciation for your environment. For example, you will understand how to select clothing that will protect you from the weather.

## Speaking Skills

Speaking is just as important in the workplace as reading and writing. Developing the ability to express your thoughts verbally will help you perform well on the job, no matter what career you choose. You can improve your speaking skills by:

- thinking before you speak in order to organize your ideas.
- speaking in a direct and straightforward manner.
- pronouncing words clearly and correctly.
- making sure that the other person understands what you are saying.
- finding a different way to express your idea if your listener does not understand you.

## Listening Skills

To be an effective listener, you need to hear, think about, and respond to what the speaker is saying. On the job, you will need to make a real effort to understand what others say to you. If you do not understand what your employer wants you to do, you may not be able to do your job correctly. See Fig. 8-3. You can improve your listening skills by:

- concentrating on what the other person is saying.
- letting the other person know that you are listening.
- allowing the other person to finish speaking without interrupting.
- listening even if you do not agree with everything the other person is saying.

**Fig. 8-3 Asking questions to better understand your job is a good idea.**

## Technology Skills

Technology makes life easier. You can stay in touch by using cell phones and email. Computers have changed the way we live and work. Knowing how to use a computer is essential.

Computers are used almost everywhere. Computers help track inventory, keep accurate financial records, manage large amounts of data, and allow companies to do business all over the world with the press of a button. At home, people use computers to manage finances, write reports, locate information, and communicate with others.

If you have not spent much time using a computer, now is a good time to practice your keyboarding skills. Most computer software is "user-friendly." See Fig. 8-4.

**Fig. 8-4 Technology helps us do our jobs. How do you think technology will help you at work?**

## ➤ Searching for Jobs

Before you look for a job, you need to get organized. If you were born in the United States, you were issued a social security card at birth. If you don't have a social security card, you must get one. You will need a copy of your birth certificate or other proof that you are a United States citizen. Depending on where you live, you may also need a work permit, or employment certificate, if you are under the age of 16 or 18.

Once you have the necessary papers, you are ready to begin your job search. First, decide what kind of job you want. Next, decide when and for how many hours you can work. Can you work after school or only on weekends? Now, decide when you should look for a job. If you want a summer job, you should start looking in the spring. See Fig. 8-5 for ways to conduct your job search.

## Searching for Job Openings

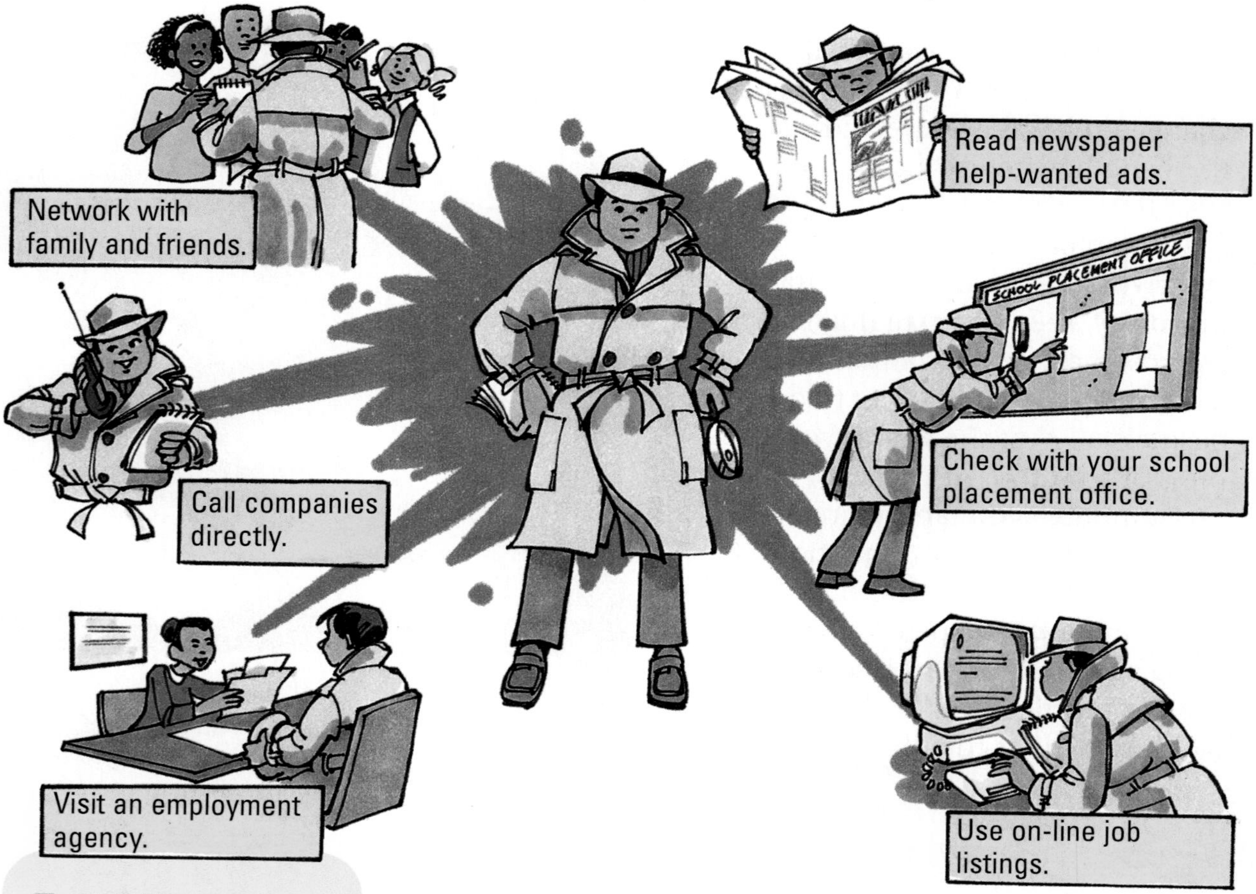
Network with family and friends.
Read newspaper help-wanted ads.
SCHOOL PLACEMENT OFFICE
Call companies directly.
Check with your school placement office.
Visit an employment agency.
Use on-line job listings.

**Fig. 8-5 Here are six ways to find job openings.** **What other sources could you use to find job openings?**

## Applying for Jobs

When you find a job opening that interests you, contact the employer to apply for the job. You will be asked to fill out a job application. You will need to write down information about your education, skills, activities, work experience, and references. If you fill out the application at the job site, you will need to have that information with you. The way you fill out a job application will make an impression on your potential employer. Here are some rules to follow:

- Read the application form carefully. Avoid putting information in the wrong place. Follow the instructions exactly.
- Print as neatly as possible, using blue or black ink.

- Check to make sure that you have answered every question. If a question does not apply, write "NA" (not applicable) in the space provided.
- Be prepared to describe your education, skills, past work experience, and references, even if you've already provided this information on a résumé.

On an application form you may be asked to list several references. **References** are people who can tell an employer about your character and quality of work. Your references should be adults who know you and like your work. You might choose teachers, counselors, coaches, previous employers, or religious leaders. Be sure to ask each person for permission before you use his or her name as a reference.

Many employers also require a résumé. A résumé summarizes your qualifications, work experience, education, and interests. References may be added to a résumé or listed as "available upon request." The *Closer Look* on pages 148-149 provides tips on putting together a résumé.

## The Interview

If the employer reviewing your application thinks that you might be suitable for the job, you will be invited to an interview. A job interview is a meeting between an employer and a job applicant to discuss your qualifications. The interviewer may ask, "Why do you think you can do this job?" The interview also gives you a chance to learn more about the job by asking questions. For example, you might ask where and when you would work and what your job duties would be. See Fig. 8-6.

After an interview, you need to follow up. Send a thank you letter, even if you don't get the job. If you are asked to contact the employer on a specific date, be sure to do so.

**Fig. 8-6 An interview provides you a chance to sell your qualifications. What questions would you ask the interviewer?**

# A CLOSER L OO K

## ...at a Résumé

A résumé is a way for employers to look at you on paper. It gives you a chance to highlight your skills, achievements and work history. The résumé that begins your career will be much different than the résumé you use after you've gained more work experience.

Your **contact information** goes at the top of the page.

**Career Objective** states what you would like to achieve in the workplace.

**Skills and Abilities** list your strong qualifications.

**Work Experience** lists your past job experience.

**Education** contains your highest level of education, plus any special training, certificates, or academic achievements.

**Activities** list extra curricular activities and achievements.

**References** list who can be contacted as a reference, or a statement that references are available upon request.

# JOE MICHAELS

208 Denver Way
Anytown, CA 55555
(555) 555-4996
joe@555email.net

## CAREER OBJECTIVE
- A professional sales position in foods industry.

## SKILLS AND ABILITIES
- Stocked groceries
- Tracked incoming deliveries
- Prepared inventory reports for supervisor
- Assisted customers in finding groceries
- Provided assembly service for bicycles
- Created customer feedback program

## WORK EXPERIENCE
- Stock person: Super Discounts, May 2003 to present

## EDUCATION
- Currently attending Chandler Junior College
- Graduate, Chandler High School, May 2003

## ACTIVITIES
- Served as Student Council Vice President
- Coordinated Student Council car wash
- Coordinated Easter Seals fundraiser, which resulted in $21,000 in donations
- Honor Roll Student in high school

## REFERENCES
- Available upon request.

# How To...

## Prepare for a Job Interview

### State the Task

- Prepare for a job interview.

### Develop a Plan

1. Find out as much as you can about the employer. Ask people who work at the business why they like to work there. Check the company Web site for background information.
2. Choose appropriate clothing for the interview. Make sure it is clean and pressed. The moment you walk through the door for an interview, you make an impression.
3. Make sure that you have a clean body, clean hair, fresh breath, and clean fingernails. An effort to appear neat and clean tells an employer that the job is important to you.
4. Know how to get where you are going ahead of time so you don't get lost.
5. Have some questions prepared to ask the interviewer about the job.

### Implement the Plan

1. Arrive at least 10 minutes early for the interview.
2. Turn off your cell phone and pager.
3. Bring your résumé and any other materials that were requested.
4. Think before you answer each question.
5. Smile, speak clearly, and be friendly and enthusiastic. Practice good posture and good manners. Don't chew gum.
6. In pairs, take turns asking questions to practice for your interview. The *interviewer* might ask about the applicant's job experience; why the applicant wants to work for the company; what the applicant wants to achieve in his or her career. The *applicant* might ask about the work schedule; what benefits are available; when the job starts.

### Evaluate the Result

1. What did you learn about the interview process during your role play?
2. In what areas of the interview process do you need to improve?

## Job Offers

When you receive a job offer, you have three options.

- **Accept the offer.** The employer will tell you when you can begin work. The employer will usually set up another interview during which you will be given details about pay, benefits, and job expectations.
- **Ask for time to consider the offer.** This is the time to bring up any unanswered questions that might affect your decision. With the employer, agree on when you will notify him or her of your decision. Do not put off responding to the employer.
- **Turn down the job offer.** You may decide the job is not right for you. Or, you accepted a better job in the meantime. Simply say, "Thank you for considering me, but I am not interested in taking the position."

## ➤ Being a Responsible Employee

The key to success in any job is to be a responsible employee. There are some responsibilities that every employee has on every job. These job responsibilities are similar to your responsibilities at school. You need to arrive on time, follow rules, and do your work. See Fig. 8-7.

- **Know your job responsibilities.** Besides general job responsibilities, every job also has specific duties. You will probably learn about some of them during your job interview. Your supervisor will explain your specific responsibilities to you. You may be given an employee manual filled with rules that employees must follow. For example, if you work in a flower shop, your job duties might include arranging flowers and processing orders from customers.

Fig. 8-7 **Working as a team shows responsibility.** How else can you demonstrate that you are responsible?

- **Fulfill your job responsibilities.** A key to success at work is to do your job. This sounds simple, and it is. You would be surprised, though, at how many people fail to follow this simple rule. For example, Sean had a part-time job as a salesperson at a music store. Sean's friends would often visit him at work. When Sean was talking to his friends, he would ignore customers. Because Sean didn't do his job, he was fired. The lesson to learn from Sean's experience is that you are at work to do your work. Arrive on time, ask questions if you do not understand something, and make your job responsibilities your top priority.

- **Evaluate yourself.** At the end of each workday, you should evaluate your performance on the job. Did you fulfill your responsibilities? How could you have done your job better? Did you use good communication skills? Because conditions on the job often change, most work situations require flexibility. **Flexibility** is the ability to adjust easily to new conditions. For example, computer technology is constantly changing, and as a result, workers must learn new skills and new ways to accomplish tasks.

Success on the job requires hard work. Following these steps will help you become a good employee and reach your career goals.

## Teamwork

Relationships are an important part of every job. You have to learn to get along with your employer, supervisor, and coworkers, and perhaps customers or clients. The better your relationships are with these people, the more you will enjoy work and experience success.

At work, you become part of a **team,** or a group of people performing work toward a common goal. As a team member, you work with and listen to others and have a helpful attitude. You build teamwork while working together to reach a goal. When coworkers cooperate with one another and share feelings of pride in their work, they get along better and can reach their goals more effectively.

# Explore

## Working in Teams

### State the Task

- Work in a team to complete the project of your choice.

### Develop a Plan

1. Make a timeline for what needs to be accomplished by the team.
2. Write down the topics you will talk about at your meetings.
3. Decide how decisions will be made, such as by majority vote, or when everyone agrees.
4. Decide who will lead the group.
5. Pick one person to remind other group members of meeting times and places, and to take notes when you meet.

### Implement the Plan

1. Set goals for your team meeting and a time limit for the meeting. Make sure all team members understand the goals.
2. Make everyone comfortable by giving each team member a chance to share his or her ideas. When a team member is silent, the leader should ask for his or her input.
3. As a team, choose a project to complete during class.

4. Write down what each person is responsible for along with any special instructions.
5. Set a deadline for the project. Work as a team to complete the project.

### Evaluate the Result

1. What did you accomplish at your team meeting?
2. How did team members interact while working on the project?

Team Goals. Sharing goals and responsibilities as a team is valuable to everyone. Follow these hints for success:

- Be flexible. Remember, there is more than one way to accomplish a task.
- Have a positive attitude.
- Focus your attention on each task.
- Speak in a pleasant tone.
- Listen attentively to others.
- Do your full share of the work.

## Work Ethic

Everyone who is successful on the job has a good work ethic. **Work ethic** is a personal commitment to doing your very best. Work ethic develops with practice. Are you responsible? Do you work well on a team? Are you flexible? Can your coworkers rely on you?

As you work, you will develop a reputation based on your work record. A **work record** is a written record of how well an employee performs on the job. Your work record shows how well you have fulfilled your job responsibilities. It mentions how often you were late and how often you missed work. You can also expect to find comments about your attitude and how well you performed your job.

If you apply for a job with a different company, that employer will probably check your work record. A good work record will improve your chances of being hired. Your work record follows you from job to job, so it pays to build a favorable one. See Fig. 8-8.

**Fig. 8-8 Your work record is of great interest to an employer. What can you do to keep a good work record?**

## ➤ Advancing on the Job

Employees who use their employability skills to do a good job are likely to be promoted. A **promotion** is a move into a job with more responsibility. For example, you might be promoted from stock clerk to assistant manager. A promotion usually includes a raise in salary. Another way to advance is to accept a job with more responsibilities and higher pay with another company.

## Internet ACTIVITIES

1. Search the Internet for the name of a company that does business worldwide. Find out about the types of jobs available in that business' global marketplace.

   **Key Search Words:**
   - global businesses
   - global markets

2. Search the Internet for tips on working in teams. Make a list of helpful suggestions and share them with your classmates.

   **Key Search Words:**
   - working in teams
   - team building

## ➤ Terminating Employment

The decision to **terminate**, or leave, a job should be made very carefully. When you decide to leave a job, try to leave on good terms with the employer. The following tips will help you leave on a positive note.

- Notice should be given soon enough for the employer to find a replacement by the time you leave the job. A two-week notice is considered minimum.
- A letter of resignation is preferred. The letter should be given to the immediate supervisor. The letter should state the exact date you expect to be your last day of employment. It should also thank the employer for his or her help during your time with the company. Be sure to give a brief explanation of why you are leaving.

# Career CHOICES

## Press-Service Reader

Reads newspapers, magazines, and other types of articles on specific subjects. Marks items to be clipped for each customer. Gathers clippings for customers.

## Mathematician

Conducts mathematical research for science, management, and other fields. Studies number theory. Tests hypotheses and alternative theories. Develops ideas for use in a variety of fields, including engineering and management.

## Bill Collector

Receives overdue payments from customers. Figures bills, itemized lists, and tickets showing amounts due. Issues notices. Calls customers for payments.

## Computer Operator

Operates computer and peripheral equipment. Processes scientific, engineering, business, and other data. Enters commands in computer following instructions and schedules.

## Scientific Linguist

Studies structure and relationships of languages. Prepares description of sounds, forms, and vocabulary. Helps develop methods of translation. Prepares teaching materials and handbooks.

**AT School**

Select three of the careers listed. Research the education, training, and work experience required for each career. Compare the results to select a career to investigate further.

**IN THE Workplace**

Make a list of all the ways you can use employability skills in the workplace.

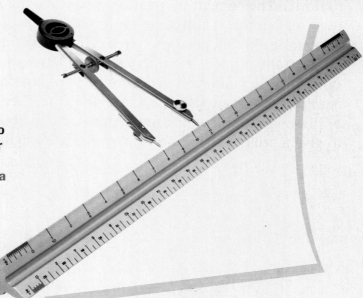

**Mathematicians use many tools in addition to the computer to do their jobs.** What tools do you think would be used by a scientific linguist?

## Chapter Summary

- The most important key to your success is developing basic reading, writing, math, science, speaking, listening, and technology skills.
- You apply for a job by filling out a job application, and submitting a résumé.
- It is very important to make a good impression during a job interview.
- Being a responsible, yet flexible, team player will help you succeed on the job.

## Words You Learned

1. What does comprehension mean?
2. What are references?
3. Why is flexibility important at work?
4. What is a team?
5. Define work ethic.
6. What is a work record?

7. Define promotion.
8. What does it mean to terminate employment?

## Check Your Facts

1. Why is it important to develop basic knowledge and skills?
2. What document must you complete in order to get a job?
3. What is the purpose of a job interview?
4. How can you demonstrate responsibility as an employee?
5. Why is teamwork important?
6. What does it mean to receive a promotion?
7. How should you terminate employment?

## Apply Your Learning

1. List three questions you can ask an employer during a job interview.
2. What are three options you have when responding to a job offer?
3. Describe good work ethic.
4. **Speak Up.** You can use several of your basic skills by preparing a speech to be given in front of your classmates. Write a one-minute speech on employability skills. Make note cards to help remind you of important points. Practice your speech in front of the mirror. Present the speech to your classmates. Ask them what they learned from it and how you could make it better.

# Chapter 9

# Caring for Children

## You Will Discover . . .

- how parenting skills can help you interact positively with children.
- how infants, toddlers, and preschoolers learn through play.
- how infants and children develop.
- what to expect when interacting with infants and children.
- how to help children learn.

𝒟o you remember who taught you to ride a bike, tie your shoes, or tell time? Was it your mother, father, grandmother, grandfather, or another adult? You can probably think of many people who have taught you what you know today. These caregivers have had a major influence on your life.

## Key Words

- parenthood
- guidance
- discipline
- child abuse
- child neglect
- developmental tasks
- attention span
- independent play
- cooperative play

## ➤ Parenthood

If you were asked to apply for a job that required a life-long commitment, 24-hour duty, and no paycheck, but extra benefits, how would you respond? That is the job description for **parenthood**, or the function of being a parent. Parent-hood is a major decision and a lifelong commitment. Effective parents must provide love, patience, guidance, and financial resources. See Fig. 9-1.

Parents are primary caregivers. They are responsible for providing a safe, loving, and stimulating environment for their children. They must fulfill a child's physical needs as well as provide emotional support.

Many new parents are surprised to find how demanding parenthood can be in terms of time, energy, and money. Parents often have to make adjustments or give up their personal desires in order to provide for their children.

Parenthood can also bring many joys, however. The special relationship that develops between a parent and child is a fulfilling experience. All over the world parents claim that parenthood brings them happiness, love, and pride.

Fig. 9-1 Parenthood is a lifelong commitment. What skills do you have that might make you a good parent?

## Responsible Parenting

Parents and other caregivers need to use good parenting skills. Parenting is the process of caring for children and helping them to grow and learn. This process can be very rewarding, but it also takes a lot of hard work.

Perhaps you help care for a younger brother or sister, or maybe you babysit children in your neighborhood. You can gain parenting skills by watching your parents and by taking a child development or parenting course. The more you know about children, the more comfortable you will be with them. You will find that the way you handle children affects the way they behave toward you. See Fig. 9-2.

Fig. 9-2 Babysitting and caring for younger brothers and sisters require basic parenting skills. How else can you learn to be a good parent?

## Children's Needs

Young children have physical, emotional, social, and intellectual needs that must be met. While you are caring for, playing with, and teaching children, it is up to you to fulfill these needs.

- **Physical needs.** All children have basic physical needs. They need healthful food, appropriate clothing, rest and sleep, and a safe and stimulating environment. Infants indicate their needs by crying. Crying is their way of telling you they are hungry, wet, tired, frightened, ill, or unhappy. As children age, they are better able to use words and sentences to communicate their needs.
- **Intellectual needs.** Children have intellectual needs, too. They need a stimulating environment and opportunities to explore. Reading books, playing with puzzles and blocks, and selecting toys of different shapes and sizes help develop intellectual abilities. See Fig. 9-3 on page 162.

**Fig. 9-3 Playing with children helps improve their intellectual skills.** What are some other ways you can meet a child's intellectual needs?

**Fig. 9-4 Children sense your feelings toward them.** How can you meet a child's emotional and social needs?

- **Emotional and social needs.** Children also need to be held, cuddled, and comforted. Sometimes a kiss, a hug, or a gentle pat is all children need to be reassured that someone cares. Children are very sensitive to your feelings about them. Speak kindly to them. They can tell by the way you touch, hold, and talk to them that they are loved. See Fig. 9-4 on page 162.

## Communicating Positively

Children, like adults, respond better to positive statements than to negative ones. For instance, say "Let's play outside for awhile," instead of "Don't play in the living room." Emphasize what the children are allowed to do rather than what they should not do. You may also need to explain why. "Try to climb on the jungle gym this way, so you won't fall and get hurt."

Praise is another way of focusing on the positive. You might say to a young child, "I think you did a terrific job finding all those marbles that spilled. You have really sharp eyes."

Fig. 9-5 Encourage children to become independent. What can you do to set a good example?

## Encouraging Independence

Children want to become independent and be able to perform tasks by themselves. As children try to do new tasks on their own, they will probably make mistakes at first. It takes practice to learn skills such as using a fork, brushing teeth, or tying a shoe. Just like you, they learn from their mistakes. See Fig. 9-5.

## Providing Guidance

Caregivers need to give children **guidance**, or direction. That is how children learn basic rules for behavior. These rules help children stay safe, learn self-control, and learn to get along with others. Children need guidance to learn appropriate behavior.

**Discipline** is the task of teaching a child which behavior is acceptable and which is not. Discipline can be effective in helping a child learn self-control. It is important to be consistent, which means reacting the same way to a situation each time it occurs. It also means that you follow through and do what you say you will do. For example, if you say that you will take away a toy the next time a child throws it, you should do so. When you are consistent, children know what to expect.

In addition to being consistent, avoid making false threats. For example, telling a child that you will leave him or her at home alone if he or she misbehaves is a false threat. You know that it would be unsafe to leave a child at home alone without supervision.

## ➤ Child Abuse & Neglect

A sad fact of life is that some parents abuse and neglect their children. **Child abuse** means physical, emotional, or sexual injury to children. **Child neglect** is failure to meet a child's physical and emotional needs. Parents who leave young children alone or don't provide adequate food or medical attention are guilty of neglect. Some children suffer from both abuse and neglect.

Abuse and neglect occur in families from all income levels and racial and ethnic groups. Unless help is found, both abuse and neglect tend to occur again and again.

### Causes of Abuse & Neglect

Why would someone injure a child? Emotional outbursts of anger and frustration are often the cause of child abuse. Adults who lose their tempers can inflict serious, life-threatening injuries on infants and children. The abuser may expect too much of a child. He or she may not be able to cope with personal problems. In some cases, substance abuse is also involved.

In some cases, parents or caregivers may incorrectly think they are actually helping to teach the child right from wrong. The adults may have been abused as children, making it seem appropriate to do so to their children.

**Internet ACTIVITIES**

1. **Search the Internet for information on building a child's self-esteem. Make a list of tips and share them with the class.**

   **Key Search Words:**
   - **self-esteem**
   - **self-confidence**

2. **Search the Internet for information on child abuse and neglect. Make a list of the signs of child abuse and neglect. Share the list with your classmates.**

   **Key Search Words:**
   - **child abuse**
   - **child neglect**

Neglect can be caused when a child does not receive basic food, clothing, shelter, or health care. Families under financial or emotional stress should seek help from agencies, friends, or extended family members.

## Preventing Abuse & Neglect

Abuse is very serious. If you ever suspect a child has been abused or neglected, tell a trusted adult. You can even make an anonymous report to a child protective services agency. If you think a child is in immediate danger, call 9-1-1. State child protective agencies require a social caseworker investigate each report. In addition, early childhood professionals, health care providers, and teachers are required by law to report child abuse and neglect.

To help prevent abuse, a child should never be left with someone who is not reliable. Relatives, neighbors, and friends can often provide help in times of need. Several helpful groups exist to provide parenting support, including parenting courses. Some communities even have crisis nurseries where parents can leave their children while they cool off. One self-help group found in many cities is Parents Anonymous. While the children are occupied with activities, parents support each other as they learn new parenting skills and attitudes.

Child abuse is illegal and should never be hidden. All types of abuse and neglect leave lasting impressions on children. The longer abuse continues, the more serious the problem becomes. There is no prescribed treatment for child abusers. Counseling and parenting courses help abusers face their problems. However, a good support system is always necessary. More information about child abuse and its prevention can be obtained from groups such as the National Committee for the Prevention of Child Abuse. Search the Internet for a list of agencies, organizations, and laws providing help for victims of child abuse and neglect in your state.

## Developmental Tasks

The concept of developmental tasks is important to understand when caring for children. **Developmental tasks** are achievements, such as walking and talking, that can be expected at various ages and stages of growth. See Fig. 9-6.

The sequence, or order, of developmental tasks follows a pattern. Infants crawl before they walk, for example. Some children achieve these milestones faster than others. Janie learned to walk by the age of 12 months, but Marta did not take her first step until 15 months.

Developmental tasks are useful for explaining what the typical child can do by certain ages. Toddlers babble sounds before they learn to say words. They say individual words before they speak in complete sentences. However, each child is a unique individual. Just as children do not grow at the same rate physically, they do not all perform developmental tasks at the same time.

Fig. 9-6 Children reach different milestones as they grow and develop. What can you do to encourage development?

## Expectations for Children

It is important to treat each child as an individual. Even children who have the same parents experience different growth rates and patterns. After you spend time with children and get to know them, you will have an idea of what you can expect from each child. See Fig. 9-7.

## Infants

Katrina, a newborn baby, eats every few hours. She sleeps 16 to 20 hours each day. As she gets older, she will stay awake longer and eat less often. In the first few months, her parents will develop a schedule so that Katrina can learn to have a regular time for eating, bathing, sleeping, and playing.

Katrina will have many developmental tasks to learn, such as how to eat, sit alone, pick up objects, and crawl. She will learn how to play with toys and be comfortable with different people and places. Katrina will also need a great deal of love and attention.

**Infant Milestones. (Birth to 1 year of age)**

- Coos, Laughs (Birth to 6 months)
- Grasps at Rattle (2 months)
- Smiles (2 months)
- Rolls Over (3 to 6 months)
- Puts Objects in Mouth (2 months)
- Sits Up Alone (4 to 6 months)
- Says Single Words (6 to 12 months)
- Crawls (7 to 9 months)
- Pulls Self Up (9 to 12 months)
- Plays Peek-A-Boo (10 to 12 months)

**Fig. 9-7 Each child develops at his or her own pace.**

## Toddlers

Toddlers are children who are 1 to 3 years old. The name comes from the unsteady way they walk, or toddle. Toddlers are usually full of energy and ideas. They are learning to be more independent by doing tasks for themselves and by being less dependent on the people who care for them. As a part of this new independence, they often use the word "no." Toddlers can learn to do these tasks:

- Come to the table for meals when called.
- Eat food without being encouraged.
- Follow safety rules such as not touching something hot.

# A CLOSER L👓K

## ...at Child Development

Children develop physically, intellectually, emotionally, socially, and morally.

❖ **Physical Development**
During the first 12 months of Anna's life, she put on weight, grew longer, and gained the muscle coordination to hold her head up, sit up, and crawl.

❖ **Intellectual Development**
During the first few years of her life, Anna developed the ability to think, reason, and solve simple problems. She learned to recognize familiar faces and places, and she learned to talk.

## Social Development

During the first weeks of life, Anna began to learn how to relate to others. She began by smiling when she saw her mother's or father's face. As a toddler, Anna learned to play with other children, make friends, and share toys.

## Emotional Development

When Anna was an infant, her needs were met as soon as she cried. Anna learned to trust her caregivers—the first stage of emotional development.

## Moral Development

Anna's parents are teaching her a system of rules to guide her behavior. They want her to develop a sense of right and wrong, and to be considerate of others.

### Toddler Milestones. (1 to 3 years of age)

- Walks
- Learns Meaning of "No"
- Follows Simple Instructions
- Feeds Self with Spoon
- Identifies Pictures
- Climbs Stairs
- Undresses Self
- Plays Beside Others
- Puts Words into Sentences
- Begins Toilet Training

## Preschoolers

Preschoolers are children who are 3 to 5 years old. Preschoolers interact more with their playmates and like to play with children of all ages. They like to talk. Preschool children may carry on a conversation with make-believe playmates. They might imitate their heroes or pretend to be superhuman.

### Preschooler Milestones. (3 to 5 years of age)

- Opens Doors
- Dresses Self
- Recognizes Colors
- Rides a Tricycle
- Repeats Rhymes, Songs
- Brushes Teeth
- Speaks in Sentences
- Begins Cooperative Play

## Children with Special Needs

Some children have special needs. Jake walks with a leg brace. Peter wears a hearing aid. Joanna has emotional problems. Each of these children has a particular disability, yet what they need most is to learn how to develop their abilities and enjoy life. For example, they need to learn to be as independent as possible, and they need encouragement to develop a positive self-concept. The attitudes of people around them are important in making this possible. See Fig. 9-8.

**Fig. 9-8** Children with special needs learn from caregivers who encourage independence.

# How To...

## Choose Age-Appropriate Toys

**State the Task**

- Choose age-appropriate toys.

**Develop a Plan**

1. Choose several age-appropriate toys and look each one over to see how it works.
2. Write down how each toy would help children learn.
3. Make a list of any dangers that each toy might have if given to a child who is not the appropriate age. For instance, are there any small parts that might be a choking hazard?

**Implement the Plan**

1. Choose a toy for a sibling, family friend, or neighbor's child, based on his or her age and interests.
2. Watch how the child plays with the toy. Make a list of all the things he or she learns from using the toy.
3. Compare the list with the one you made above and see how many matches you have.

**Evaluate the Result**

1. What types of toys were the favorites among infants, toddlers, or preschoolers?
2. What did you learn about choosing toys for children?

**Birth to 6 Months**
- Crib mobiles
- Rattles
- Stuffed toys
- Clutch balls

**7 to 12 Months**
- Nesting toys
- Stacking toys
- Cloth ball
- Blocks

**1 to 2 years**
- Take-apart toys
- Push-pull toys
- Riding toys
- Balls
- Dolls

**2 to 3 years**
- Crayons
- Books
- Large blocks
- Sandbox

**3 to 5 years**
- Modeling clay
- Finger paint
- Educational card games
- Books
- Puppets
- Puzzles

# How Children Learn

Young children learn from exploring their environment with their five senses—sight, hearing, taste, touch, and smell. Children learn something from everyone and everything around them, including toys. Their first toys might help develop their coordination or help them learn to focus on brightly colored objects. As children grow, activities and toys can help them improve their intellectual abilities. Some toys teach shapes, colors, letters, and numbers.

Young children also learn by practicing tasks over and over again, observing and imitating others, and exploring their environment. Children learn from being exposed to aquariums, science museums, historic houses, and a strawberry patch.

**Fig. 9-9 Young children learn by using all five senses. How can you provide hands-on experiences?**

# Learning Through Play

Although every child is unique, most children go through a similar pattern of growth and development. As an older brother or sister, or as a babysitter, you can help children learn and discover new things by interacting with them. Show children that you are interested in them and that what they say matters to you. See Fig. 9-9.

## Infant Playtime

Baby Nicholas is happy waving his arms and kicking his legs. He likes to have someone play with him and enjoys being moved from place to place so he can look at new sights. A walk outside or to the grocery store is very interesting to him. Nicholas does not stay with one toy for very long. He, like other infants, has a short

**attention span**, the length of time a person can concentrate on any one thing. This means that toys and other objects hold his interest for only a short amount of time.

When infants discover their hands and can hold a toy, play becomes more important to them. They gradually learn to pick up a toy and hold it. It is natural for infants to play happily, first picking up one toy, then another. Playing with toys is one way babies learn about the world around them.

Infants playing alone and showing little interest in interacting with other children are engaging in **independent play**. Infants play with their hands, toes, toys, or other objects. See Fig. 9-10. Toys that are easy to pick up and hold with tiny fingers are best for first toys. Infants like toys that are pleasant to touch, see, and chew on. Musical toys, squeeze toys, and stacking and nesting blocks are good toys for infants. Even small kitchen items, such as plastic measuring cups and spoons and pots and pans, can be entertaining toys.

Fig. 9-10 Mobiles fascinate infants. Which senses are stimulated by mobiles?

## Toddler Playtime

Play is toddler's work, and toys are their tools. Playing helps develop their minds, bodies, and social skills. Toddlers are curious about everything and spend much of their time exploring. They pull out various toys, look them over, and go on to something else. Most toddlers play alone or watch others play. They engage in parallel play—play that occurs alongside of, rather than with, a friend. They are just beginning to learn to share toys with others.

Toddlers need toys for both active and quiet play. Their toys should help them develop socially and physically. The toys you choose for toddlers should also help them think and use their imagination. Toddlers like toys that move, but toys like a jack-in-the-box or toys that move too fast may startle them. Action toys, such as riding toys and balls, help toddlers develop skill and coordination. Toy cars, bulldozers, and airplanes will capture their attention and stimulate their imagination.

## Preschooler Playtime

Preschoolers engage in **cooperative play**—playing together with one or two other children and sharing toys. Play helps preschoolers learn to take turns, share, and make friends with other children. As they get older, they enjoy playing with several other children, especially those their own age. The benefits of playtime for preschoolers include taking turns, sharing with others, and learning how to get along with a group.

As children develop, their interests gradually change. New toys help keep pace with their natural development. Preschoolers enjoy action toys that encourage physical exercise, such as tricycles and climbing equipment. Toys for pretend play include briefcases, dress-up clothes, and nontoxic art materials. See Fig. 9-11.

**Fig. 9-11**
**Preschoolers learn to cooperate through play.**

# Explore

## Quiet Play Activities

### State the Task
- Discuss how children react to quiet play activities.

### Develop a Plan
1. Create several quiet play activities for young children you know. Making up stories, reading books aloud, or listening to music are good activities for infants and toddlers. Drawing with crayons or markers, painting, making collages from old magazines, and playing with clay are quiet activities for preschoolers.
2. Fill a craft box or plastic tub with paper, scissors, school glue, old magazines, crayons and markers, and modeling clay. Add your favorite children's books and CDs of soothing children's music.
3. Make up stories of your own, if desired. Draw pictures, write out a story and bind the book with ribbon. Add the book to your activity box.

### Implement the Plan
1. Take your quiet-play activity box to a babysitting job. Choose one or more age-appropriate activities to use.
2. Watch how the child reacts to each quiet activity. Write down what you learn by watching the child's response to each activity.

### Supplies
- Paper
- Child-safe scissors
- School glue
- Non-toxic crayons or markers
- Old magazines
- Modeling clay
- Storybooks
- Music tapes
- Craft box or plastic tub

3. Make a list of how the child used his or her senses during each activity.
4. Did the child settle down for a nap or bedtime more easily after a quiet activity? Why or why not?

### Evaluate the Result
1. List the ways that quiet activities differed from active play activities. What conclusions can you draw?
2. What other activities could you add to your activity box?

# areer CHOICES

## School Nurse

Provides health care services to students. Plans school health program, in cooperation with medical authority and school. Evaluates health of students and establishes policies for health emergencies.

## School Cafeteria Cook

Prepares, cooks, and serves food in school cafeteria. Plans varied menus to ensure that food is appetizing and nutritionally appropriate for children. Orders food and supplies as needed.

## Pediatrician

Plans and carries out medical care program for children from birth through adolescence. Examines patients to determine presence of disease and to establish preventive health. Determines nature and extent of disease or injury. Prescribes and administers medicine.

## Playground Equipment Builder

Builds playground equipment for schools and community playgrounds. Assembles swings, horizontal ladders, basketball hoops, slides, and other equipment. Checks to see that equipment meets safety standards.

## Toy Builder

Designs children's toys. Assembles parts to produce toys. Inspects and tests toys to ensure they work properly.

**AT** School

Select three of the careers listed. Research the education, training, and work experience required for each career. Compare the results to select a career to investigate further.

**IN THE** Workplace

Make a list of 10 different jobs that involve caring for children. What school subjects would you need to take to be prepared to do these jobs?

**Tools used to build toys and playgrounds range from a hammer to robotic equipment.** What tools would you use when caring for children?

# Chapter 9 Review & Activities

## Chapter Summary

- Parenthood means providing love, patience, guidance, and financial resources.
- Play activities are dependent on the age of the child.
- Infants and children develop physically, intellectually, emotionally, socially, and morally.
- Help children learn by repeating and practicing tasks over and over.

## Words You Learned

1. Why is parenthood so important?
2. What is another word for guidance?
3. What is discipline?
4. Define child abuse.
5. Define child neglect.

6. What skills do developmental tasks foster?
7. What is meant by a child's attention span?
8. Define independent play.
9. At what age are most children ready for cooperative play?

## Check Your Facts

1. Give three examples of people who could be caregivers.
2. Name some ways that you can help fulfill a child's emotional and social needs.
3. Why is it important to be consistent when guiding children?
4. How do children learn?
5. How does play benefit preschoolers?

**Apply Your Learning**

1. Explain the difference between independent play and cooperative play.
2. Name three toys for infants, toddlers, and preschoolers that are beneficial to the children's development.
3. **Sensory learning.** Create "musical shakers" for children. You'll need two paper plates to make each shaker. Use colored markers to decorate the backside of each paper plate. Fill one plate with mini cookies or crackers. Use masking tape to attach two plates together so the food is sealed between the two plates. Encourage children to use their shakers to keep pace with their favorite music. After the music ends, help the children open their "shakers" to enjoy a tasty treat.

# Chapter 10

# Babysitting Basics

## You Will Discover . . .

- how to keep children safe.
- how to prevent common accidents.
- how to prepare for babysitting jobs.
- how to care for infants, toddlers, and preschoolers.

## Key Words

- childproof
- intruder
- redirect

Babysitting is usually the easiest kind of job for young people to find, and it provides good experience. However, caring for children is a big responsibility. You will be better able to handle it if you prepare in advance. The more frequently you care for children, the more you will know about keeping them safe.

## ➤ Keeping Children Safe

Children do not understand the dangers that surround them. In their eagerness to explore, they can easily hurt themselves by playing with a dangerous object or substance. There are precautions you can take, however, to help prevent children from getting hurt.

Fig. 10-1 Infants put things in their mouths. Toys should never be small enough to swallow.

Families can make their homes **child-proof**, or a safe environment for children to play and explore. Here are some ways to childproof a home.

- Put safety latches on cabinet doors and drawers.
- Use safety gates at the top and bottom of stairs.
- Put safety covers on electrical outlets.
- Move cleaning supplies and other dangerous items out of children's reach.
- Remove poisonous plants.
- Check all toys to be sure they are nontoxic and don't have any broken parts.

Even if a home has been childproofed, you still need to watch children carefully to make sure that they are safe. Because infants put objects in their mouths, you need to make sure that anything small enough to be swallowed is kept out of reach. See Fig. 10-1. Toddlers must be watched every minute because they move quickly and get into everything. Although preschoolers have a better idea of what they should not do, they may still get into dangerous situations. You should monitor their behavior closely.

Keeping children safe involves protecting children, and yourself, from intruders. An **intruder** is someone who uses force to get into a home. Caregivers need to take the following precautions:

- Make sure that all doors and windows are locked.
- Do not open the door for any stranger.
- Call a neighbor, another trusted adult, or dial 9-1-1 if a stranger does not go away.

**SAFETY FIRST**

Never tell a caller that you are the babysitter and alone with children.

- - - - - - - - - - - -

## ➤ Preventing Accidents

When caring for young children, you need to take precautions to prevent accidents. Some common accidents are falls, injuries, fires, and poisoning. To learn how to take care of basic injuries, such as a small cut or a nosebleed, consider taking a first-aid course. If a child gets hurt and you do not feel capable of handling the situation, stay calm and call for help. A broken bone, serious bleeding, a burn, or an animal bite can be dangerous. Call the child's parents, a neighbor, or dial 9-1-1 for help.

### Falls & Injuries

Falls are the leading cause of accidental death in the home in the United States. When caring for children, follow these guidelines to prevent falls and other common injuries. See Fig. 10-2.

**Fig. 10-2 You should be able to perform basic first-aid.** How can you avoid injury to children in your care?

- Never leave an infant alone on a changing table, sofa, or bed. The infant may roll over and fall off.
- Restrict crawling infants and toddlers to places that they can explore safely.
- Keep all young children away from electrical wires and outlets.
- Remove all breakable or dangerous objects out of children's reach.
- Make sure that toys are age-appropriate and free of loose parts.
- Keep plastic bags away from children. This will prevent suffocation.
- Keep knives and breakable items away from children.
- Always watch children to prevent them from running into the street.
- Children should always ride in a secured, child car seat.
- Never leave children alone in a car or a home.

# A CLOSER LOOK

## ...at Giving a Child CPR

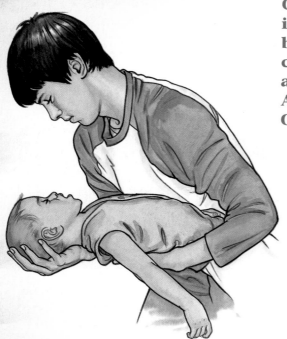

CPR, cardiopulmonary resuscitation, is a life-saving technique. It can also be life-threatening if not performed correctly. Only certified people should administer CPR. The American Heart Association and the American Red Cross offer CPR training.

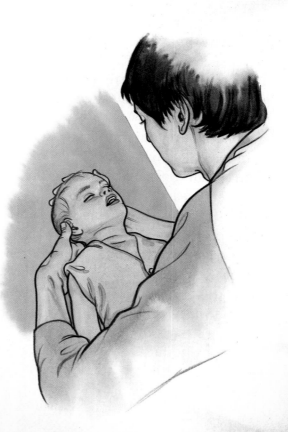

**1** Make sure the child's throat is clear of any obstructions. Gently tilt the child's head back and lift the chin. Feel inside the mouth for obstructions.

**2** Check to see if the child is breathing. If the child is not breathing, position him or her gently on his or her back to administer CPR.

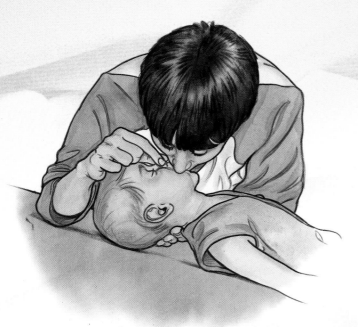

**3** Cover his or her nose and give two short breaths into the mouth. You should see the child's chest rise with each breath.

giving CPR

**4** Gently press the child's chest at the center with the heel of one hand. Press down only 1" to 1½". This is a chest compression.

**5** Repeat the procedure using one breath and five chest compressions. Continue giving breaths and chest compressions until help arrives or the child begins breathing again.administer CPR.

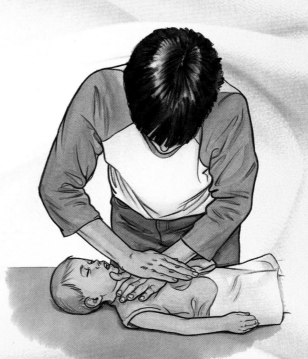

**House Fires. According to the National Fire Protection Association (NFPA), it takes less than five minutes for a fire to spread throughout a house.**

## Fires

Fires are the second leading cause of accidental death in the United States. Follow these guidelines to prevent fires:

- Be sure that there are smoke alarms on every floor of the home.
- Keep all matches and lighters away from children.
- When cooking, avoid wearing clothing with long, full sleeves. Turn pot and pan handles away from the edge of the stove. Keep the oven door closed.

If you smell smoke or see a fire while you are caring for children, get the children out safely first. Then call the fire department from a neighbor's home. Do not try to put out the fire yourself.

Try not to panic if you are trapped by smoke or fire. Stay close to the floor. If you can, put a wet cloth over your nose and mouth and crawl to safety. If you cannot get out, close the door to the room and stuff wet towels around the cracks in the door. Call for help immediately.

**Fig. 10-3 Many household items are dangerous. Keep them out of a child's reach. What should you do to prevent poisoning while you babysit?**

## Poisonings

Common sense is the best way to keep children away from dangerous household substances. All poisonous items should be kept in locked cabinets. If that is not possible, keep the items on a high shelf, out of children's reach. See Fig. 10-3.

The first step to take if you suspect a child has been poisoned is to call the poison control center. You can find the number of the nearest poison control center in the telephone book or by calling directory assistance.

## ➤ Babysitting Responsibilities

When you babysit, you are totally responsible for the safety and well-being of the children in your care. If you do your job well, you will gain valuable experience and earn money. You will also have an opportunity to play with children and teach them new things.

Before you begin looking for a babysitting job, you should take a course in first-aid through a local hospital, a community center, or the American Red Cross. See Fig. 10-4. You could also volunteer as a parent's helper—someone who cares for an infant or a young child under a parent's supervision.

When parents ask you to babysit, find out the following information before you accept the job.

- The number and ages of the children.
- The time you will need to arrive.
- How long the parents plan to be gone.
- The rate of pay you will receive.

If everything about the job is agreeable to you, check with your parents to make sure that the job meets with their approval. After you accept the job, write down the date, time, and place. Give your parents the telephone number where you can be reached.

**DID YOU know?**

**Putting children at ease.** Follow these tips to help children feel comfortable with you:

- When talking to children, sit or kneel so that you are at their eye level.
- Ask children how you can join in their play. For example, "How about if I be the letter carrier who delivers mail to your store?"
- Be patient—don't jump in to finish their sentences.

**Fig. 10-4** Taking a first-aid course will help you prepare for emergencies.

# Explore

## Making a First-Aid Kit

### Supplies

- Small plastic tub with lid
- Bandages (various sizes)
- Gauze pads
- Anti-bacterial cream
- Crayons
- Paper

### State the Task

- Make a first-aid kit to take on baby-sitting jobs.

### Develop a Plan

1. Gather the supplies for your kit.
2. Research basic first-aid instructions in your school or community library, on the Internet, or by asking your school nurse.
3. Write down the first-aid instructions in the notebook. Alphabetize the instructions. Include choking, cuts, minor burns, poisoning, scrapes, and others.
4. Write down the telephone numbers for the poison control center and local hospitals.

### Implement the Plan

1. Place the first-aid supplies in your plastic tub so that you can reach each item easily.
2. Place the first-aid notebook in your tub as a reference.
3. Add paper and crayons. After you take care of a child's first-aid needs, give him or her paper and crayons. Ask the child to draw a picture of something happy.

### Evaluate the Result

1. What else can you add to your first-aid kit?
2. What were the most interesting first-aid instructions you learned? Why?

## Babysitting Job Tips

The first time you babysit for a family, ask the parents if you can arrive a little early. That way, you will have a chance to get to know the children while the parents are still at home.

It is a good idea to ask the parents to go over a few of the family rules in front of the children. Be sure to ask about:

- television viewing.
- homework.
- visits from friends.
- snacks.
- bedtime.

Discuss any rules or limits that might cause problems later. Meet the family pets. Find out if the family has a swimming pool. Take a walk through the house with the parents to become familiar with the layout and emergency exits.

If you are friendly and caring with children, they will feel comfortable with you in charge. Show the children that you enjoy being with them and that you are interested in what they would like to do. Try to get them involved in something enjoyable so that they stay happy and busy. This way they won't have the opportunity to behave inappropriately.

Reliable babysitters get asked back again and again. They establish good relationships with the parents and children. Show that you are reliable by:

- keeping a constant, careful eye on the children.
- keeping an accurate list of telephone messages.
- leaving the house as neat as you found it.
- not allowing your friends to visit.
- not opening the door to strangers.

Being responsible for children is a serious and important task. It can also be enjoyable. Children of different ages have different needs and require different types of care. Learning how to take care of infants, toddlers, and preschoolers will help you meet their needs and enjoy your time with them. See Fig. 10-5.

**Fig. 10-5 Involve children in activities while you babysit.** What creative ideas do you have for playtime?

# How To...

## Create a Babysitter's Resource Guide

**State the Task**

- Create a resource guide for babysitting.

**Develop a Plan**

1. Divide your guide into three sections. The first section will contain the names of all of the people for whom you babysit. The next section will contain first-aid information. The last section will contain entertainment ideas, tips, and meal suggestions for children.
2. Gather first-aid information on burns, CPR, choking, poisons, and any others you may need.
3. Gather meal and entertainment ideas and any special tips on caring for children.

**Implement the Plan**

1. Mark each section of your Babysitter's Resource Guide so you can easily use the information.
2. Write down the names of all the adults for whom you babysit in alphabetical order. Include their addresses, phone numbers, and children's names. Write down any special instructions for each child, including allergies, bedtimes, television guidelines, and approved snacks. Include the name and phone number of each child's doctor.
3. Organize your first-aid information by topic. Include telephone numbers for your local fire, police, and rescue units, as well as the poison control center and local hospitals.
4. Organize your entertainment ideas, meal suggestions, and child care tips by topic and in alphabetical order.
5. Take your guide with you on each babysitting job and use it as a reference.

**Evaluate the Result**

1. What other information could you add to your guide?
2. How can having this information help you on babysitting jobs?

# ➤ Caring for Infants

Infants are cute, fun to cuddle, and easy to entertain. Because they cannot do things for themselves, they rely on their caregiver for all their needs. Infants communicate their needs for sleep, food, comfortable clothing, and attention by crying.

When infants cry, check to see if they have dirty diapers or are hungry. Sometimes they may be too hot or too cold, or may need to be burped. If none of these problems exists, try holding, rocking, or walking them. See Fig. 10-6.

When caring for infants, you need to pay attention to the following needs:

- **Holding.** Infants can't hold their heads up without help. To support an infant's head, place one hand under the head and the other hand and arm under the lower part of the infant's back. Then you can lift the infant safely to your shoulder or cradle the infant in the bend of your arm and elbow area.

- **Changing.** Ask the parent to show you the diaper-changing procedure and where to put dirty diapers. When you change a diaper, assemble everything you need before you begin. Infants can roll off changing tables and beds, so never leave them unattended.

- **Feeding.** A young infant drinks milk or formula. Cradle the infant in your arm when you give a bottle. After the infant stops drinking, hold the infant over your shoulder, and lightly pat his or her back until you hear a burp. It may take a minute or two for the burp to come. Be patient. Also know that infants do not always burp.

- **Sleeping.** To put the infant to sleep, place the infant on the side or back, never on the stomach. Be sure to pull up the side of the crib and fasten it securely. When the infant is sleeping, check frequently to make sure that everything is all right.

**Fig. 10-6 When you hold an infant, support the entire body. Hold the body firmly against your shoulder or cradle the infant in your arms.**

# Internet ACTIVITIES

1. **Search the Internet for information on basic first-aid techniques. Look for information on burns, choking, cuts, poisoning, and others.**

   **Key Search Words:**
   - **first-aid**
   - **emergency aid**

2. **Search the Internet for information on babysitting classes.**

   **Key Search Words:**
   - **babysitting**
   - **child care**

## ➤ Caring for Toddlers

Toddlers require a lot of attention. They need help and understanding as they grow and make new discoveries. They also demand a lot of attention because they are busy moving from one thing to another.

While toddlers enjoy showing off their budding independence, most will need comforting when their parents leave. See Fig. 10-7. You may need to redirect them with a favorite toy, puzzle, or game. When you **redirect** children, you turn their attention to something else. They will usually get over missing their parents in a few minutes.

If the toddler has learned to use the toilet, you may have to help him or her in the bathroom. Unfasten the toddler's clothes, and help him or her get onto the toilet or potty seat. Afterwards, help the child wash his or her hands.

Fig. 10-7 **Toddlers often need extra comfort when their parents leave for the evening.** How can you comfort an unhappy toddler?

## ➤ Caring for Preschoolers

Preschoolers are curious and often look forward to being with caregivers they like. You can share activities such as reading, coloring, and pretend play with pre-schoolers. They like to be kept busy and often enjoy your company.

Babysitting preschoolers can be exhausting. Their creativity seems endless and their curiosity endless. It is important to have a lot of back-up activities planned to keep them entertained. Bedtime can be an issue with preschoolers. You can often avoid this problem if the preschooler is tired. Babysitting preschoolers is a lot of fun and good experience.

# Career CHOICES

## Child Care Worker

Cares for children, overseeing their recreation, diet, health, and general care. Teaches children good health and personal habits. Communicates child's behavior and activities to parents.

## Child Care Instructor

Organizes and leads activities of preschool children in nursery schools and daycares. Organizes games. Reads to children. Teaches simple painting, drawing, songs, and other activities. Directs snack time, nap time, and toileting. Helps children learn to care for their own clothing and to put away toys and books.

## School Bus Monitor

Monitors conduct of students on school bus to maintain safety. Directs students to prevent altercations and damage to bus. Participates in school bus safety drills.

## Special Needs Aide

Attends to personal needs of disabled children. Wheels children to classes and other areas of buildings as needed. Secures children in equipment and places or hoists children into baths or pools for therapy. Helps children walk, board buses, put on prosthetics, eat, dress, bathe, and perform other physical activities as needed.

## School Music Director

Plans and develops music education program. Coordinates vocal and instrumental music activities. Evaluates and recommends changes in work of teaching staff to strengthen teaching skills in music classroom.

### AT School

Select three of the careers listed. Research the education, training, and work experience required for each career. Compare the results to select a career to investigate further.

### IN THE Workplace

Make a list of jobs in the field of child development and care. Compare your list with those of your classmates.

**Working in child care can be very satisfying.** What type of job will make you feel satisfied?

# Chapter 10 Review & Activities

## Chapter Summary

- Keep children safe by childproofing the area, preventing falls, and constantly being aware of where the children are.
- Prevent common accidents like falls and injuries by never leaving an infant alone, keeping young children away from electrical wires and outlets, choosing appropriate toys, and keeping plastic bags and balloons away from them.
- Care for infants, toddlers, and preschoolers by recognizing that each age group has different needs and will require a different type of care.

## Words You Learned

1. Why do parents childproof their home?
2. How does a babysitter protect against an intruder?
3. What does it mean to redirect a child?

## Check Your Facts

1. Where can you call for help if a child swallows poison?
2. What questions should you ask before you accept a babysitting job?
3. As a babysitter, what could you do to learn children's family rules?
4. How do babies communicate their needs?

## Apply Your Learning

1. What should you do if a child becomes seriously injured while in your care?
2. How can you prevent children from getting into poisonous substances?
3. Describe a reliable babysitter.
4. **Puppet Play.** Children love to become pretend characters and tell stories. The next time you are babysitting, take supplies to make puppets: old, clean socks; yarn, ribbon, buttons, markers, and pieces of scrap fabric. Create your puppets, then let the kids tell stories. *Note:* Do not let very young children handle small buttons. They could choke on them.

# Chapter 11

# Managing Your Money

## You Will Discover . . .

- how to evaluate advertisements.
- how to compare price and quality.
- sources of income and expenses.
- how to develop a plan for spending and saving money.
- how to manage your money.

## Key Words

- consumer
- advertisement
- comparison shopping
- warranty
- redress
- shoplifting
- income
- expenses
- budget
- credit

Do you ever think about how you spend your money? Do you buy a new DVD or go to a movie? Do you save money to buy a birthday present for your mother or perhaps for your college education? The way people manage their money reflects their needs and wants. How do your needs and wants influence your spending?

## Teens as Consumers

Teens spend their money to buy goods and services. Goods are products made for sale, such as in-line skates, computer games, or jeans. Services, or work performed for others, include the work done to repair your bike, or teach you karate. Even if you don't spend a great deal of money, you can be a smart shopper if you know what factors influence your buying decisions. A **consumer** is a person who buys goods and services.

As a consumer, you have many decisions to make. You must decide what to buy, where to buy, and when to buy. You have to decide how to get the best value for your money. By making wise purchases, you will be a satisfied consumer. See Fig. 11-1.

**Fig. 11-1** As a consumer, you have many choices when it comes to spending money.

## Buying Decisions

When you bought your last pair of athletic shoes, what influenced your decision? Did your friends convince you that you needed the shoes? Maybe your decision was based on price. Perhaps you saw an advertisement that encouraged you to purchase the shoes. An **advertisement** is a message that persuades consumers to buy a product or service.

Have you ever tried out a new shampoo because some of your friends were using it? Have you ever decided to buy a new backpack because a friend bought one? Your friends influence your buying decisions. See Fig. 11-2.

Sometimes a buying trend can be started by a movie, concert, or sports event. Other students may carry a certain kind of bag or wear a certain brand of shoes that a celebrity wears. These items may even become status symbols, or signs of popularity and importance.

Before you make a purchase, evaluate the product. You may choose to wait or to buy something else. Do what is best for you, and be proud of your individuality.

Fig. 11-2 Before buying goods or services, think about why you want to make the purchase. Who influences your buying habits?

## Buying Habits

As you have probably discovered, many of your buying decisions are influenced by your habits. If you always shop at the same store, you may be passing up good prices offered at another store. Sometimes you need to evaluate your habits to make sure that you are being a careful shopper.

## Internet ACTIVITIES

1. **Search the Internet for an example of a brand ad and an information ad for a product such as a running shoe. Compare the two ads. Write down the differences between the two ads.**

   Key Search Words:
   - **information advertising**
   - **brand advertising**

2. **Search the Internet for resources that could help you make a wise product choice. Create a list of buying tips to share.**

   Key Search Words:
   - **comparison shopping**
   - **buying guidelines**

Fig. 11-3 You are surrounded by advertisements for products and services.

# Advertising

Advertising is another important influence on people's buying decisions. Advertising is everywhere you look—in newspapers and magazines, on television and radio, on clothing and buses, and on the Internet.

Advertisements, or ads, are designed to catch the attention of consumers and convince them to buy a product or service. Ads influence consumers by presenting goods or services in an attractive way.

Ads introduce new products and point out their benefits. In addition, they let you know about sales. Looking at the weekly advertising circulars is a great way to compare prices. See Fig. 11-3.

Some ads deliver a public-service message. They may warn people about the dangers of tobacco, alcohol, and other drugs. Other advertisements ask people to conserve resources or donate money to charitable organizations.

There are also disadvantages to advertising. Some ads persuade people to buy items they don't need, especially if the product is endorsed by a celebrity the consumers like or admire. Ads can also be misleading or make exaggerated claims.

## Types of Advertisements

Advertisements generally fall into one of two categories: information ads and image ads. Each type of ad sends a different kind of message.

- **Information ads** are ads that describe the features of a product or service and give facts about its price and quality. Information ads send the message that an item is a good buy for the price or because of its high quality.

- **Image ads** connect a product or service to a lifestyle that consumers would like to have. Image ads often use celebrities to endorse, or recommend, a product. They send the message that consumers will be more attractive or popular, or perhaps smarter or healthier, if they use the product or service. Image ads are often used to promote fashions, cosmetics, and other items that a person may want but does not actually need.

## Evaluating Advertising

Before you decide to buy a service or product, be sure to analyze the advertising claims. See Fig. 11-4.

- **Ads mention only the best features of a product.** Before buying, think about what you need to know about the product to decide which brand is best for you.

**Fig. 11-4 Advertising techniques are used to send messages.** Which of these advertising techniques have you experienced?

**Slogans.** Advertisers use slogans and jingles to remind people of their products.

**Endorsements.** Advertisers use famous people, including actors, athletes, and musicians, to promote their products.

**Product Characters.** A popular technique is to use cartoon characters to advertise products.

**Emotional Appeals.** With this technique, advertisers tell you that you will be happier, healthier, and more popular if you use their products.

# A CLOSER L**OO**K

## ...at Types of Media

### Electronic Media

The Internet, radio, and television are examples of electronic media. Internet advertising appears on the computer screen when users are on-line. The ads that you hear on the radio and see on television are called commercials. A special kind of television commercial called an infomercial is a lengthy product information commercial.

### Print Media

Newspapers and magazines are examples of print media. Food and clothing stores often place ads in newspapers to reach their local customers. Companies that sell products nationwide may take out ads in national magazines. Items that appeal to a specific audience are often advertised in specialty magazines.

## Signs & Displays

Signs and displays are two other types of media that you have seen many times. Advertising signs can appear on billboards, buses, taxis, and storefronts. Window displays as well as product displays inside stores attract buyers.

## Direct Mail

Mail-order catalogs and coupons are examples of direct mail. Catalog retailers and wholesalers use direct mail. Some companies use only direct mail to advertise their products.

## Telemarketing

Telemarketing means calling a person's house to discuss a product or service. Telemarketers use this means to reach people they think will respond to telephone offers.

- **Separate emotional appeals from facts.** Does the ad suggest that the product will make the buyer healthier, more attractive, or even happier than is realistic?
- **Don't trust endorsements.** Famous people appear in ads to get your attention, but they are seldom experts in nutrition, medicine, or fashion.
- **Beware of slogans.** They may make certain items memorable, but they are not a guarantee of quality.

## Getting More Information

Although the federal government requires advertisers to make truthful claims, companies often exaggerate how good their products are. You don't have to depend on advertisements for all your information about a product or service, however. Other sources of useful information are also available to you.

One of the most reliable sources of information is the people you know. Ask your family and friends what brand of a product they use, whether it works well, and if the item was worth the money they paid. Another good source is consumer magazines. Consumer organizations test products, survey the people who use them, and then report their findings. See Fig. 11-5.

A third source of information is product labels. Learning what a product is made of, and how much care it needs, can help you determine if it is the right one for you.

**Fig. 11–5 When you plan to make an important purchase, ask your family members for recommendations. How else can you research a purchase before making a decision?**

## ➤ Shopping Skills

Skillful shoppers get the best value for their money. As you develop your shopping skills, you will get greater satisfaction from the purchases you make and save a great deal of money over the years.

Now is the time to learn how to be an informed shopper. Begin by reading labels. Compare prices at different stores and among different brands. Look closely at merchandise to judge its quality. Check to see whether the manufacturer will replace or repair the item if it breaks.

Fig. 11-6 Smart shoppers compare price and quality.

It is possible to find out some of this information before you even walk into a store. See Fig. 11-6.

Impulse buying means making a sudden decision to buy. Did you ever decide to buy candy or a magazine while you were standing in the checkout line? When people buy on impulse, they often purchase things they don't need, that are not worth the money, or were not budgeted. See Fig. 11-7.

Collect information about products from friends and family members and advertisements. Word of mouth is a great way to find out about products and services. Ask friends and family such questions as:

- Are you satisfied with the product?
- What do you like or dislike about it?
- Would you purchase the product again?

Fig. 11-7 Impulse buying leads to the purchase of items you do not need or cannot afford. How can you avoid impulse buying?

## Selecting a Store

What types of stores are familiar to you? Different kinds of stores carry different selections of merchandise. The best store for you depends on the particular item you want to buy, the price you are willing to pay, and the service you need. See Fig. 11-8.

Prices for the same item often vary among stores. Suppose that you are looking for a DVD player. You may go to a department store that carries a wide range of merchandise. Most department stores sell clothing, shoes, household items, and electronic equipment. Department stores usually offer many services, such as gift-wrapping and delivery.

You may choose a specialty store, a store that carries only a specific type of merchandise. In a store that specializes in electronic equipment, you will probably find a large selection of DVD players. The prices in a specialty store may be higher than in a department store, unless the store is very large or part of a chain.

**Fig. 11-8 Choosing where to shop can be difficult. How do you decide where to shop?**

Chain stores are stores that bear the same name and carry the same merchandise. There are chains of department stores as well as of specialty stores. Some chain stores cater specifically to teens.

Another type of store is the factory outlet, a store that carries only one manufacturer's products. Outlets have a limited selection of styles and some items may be imperfect, but you will find low prices.

Discount stores are stores that carry a selection of items at low prices. Some discount stores specialize in a particular kind of merchandise, such as household linens, or athletic shoes. Few customer services are provided, but the prices are among the lowest available. Other stores that sell merchandise at discounted prices include membership warehouses and thrift shops.

Another shopping option is to buy products from catalogs. Some catalogs are associated with stores and carry merchandise that the stores cannot keep in stock. Other catalog companies do business only by telephone and mail.

Electronic shopping is available on the Internet. Consumers can view pictures and descriptions of the merchandise offered by many different stores and manufacturers. While on-line, you can place an order that will be received instantly.

When choosing a shopping option, you may want to consider how important it is to you to see and inspect the merchandise yourself. Also keep in mind how convenient it is to get to the store and whether it is a pleasant place to shop.

## Checking Quality & Price

After you have decided where to shop, you will need to consider certain factors before making your purchase. **Comparison shopping**, or checking quality and price and reading labels and guarantees, will help you get the best value for your money. See Fig. 11-9.

Some people think that price is an indicator of how good a product is. They think that a more expensive product must be superior. That is not always the case.

**Fig. 11-9 Prices vary among brands and stores.** How can reading labels and comparing prices get you the best value?

Items that are on sale may be less expensive than regular-priced items, but may not be of the same quality. Stores sometimes sell products that they have bought at special, lower prices. The quality of these items may also be lower than that of their regular merchandise. You need to look carefully at products on sale to see if they really are bargains.

Higher-priced items may be of good quality, but they may also contain features that you don't need. For instance, having an additional five speeds on your bike may not be a feature you consider worth the extra money.

## Reading Labels

Labels give useful information about the features and the use and care of the product. Labels also give information required by law on products such as clothing and food. A clothing label must contain the name of the manufacturer, country of origin, fiber content, and instructions for care. Labels on foods list ingredients by weight, from greatest to least. If a can of chili lists beans before meat, you can expect to see more beans than meat when you open the can. Food labels must also contain the name of the product, the name and address of the manufacturer, weight of the contents, and a nutrition label on all processed foods. Food labels also give information on how to prepare the food.

## Checking Warranties

Many items come with a guarantee or a warranty. A **warranty** is the manufacturer's written promise to repair or replace a product if it does not work as claimed. Be sure to read the warranty so that you know what is promised. Some warranties apply only to certain parts of the product or only under specific conditions.

Regardless of the way you pay for an item, however, remember to keep the receipt and tags as proof of your purchase. Keep the receipt and the warranty in a safe place. If you decide to return the item, you will need the receipt.

# Explore

## Consumer Reports Magazine

### State the Task

- Use *Consumer Reports* magazine as a research tool when buying a product.

### Develop a Plan

1. Choose an electronic product that you want to purchase. Some ideas include a DVD player, palm-size organizer, or computer.
2. Make a list of the features that you want the electronic product to have.
3. Make a list of local electronic and department stores and look up their telephone numbers.

### Implement the Plan

1. Use *Consumer Reports* magazine to look for comparison information on your chosen electronic device. Make a list of the brands and models that have the desired features.
2. Compare the prices, quality, and features of all the models on your list to determine which is the best value.
3. Call the local stores on your list to find out if they carry the product you desire. Ask for the price and write it down.

### Evaluate the Result

1. How many choices did you have that offered your list of desired features?
2. How did the prices compare?
3. How many stores in your community carried the desired brand or model?
4. How else could you purchase the product if a local store didn't carry it?

# ➤ Your Consumer Rights

Consumers have rights that protect them from false advertising and unsafe products. The law requires manufacturers to put labels on food and clothing and to make products that are safe to use. Your rights make it possible for you to voice a complaint if you are not satisfied with a product or service.

Your consumer rights may have helped you already. For example, if you returned a shirt that didn't fit, you exercised some of your rights. See Fig. 11-10. The following are included among your specific rights as a consumer:

- **The right to safety.** Products must be well designed and, if used properly, must not cause harm or injury.
- **The right to be informed.** Labels give you information about products. Laws protect you from false or misleading advertisements.
- **The right to choose.** Consumers are entitled to choose from a variety of products. They have the right to select the items that fit their needs.
- **The right to be heard.** Consumers can speak out about a product if they are not satisfied with it.
- **The right to redress.** Action taken to correct a wrong is called **redress**. Consumers can seek redress if they have a problem with a product.

Fig. 11-10 As a consumer, you have the right to return items that do not fit your needs. Return policies vary by store.

- **The right to consumer education.** Consumers are entitled to learn about their rights. Consumer rights protect you and help you get the best product for your money. However, along with those rights you also have responsibilities.

## ➤ Your Consumer Responsibilities

Do you consider yourself a responsible consumer? Being courteous, counting your change, handling merchandise carefully, and getting the information you need are all part of being a responsible consumer.

### Being Courteous

When you have to return an item to the store, you should do so in a polite way. Calmly explain to the salesperson what the problem is and how you would like to resolve it. For example, do you want your money back, or do you want to trade the item for another size or color? Remember to bring your receipt with you.

### Behaving Responsibly

The manufacturer also has responsibilities—to produce a product that is good, safe, and reasonably priced. As a responsible consumer, you need to read and follow the instructions. Experts who understand the product prepare instructions that provide for your safety and satisfaction. It is important to follow them. See Fig. 11-11.

Another way to behave responsibly is to handle merchandise with care. This applies to more than breakable items. Clothing can also be easily damaged while you are trying it on. Remove your shoes before trying on pants. Return clothes that you have tried on to their hangers and leave the dressing room neat.

**Fig. 11-11** As a consumer, it is your responsibility to follow the manufacturer's instructions. How else can you show consumer responsibility?

If you get a warranty card with a product, fill it out and send it to the manufacturer. The date on the card lets the manufacturer know when the warranty expires, or runs out. Keep your warranties together in one place.

## Being Honest

When paying cash for your purchases, pay attention to the change you receive. If you receive too much change, return it to the salesperson. Otherwise that person may be responsible for replacing the money.

Some teens do not realize the seriousness of shoplifting. **Shoplifting**, or taking items from a store without paying for them, is stealing. Some teens look at shoplifting as a prank. Their friends may dare them to do it. Shoplifting is a serious crime for which a person may go to jail. It is a crime that remains on that person's record. Shoplifting costs businesses billions of dollars each year. These losses are passed on to customers as increased prices.

## Refunds & Exchanges

Like most people, you have probably purchased a product that did not work properly. What did you do? You may have asked for an exchange—a trade of one item for another—or a refund, the return of your money in exchange for the item. Whenever you make an exchange or ask for a refund, follow these guidelines:

- **Know the store's policy.** Every store sets its own return-and-exchange policy. The policy is usually posted where you pay for the item. Read the policy. If you don't understand it, ask the clerk before paying for the purchase. Never assume that you can return an item.

- **Keep proof of your purchase.** The store receipt is proof of the price, date of purchase, and store where you bought an item. Most stores require you to show your receipt in order to receive a refund.

- **Determine whether you are entitled to a refund.** Some items that are defective or on sale are marked "As Is" or "All Sales Final." In these cases you are not entitled to a refund. Certain products such as bathing suits, underwear, and pierced earrings are usually not returnable because of health codes.

- **Be ready to process your claim.** Take your merchandise and sales receipt to the store if you are entitled to a refund. You may be asked to complete a form giving a reason for returning the item. When the item is defective, be sure to provide this information so that the store can notify the manufacturer.

**Fig. 11-12** How you spend your money is more important than the amount you have to spend.

## ➤ Money Management

You will be earning, spending, and saving money all of your life. The key to managing your money is to remember that the amount you have to spend is less important than how you spend it. Even if you have only a small amount to spend, you can stretch your buying power by learning to buy and save wisely. See Fig. 11-12.

To manage your money wisely you will need to:

- know the source of your income.
- determine how much money you will have.
- look at how much money you are spending.
- evaluate what you are buying.

Your **income** is the amount of money you earn or receive regularly. Your **expenses** are the monies you spend to buy goods and services. If you manage your money well, you will not spend more on expenses than you receive as income. What are your sources of income? What are your expenses?

**DID YOU know?**

**Snacks Cost.** Imagine that you spend $5 a week on snacks. Did you know that over five years your snack habit would have cost you $1,300?

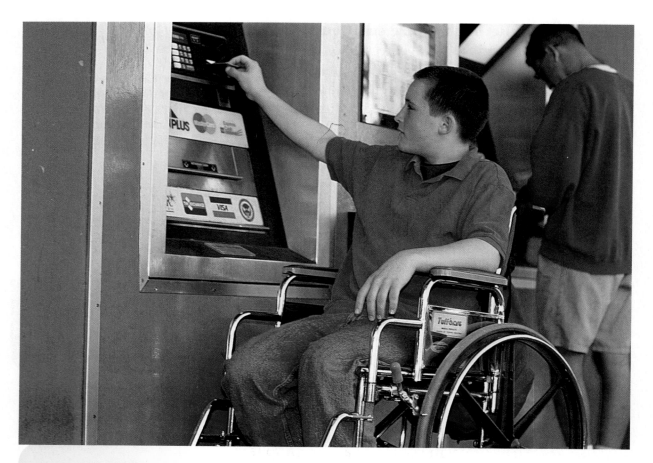

**Fig. 11-13** Budget your money so that you will be able to buy what you need and want. Do you follow a budget?

## Planning & Budgeting

Before you set up a **budget**, or plan for using your money, you need to examine your goals. Do you want to save enough money for a new skateboard? Do you want to pay for singing lessons so that you can try out for the musical at school? Are you saving money to buy your parents an anniversary gift?

Once you have an income, record your expenses, and understand your goals, you can plan a budget. Begin by setting aside enough money to cover your expenses. When your income does not cover your expenses, you will need to make some adjustments. You may choose to cut back on some of your expenses or to find new ways to add money to your weekly income. See Fig. 11-13.

Your budget should include a savings plan. A savings plan helps you put money aside for unexpected needs

## Making Connections

**Math.** When you put money in a savings account, the money earns interest, a fee the bank pays to use your money. The interest is added to the principal, or the money in your account.

### Get Involved!

Imagine that instead of buying junk food you put $15 a week in a savings account that pays five percent interest. How much would you have after one year? Contact a local bank to find out what types of savings accounts are available and the rates of interest.

and for future use. Many people find it easier to save when they set goals, such as having money for holiday activities. Some teens begin saving for a car or a college education. Unless you plan ahead and save regularly, it might be difficult to achieve your goals.

It's a good idea to loan the money you save to a bank. The interest your bank pays is added to the money in your account. In this way your money grows.

## Paying for Purchases

Teens generally pay for their purchases with cash. You may not always have enough cash to buy what you want, however. Here are some other payment options:

- **Layaway plan.** A layaway plan is a scheduled payment plan in which you put a small amount of money down and make regular payments until you have paid for the item. When the item has been paid for in full, you take it home. See Fig. 11-14 on page 214.

**Fig. 11-14** Layaway plans can help you purchase items within your budget.

- **Check.** A check is a written order directing a bank to pay the person or business named on the check. In order to pay by check, a person must open a checking account and deposit enough money to cover the checks you write. A checking account is a convenient way of handling money without keeping cash on hand.
- **Debit cards.** A debit card is used to withdraw money directly from a person's bank account. For example, people can use debit cards to pay for groceries.
- **Credit cards.** You can buy now and pay later using a method of payment called **credit**. Either the seller or a bank must trust in your ability to make payments until the item is paid in full. Interest on the unpaid balance is charged for the use of a credit card. Credit is often used to buy expensive items such as furniture or large appliances.

 How To...

# Recognize Your Expenses

### State the Task

• Create a spreadsheet to track your expenses.

### Develop a Plan

1. Make a list of all of the expenses you have for one month. By looking at your expense record, you can evaluate how you spend your money. You can decide whether you should improve your buying habits.
2. Identify whether they are necessary expenses (such as lunch), or discretionary expenses (such as going to the movies).
3. Develop a chart using the sample on this page as a guide. Each day list the date, the items you buy, and the amount you spend. Use a spreadsheet program to create the chart on the computer.

### Implement the Plan

1. Total up the amounts at the end of each day and at the end of each week.
2. Note whether the expenses are necessary.

### Evaluate the Result

1. What does your spreadsheet say about your spending habits? Will you make any changes? Explain your answer.
2. Make a list of items you could have purchased later when you have the money.
3. Make a list of items that cost you more than you expected to pay.

| Expense Worksheet | Date | Purchase |
|---|---|---|
| Savings | | |
| Clothing | | |
| Food | | |
| Recreation | | |
| School Supplies | | |
| Grooming Supplies | | |
| Other | | |

# Career CHOICES

## Accountant

Prepares financial reports. Prepares entries to accounts documenting business transactions. Details assets, liabilities, and capital. Prepares balance sheets, profit-and-loss statements, and other financial statements.

## Tax Accountant

Prepares federal, state, or local tax returns for individuals, businesses, or organizations. Computes taxes owed according to laws and regulations. Suggests ways to lower taxes.

## Ad Space Reservationist

Measures and draws outlines of advertising space and records data. Adds up total inches of advertising and news copy. Arranges advertisements on each sheet so that competitive ads do not appear on the same page.

## Debt Collector

Collects debts by phone, mail, and in person. Contacts people at home or work to set up payment arrangements. Reports delinquent accounts to the proper authorities.

## Personal Shopper

Selects and purchases merchandise for clients. Shops in department stores and on-line to find items requested. Processes mail orders and merchandise returned for exchange.

---

**AT** **School**

Select three of the careers listed. Research the education, training, and work experience required for each career. Compare the results to select a career to investigate further.

**IN THE** **Workplace**

Make a list of the buying decisions that might need to be made on the job. Compare lists with your classmates.

---

**Communication skills are critical in financial careers. Consider job shadowing someone with a financial career.**

## Chapter Summary

- Evaluate advertising messages by deciding what you want from a product; separating emotional appeal from facts; not overly trusting endorsements; and being wary of slogans.
- A careful shopper compares price, quality, labels, and warranties.
- Keeping an expense record, setting up a budget, and starting a savings plan are smart methods of money management.

## Words You Learned

1. Why is everyone a consumer?
2. What is an advertisement?
3. Define comparison shopping.
4. What is a warranty?
5. Define shoplifting.
6. What is meant by right to redress?

7. Define income.
8. Define expenses.
9. What is a budget?
10. Explain why credit is not free.

## Check Your Facts

1. What choices do you have as a consumer?
2. Name three factors that influence your buying decisions.
3. Name three ways to get product information before you go to a store.
4. What factors should you consider when selecting a store?
5. Explain how shoplifting affects the price you pay for goods.
6. What is the purpose of keeping an expense record?
7. Why should you have a savings plan?

**Apply Your Learning**

1. Make a list of eight items that you purchased recently. Next to each item, identify what most influenced your buying decision—friends, family, habit, or advertising. Compare your list with those of your classmates.
2. What is the relationship between price and quality? What should you consider when comparing price and quality?
3. Name four ways to pay for purchases.
4. **Create an Ad.** Create a fictitious product and make a print ad to advertise it. Color your ad or create it on the computer so it will draw attention. Ask your teacher's permission to post your ad on the bulletin board.

# Chapter 12

# Managing Your Resources

## You Will Discover . . .

- the management process.
- personal, material, and community resources to help you reach your goals.
- time-management tools and techniques.
- how to improve your study skills.
- the effects of stress.

## Key Words

- management
- resource
- prioritize
- procrastinate
- stress

*M*egan and her friend Theresa are opposites. Theresa always has her homework done on time, while Megan is often working on hers until the last minute. Theresa gets more accomplished than Megan because Theresa practices good management skills. **Management** is using what you have to accomplish something. Being organized and planning ahead will help you manage your resources.

## ➤ The Management Process

People who manage well accomplish more with greater ease. They use their time and energy wisely. Katie and Hassan are good managers. Katie has learned to multi-task in order to get more accomplished. Hassan gets to school a half-hour early so that he can work in the computer lab.

You can be a good manager if you learn to follow a few basic steps. These steps work whether you are writing a report or organizing a fundraiser for the school band.

- **Step 1—Decide on your goal.** Write it down on a piece of paper. Maybe you need to finish your science project by a certain date. Writing down your goal helps you commit to it. See Fig. 12-1.

Fig. 12-1 The key to management is planning. Writing down goals makes planning easier.

- **Step 2—Make a plan.** Decide how you want to achieve the goal. Maybe the goal can be broken into smaller, short-term goals that are easier to reach. For example, if you want to finish the project in two weeks, you could work on research this week and writing next week.

- **Step 3—Put the plan into action.** Begin working on your plan. If you are going to try out for the cheerleading squad, don't just talk about it—practice!

- **Step 4—Evaluate the results.** When you evaluate the outcome of your plan, you determine the value of what you accomplished. Are you satisfied with the way your plan worked? If not, what would you do differently the next time?

# Internet ACTIVITIES

1. **Search the Internet for tips on time management. Write down at least 10 tips and describe how each one would help you.**

   **Key Search Words:**
   - **time management**
   - **saving time**

2. **Search the Internet for ideas on organizing your study space. Make a list of five tips or suggestions and share them with your classmates.**

   **Key Search Words:**
   - **organizing space**
   - **study space**

## ➤ Resource Management

To be a good manager you must make full use of your resources. A **resource** is a source of information or expertise that you can use to help you meet your goals. The three types are personal resources, material resources, and community resources.

### Personal Resources

Personal resources are time, energy, knowledge, skills, and people. How well you use your personal resources will make a difference in how much you accomplish.

- **Time.** Everyone has 24 hours each day. Much of this time is spent sleeping, eating, grooming, studying, working, and playing. The time that is left over can be used for special activities. Learn to use your time wisely. See Fig. 12-2.
- **Energy.** Energy is the power or ability to be active. It has to do with the strength of the body and mind to work and play. Keep your energy level up by getting enough sleep, eating nutritious foods, and following a regular exercise program. Your attitude toward what has to be done also affects how energetic you may feel.

**Fig. 12-2 Time does not stop for anyone. How do you manage your time?**

- **Knowledge.** Knowledge is information and understanding. Throughout your life you will continue to learn. Knowledge is a powerful personal resource.
- **Skills.** A skill is an ability that comes from training or practice. You have reading, writing, and computer skills. You may also have other skills, such as the ability to play tennis, which you learned by taking lessons. Talents are different from skills. A talent is a natural ability, such as being able to draw, sing, or dance. What are your talents?
- **People.** People are valuable resources. Strong relationships with family and friends will provide support all your life. The encouragement of family and friends can help you gain confidence and strengthen your self-concept.

## Material Resources

Material resources are possessions, objects, and money. They make it easier to do what you want to do. Your personal possessions might include a bike, a stereo, or books. Objects might include a refrigerator, a table, or a microwave oven. How do these possessions and objects help you do what you want to do? What role does money play in reaching your goals?

Personal possessions give you enjoyment and satisfaction. Riding your bike and listening to your stereo are two ways that you gain enjoyment from your possessions. Objects make life easier. For example, using a washing machine to wash clothes is easier than washing them by hand. Buying a cake is quicker than baking one yourself.

## Community Resources

Every community provides a variety of resources for its citizens to use. These include schools, hospitals, and police and fire departments. Some communities have interesting places to visit, such as museums or important historic buildings. Among other community resources are youth programs, parks, and recreational facilities. See Fig. 12-3.

**Fig. 12–3 Community parks allow you to enjoy many outdoor activities.** What resources are provided by your community?

Communities also provide resources for people who have special kinds of problems. Most communities offer programs for the homeless, the elderly, people with low income, and people who have problems with alcohol and other drugs. There are also programs to protect battered spouses and abused children.

## ➤ Time Management

Using good time-management skills will help you in all areas of your life. You will have more time for special activities, such as playing basketball or starting a stamp collection. You won't constantly be late or forget to do important tasks. You will have more time for yourself and others.

Time management also includes dealing with problems that may arise. You may find that two activities occur at the same time. You may have to make a choice between two things you really want to do. Think about what is more important to you, and make a choice. Then act on your decision.

### DID YOU know?

**Time-saving Techniques.** Here are some ways to save time.
- Divide big jobs into small tasks.
- Do two tasks at the same time.
- Try to avoid interruptions.
- Stick with a task until it is done.
- Establish routines for daily tasks.

Sometimes you have several things you want to accomplish during a day. It may be difficult to know where to begin. In this case, you can rank the tasks in order of importance, or **prioritize** them. If you are using a to-do list, put an *A*, *B*, or *C* next to each task. Activities marked with an *A* are top-priority items. They need to be done first. The *B* activities are completed next. The *C* activities are the least important activities. If these activities are not done, they can wait until the next day. As you complete each task, cross it off the list and see how much you have accomplished.

Another challenge is dealing with unexpected changes. Sometimes schedules and lists do not work out exactly as planned. A friend may have to cancel a shopping trip to the mall you had scheduled. The rain may prevent you from raking leaves. Whatever the case, stay flexible. Make the most of your time by having ideas for alternate activities. See Fig. 12-4.

Fig. 12-4 Studying for a test is a good use of time when you get a good grade. How can you prioritize your study time to make it count?

## Making Time Count

Have you ever turned on the television to watch one show and later realized that you were watching television for hours? Perhaps you have spent a lot of time looking for your math book, only to find it under a stack of papers. Here are some ways to avoid wasting time.

- **Avoid putting things off.** If you **procrastinate** (PRO-cra-stuh-nayt), or put things off, you can waste a lot of time thinking and worrying about the task you need to do. Usually you will find the job itself doesn't take very long when you finally do it.

- **Get organized.** Almost any task goes faster when you are organized. Before you begin the task, gather the tools or equipment you need and find out how to do the task. See Fig. 12-5.
- **Take care of yourself.** You may think that you can make more time by sleeping less. You will find out it doesn't work that way. Often you end up getting less done, instead of more, because you are tired.

## Study Skills

As a student, you will find much of your time is spent studying. Make sure the time is well spent by organizing and prioritizing your studies. Here are a few tips:

- **Make a "to-do list."** What goals do you want to reach? List what you want to accomplish.
- **Set the time.** Decide how much time you are going to spend studying. Prioritize your tasks to fit that block of time. Try to study at the same time every day.
- **Set the atmosphere.** Choose a quiet place to study. Make sure the space has enough light and enough space to spread out.
- **Remove distractions.** Turn off the television, and don't use the telephone while you study. Send friends home, and siblings out of the room.
- **Gather supplies.** Gather all of your pens, pencils, erasers, and books before you begin.

Effective study skills include good reading skills, note-taking skills, test-taking skills, listening skills, and time-management skills. Keep track of the areas where you need to improve your study skills. Consider taking courses on how to study. Ask for help when you need it. You could also get tutoring help. It is important that you continue to improve your study skills. You will use them at home, at school, on the job, and in the community.

Fig. 12-5 Organizing the tools you need before beginning a task will save you time. What are some other ways to save time?

# How To...

## Create a Schedule of Activities

### State the Task

• Make a monthly schedule of activities.

### Develop a Plan

1. Determine how you spend your time by making a daily list of your activities and the approximate amount of time you spend on each one. Include the time you are at school, family time, study time, chores, volunteer activities, sports, extracurricular activities, and clubs or organizations.

2. Divide a sheet of paper in two columns. In one column list all of your routine activities, such as sleeping, eating, and grooming. List the amount of time you spend on each of these activities.

3. In the other column, list activities that are not routine and the amount of time you spend doing each. For example, are you attending a birthday party or participating in a music recital?

4. Add up all of the hours and divide them by the number of days in the week.

### Implement the Plan

1. Divide a second sheet of paper into seven columns and five rows to show an entire month. Label each with a date.

2. List your activities on each date.

3. Prioritize your activities and add up the hours for each day.

4. Decide what you would like to do with your unscheduled time.

5. Refer to your calendar for any special activities.

6. Post your schedule in a prominent place and check it each day.

### Evaluate the Result

1. Did you have more activities scheduled than there were hours in the day? If so, how did you adjust your schedule?

2. Are you spending more time on activities than studying? How can you adjust your schedule?

3. Did you find that any of your activities were scheduled at the same time? If so, how did you solve this problem?

## ➤ The Stress Connection

When you try to do too much, you will experience stress. **Stress** is the body's reaction to changes around it. Both pleasant and unpleasant events cause stress. For example, performing a solo in a school concert may be stressful even though you enjoy singing. Whatever the situation, remember that stress is a natural part of life. See Fig. 12-6 on page 228.

How much stress you feel depends on how much is going on in your life and how you see events. For instance, adjusting to a new class and making new friends would be somewhat stressful to most people. If you are handling

**The Stress Factor. Stress triggers the release of adrenaline, which speeds up your heart rate and blood pressure. Prolonged stress on the heart can affect the body's immune system.**

## Making Connections

**Language Arts.** Netiquette is the accepted rules of conduct for Internet users. Be aware of these rules:
1. Always complete the subject line when sending a message so that the person receiving your message can identify your subject.
2. Do not use offensive language. Do not type anything that you would not show your teacher, your parents, or your boss.
3. Do not copy other people's messages without their permission.
4. Do not type in all caps because that is considered shouting.
5. Be careful when using humor as others may not be able to tell when you are "just kidding."
6. Do not forward messages from an unknown source.
7. Do not share another person's email address without his or her permission.

### Get Involved!

Write an email message to a friend that explains what you are learning about managing resources in this class. Be sure to follow netiquette!

another major life change at the same time, such as changing schools, the stress would be even greater. Here are some tips for managing stress.

1. Talk to someone you respect and trust.
2. Spend time on a hobby, such as painting or writing song lyrics.
3. Exercise by walking or riding a bicycle.
4. Participate in a sport, such as soccer or basketball.
5. Eat nutritious food.
6. Get plenty of rest.
7. Take quick breaks by closing your eyes for a minute or doing stretching exercises.
8. Practice taking deep breaths to calm yourself.
9. Plan ahead for events that you can anticipate.
10. Think positive.

Stress can also motivate and challenge you. It can help you accomplish your goals in life. The stress of wanting to make the soccer team, for example, would motivate you to exercise and practice.

Constant stress, however, can have a negative effect on you. It can cause depression and a lack of physical or mental energy. People who are unable to cope, or adjust to a difficult situation, may become depressed or seriously ill. Sometimes they try to run away from their problems by turning to alcohol or other drugs. By managing your time, and the changes in your life, you will be equipped to better handle stress when it occurs. *A Closer Look at Handling Stress* on pages 230-231 offers some available resources to help you handle stress in a positive way. Search the Internet for a list of tips, techniques, and support organizations that address various forms of stress.

**Fig. 12-6 When you try to do too much, you feel stressed out. How can you cope with stress?**

# Explore

## Reducing Stress

### State the Task

- Identify sources of stress and learn techniques to reduce stress.

### Develop a Plan

1. Write down the sources of your stress or the stressful situations in your life.
2. Divide the list into three columns: time stressors, people stressors, and "other" stressors.
3. On another sheet of paper, make a list of ways you could reduce stress.

### Implement the Plan

1. Match one of your stressors with one of your ideas to reduce stress.
2. Continue through your list, matching each stressor to a stress-reducing technique.
3. Tackle time stressors first. For example, could you lay your clothes out and pack your book bag at night in order to save time in the morning?
4. Tackle people stressors next. For example, if your sister borrows clothes and doesn't launder them before returning them, tell her she won't be allowed to borrow them in the future.
5. Finally, consider "other" stressors. If you get nervous before a big test, practice deep breathing exercises to help you calm down and focus.

### Evaluate the Result

1. What was the most significant change you made to reduce stress?
2. Did you have to re-schedule any of your time? How did this help you reduce stress?

---

**To de-stress:**

- **Breathe deeply.** Breathe in through your nose and out through your mouth, slowly and evenly. Do this for several minutes to relax.
- **Exercise.** Go for a walk, play a game of basketball, or go jogging. Exercise will help clear your head.
- **Make a list.** When you feel overwhelmed, make a "to-do" list and prioritize your tasks.
- **Picture perfect.** Visualize a beautiful scene in your mind to help you relax.
- **Take time.** Use your time wisely and don't over-schedule yourself.

# A CLOSER LOOK

## ...at Handling Stress

**Stress can affect your life in many ways. Symptoms may include changes in appetite, headaches, mood swings, and the inability to concentrate. Learning to manage stress means controlling events and situations using proper techniques.**

**Great Getaway**
Remove yourself from stressful situations, even if it's just a short break. Take a walk or listen to some relaxing music. Deep-breathing exercises can stop a racing heart and help clear your mind.

**Top Priorities**
Decide what tasks or activities are the most important and prioritize them. Make sure your goals are realistic.

### Health Check

Don't let your health suffer when you are feeling stressed. Work out to decrease your stress. Also, get plenty of sleep, eat a balanced diet, and take time to relax.

### Support Scene

Go to the people in your life who can provide support, encouragement, and advice. Friends and family who care about you can help in times of stress.

### Attitude Adjustment

Be positive about your situation. Remind yourself that stress is a part of life and you can work through the situation.

# Career CHOICES

## Human Resources Coordinator

Provides assistance in identifying and evaluating human-relations and work-performance problems. Works to achieve better communication. Develops and conducts training in conflict resolution, communication, and group interaction.

## Librarian

Maintains collections of books, magazines, documents, and other materials. Assists groups and individuals in locating and obtaining materials. Explains use of reference sources to find information. Helps people use library computers and programs.

**Computer skills are used on most every job.** How do you keep your computer skills up-to-date?

## Time–Study Manager

Directs time-and-motion studies to promote efficiency. Analyzes time-and-motion requirements of job duties. Analyzes equipment specifications to establish time and production standards.

## Transportation Scheduler

Prepares schedules for transportation systems. Determines number of vehicles and trips to be run. Arranges number of stops, length of routes, and runs per shift. Studies passenger riding patterns and traffic conditions. Establishes emergency routes.

## Production Manager

Trains and supervises employees engaged in production of radio or television programs. Makes sure the program follows station or network policies and regulations. Operates broadcasting equipment.

### AT School

Select three of the careers listed. Research the education, training, and work experience required for each career. Compare the results to select a career to investigate further.

### IN THE Workplace

Make a list of your computer skills and the software you have used. Find out ways you could improve your computer skills on the job.

## Chapter Summary

- To manage: 1) decide on your goal; 2) make a plan; 3) put the plan into action; 4) evaluate the results.
- Personal resources are time, energy, knowledge, skills, and people.
- Time management involves prioritizing tasks.
- You can make time count by getting organized and taking care of your own needs.
- Constant stress can cause a lack of physical and mental energy, depression, or serious illness.

## Words You Learned

1. What is the purpose of management?
2. How is a resource helpful?
3. What does it mean to prioritize?
4. Why do you waste time when you procrastinate?
5. What is stress?

## Check Your Facts

1. What are three types of resources?
2. What does it mean to prioritize tasks?
3. What are the benefits of good time management?
4. List three time-management tools.
5. Name four time-saving techniques.
6. Explain how stress can be a motivator.

## Apply Your Learning

1. Name five types of personal resources.
2. Describe a situation in which you used a community resource. Explain how you used the resource and how you benefited.
3. Describe a situation in which you felt stress and explain how you managed the stress.
4. **Get Organized.** Create organizers for each school subject you have. Start with empty cereal boxes. Cut out and discard the top and half of one wide side. Cover the remainder of the box with construction paper, wrapping paper, or wallpaper. Fill each box with an assignment notebook and the supplies you need for each class. Arrange the organizers in your study area.

# Chapter 13

# Your Living Space

## You Will Discover . . .

- how a home provides shelter and security.
- how to organize and share your living space.
- how design elements and principles are used.
- the value of keeping your home clean and safe.

## Key Words

- floor plan
- traffic pattern
- design
- accessories

People live in many types of homes—apartments, manufactured homes, duplexes, town homes, single-family houses, and condominiums. Homes come in all shapes, sizes, and colors, but all of them have one common feature. To the people living there, each one is called "home."

## Your Home

Homes satisfy the basic need for shelter. They are built to protect people from the weather—rain, snow, wind, and extreme temperatures. Homes also provide a place for you to take care of your personal needs. In your home you can bathe, prepare meals, and sleep comfortably. You also have a place to keep your clothes and personal possessions.

You get a sense of well-being and a feeling of security in your home. It is a place to relax and be yourself. Home is a place where you can enjoy listening to music, playing video games, or reading. It is a great place to spend time with family members and friends. See Fig. 13-1.

You also can use your home to express yourself. Take a look at your room. What do the objects in your room reveal about your interests? Does your room reflect your personality?

Fig. 13-1 Home is shelter and a place to relax with your family and friends.

## Living Areas

Most homes are divided into living areas in order to meet people's needs and interests. Some areas, such as bedrooms, are designed for privacy. Other areas, such as family rooms, are used for gathering with family members and entertaining friends. Dividing space into special areas makes the home more convenient and easier to manage.

Some areas serve more than one function. By organizing rooms for more than one function, you can make the best use of space, equipment, and furniture. For example, you probably use your bedroom not only for sleeping but also for studying, reading, and listening to music.

## Making Connections

**Technology.** Many homes are equipped with features that make life easier. Lights and appliances can be programmed to turn on and off at set times. Heating and cooling systems can be set to operate automatically. People can stay in touch by computer.

***Get Involved!***

Explain what role you think that computers play in home automation. Make a list of other types of automation that you expect to see in homes of the future.

## Organizing Your Space

To organize the space within your home, begin by thinking of the various activities of all your family members. What area would be best for each activity? For example, would exercise equipment be better located in a bedroom, the basement, or the family room? Should the computer be set up in a bedroom or in the den? See Fig. 13-2.

How do you and your family use the living space now? Are there improvements that could be made? If a shelving unit or different lighting were added, could the space be expanded to serve an additional function? A **floor plan** is a drawing of a room and how its furniture is arranged. It allows you to see how furniture fits together without physically moving furniture.

**Fig. 13-2** **Organize your living space to suit your needs.**

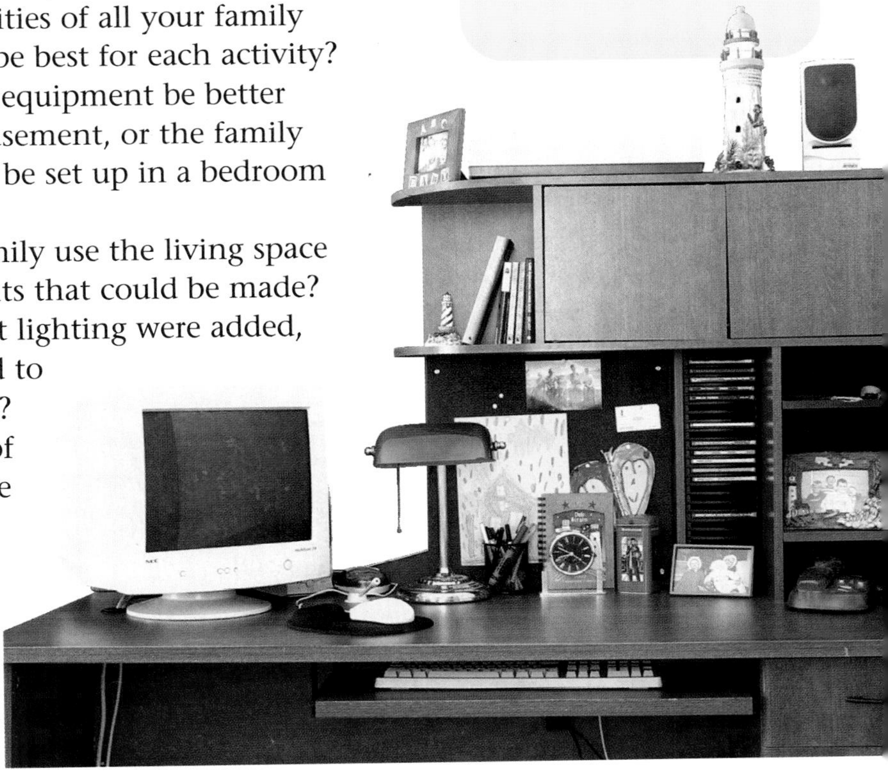

# How To...

## Create a Floor Plan

### State the Task

- Arrange a floor plan for your room.

### Develop a Plan

1. Measure your room and the furniture in it.
2. Draw the dimensions of your room on a piece of graph paper. One or two squares should equal each foot of space in the room.
3. Show where the doors and windows are located. Draw a dashed line to show which way the doors open.
4. On another sheet of graph paper draw the dimensions of each piece of your furniture using the same scale as the room. Cut out and label each piece.

### Implement the Plan

1. Place the furniture pieces on the room graph. Move the pieces of furniture around on the floor plan until you are satisfied with the new arrangement. Allow space for drawers and doors to open and for you to walk.
2. Make notes of the different ways you could arrange your furniture. How does each arrangement affect the traffic pattern?

### Supplies

- Tape measure
- Ruler
- Graph paper
- Pencil or pen
- Scissors
- Tape

### Evaluate the Result

1. Choose a final design and tape down the furniture pieces. Explain why you chose that particular arrangement.
2. How does it differ from the way you currently have your furniture arranged?
3. List any furniture that doesn't fit well in your new room design.

The way you organize your living space depends on the activities in which you and your family participate.

- Consider the traffic pattern in the room. The **traffic pattern** is the path people take to move around within a room as well as enter and exit the room. Furniture should be placed so as not to get in the way. If you find that you have to constantly walk around a chair, you should try a different arrangement.
- Leave space around furniture so it can be used comfortably. Drawers and doors require extra space for opening and closing.
- Place furniture in groupings that are functional, or useful, and convenient. For example, a small table and a lamp placed next to a bed create a functional grouping.
- Group related items together. For example, by storing cassettes next to a tape player, your music is organized and easily accessed.

## Selecting Furniture

Furniture style is a matter of personal taste. You may like furniture with sleek, modern lines. Your sister may prefer country-style furniture. Try looking in magazines and books to find the furniture styles you like best. Some furniture can serve more than one purpose. A desk that has a large surface area may be used as a computer station or a drawing table. See Fig. 13-3.

**Fig. 13-3 Furniture is available in many styles.** How can you select the best style for your home?

## Storage Space

Having enough storage space is essential for a functional room. Decide what objects should be stored in a given space. For example, paper, pens and pencils, and a dictionary should be stored in a study area. Items that would not be used in this area, such as videotapes, should be stored elsewhere.

# A CLOSER LOOK

## ...at Closet Organization

You can best utilize a closet by organizing the space and contents. Begin by cleaning out your closet. Pull out everything that you don't wear or want. Donate these items to charity, give them to a younger brother or sister, or sell them at a yard sale. Then try the following techniques:

### Hang Time
Add extra rods to the closet for hanging clothes. Double up rods for shirts, vests, and shorter items. Leave one space open to hang longer items such as dresses.

**Top Shelf**
Add a shelf along the top of the closet for items you don't use very often. If space allows, build shelves for shoes, accessories, and storage containers.

**Boxed In**
Store loose items like socks and baseball hats in plastic storage boxes or shoeboxes.

**Floor Exercise**
Place boots and shoes on the floor of the closet, along with any storage boxes that do not fit on the shelves.

## ➤ Your Room Design

Why do some rooms look more inviting than others? How can a room seem large, even though it is actually small? The way a room looks depends a great deal on how design was used—or not used—to create an overall effect. **Design** is the art of combining elements in a pleasing way. You can use design to create the type of look you want in a room. See Fig. 13-4.

**Fig. 13-4 Design your space to reflect your personality.**

## Design Elements

The elements of design are space, shape, line, texture, and color. Each contributes its own special effect to the final design.

• **Space.** Space helps draw attention to objects. For example, a vase on a shelf will stand out and be seen if some space is left on either side of it. On the other hand, too much space between objects can result in a bare, empty look. You can create many looks just by dividing space in various ways.

• **Shape.** Shape refers to the outline or form of solid objects. For example, a bed has a rectangular shape. A table may be rectangular, square, oval, or round. Attractive designs use shape effectively. Too many different shapes in one room can be distracting.

• **Line.** Lines are very important to design. Look around a room, and you can see them in the legs of a table, the frame of a door, or the stripes on a curtain. Straight lines make objects seem strong and dignified. Curved lines make objects seem softer and more graceful. Vertical lines, that go straight up and down, suggest height. They can make objects look taller. Horizontal lines move straight across and seem to widen objects. Lines that move at a diagonal, or on an angle, suggest action.

Fig. 13-5 By using different textures, you can change the look of a room. How many different textures are used in your room?

- **Texture.** Texture is the way something feels or looks as if it would feel. Texture provides visual interest in a room, and you can add more interest by using a variety of textures. A rug might feel soft and fuzzy. A polished table feels hard and smooth. Textures can also affect the mood of a room. Soft and nubby surfaces make a room look cozy. Smooth, hard surfaces create a clean, cool effect. See Fig. 13-5.
- **Color.** Color probably has the greatest effect on the appearance of a room. A change of color can make a room look completely different. For example, white or light colors on the walls make a room look larger. Using darker colors will make a room seem smaller. Colors are often described as warm or cool. Red, yellow, and orange are warm colors. If a room does not get much sunlight or is cold in winter, warm colors can make the room seem more comfortable. Blue, green, and violet are cool, restful colors. A cool color is a good choice for a room that gets a lot of sunlight. Cool colors are also used to set a relaxing mood. See Fig. 13-6 on page 244.

**DID YOU know?**

**Plants.** Decorating with plants—living or artificial—is an inexpensive way to add color to a room.

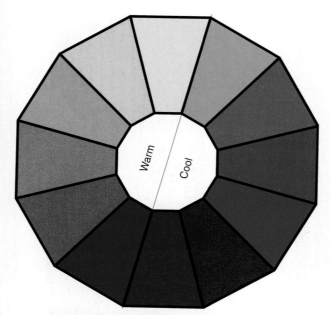

**Fig. 13-6** The color wheel shows the relationship among colors. How can you use the color wheel to help you design your room?

## Design Principles

The principles of design are rules that govern how the elements of design are organized. Here is how to use them:

- **Balance.** Use elements, such as two similar shapes, to provide equal visual weight, or balance. Toss a couple of small throw pillows on your bed to give balance.
- **Emphasis.** Create contrast by using one element to dominate the others. Try a red pillow on a blue sofa to provide interest, or emphasis.
- **Unity.** Combine similar elements to accent their similarities. For example, use several framed photos of the same size or arrange a collection of your favorite books on a shelf.
- **Scale.** Use larger pieces of furniture in large rooms. This will keep your furniture in scale with the room.
- **Rhythm.** Create a visual pattern by placing elements carefully. Hang posters on the wall to create a pattern, or rhythm.
- **Proportion.** Keep an eye on the relationship of each element to the whole and to other elements. For example, a very large poster next to a very tiny picture will be out of proportion.

## ➤ Your Own Style

Before you start planning a room makeover, you need to think about the look you want for your space. In part, that depends on what you have to work with, but it also depends on your personal taste. Of course, if you share a room you will also need to consider the taste of the other person. The elements of design and principles can be used in many ways with pleasing results, but not all of them will appeal to you.

First, consider what kind of mood you want to create. What are your interests? Do you want a sports theme? Do you want your space to be restful or lively? Are you looking for ways to make the room seem larger? Keep in mind that you will probably have to live with your changes for a long time. Be sure of your decisions before starting any work on a new look. See Fig. 13-7.

## Creating a Look

Once you have decided on the mood and style, you can plan how to achieve that look in your room. Making a plan before you start will help your project go smoothly.

Perhaps you would like a new color scheme. What parts of the room will be easiest to change? Walls can be repainted, and you can hang new pictures. Carpet, on the other hand, is difficult and expensive to replace.

If you decide to paint the walls, check with your parents first. Then choose your new color carefully. Paint a small section of the wall to be sure that the color will create the effect you want.

Fabric can also add interest to a wall or turn a sturdy carton into a covered table. You can make a simple slipcover and matching curtains, and use leftover fabric to make pillows, chair pads, and many other items.

**Fig. 13-7 Magazines contain a lot of decorating ideas.** How can magazines give you decorating ideas?

**Internet ACTIVITIES**

1. **Search the Internet for different decorating styles. Choose your favorite and describe how you could use that style to decorate your room.**

   Key Search Words:
   - **decorating styles**
   - **interior design**

2. **Search the Internet for cleaning tips. Make a list of cleaning tips and then share the list with your classmates.**

   Key Search Words:
   - **cleaning tips**
   - **house cleaning**

**Curtains**

**Handmade items**

**Posters and pictures**

**Collections**

**Lamps**

**Pillows**

**Trophies and awards**

**Quilts**

**Soccer ball**

**Baskets**

**Rugs**

**Plants**

**Fig. 13-8 Accessories can personalize your room.** What kinds of accessories express your personality?

## Using Accessories

No room is complete without accessories. **Accessories** are interesting items added to make a space more personal. You can make your own accessories, such as storage organizers, or buy accessories like lamps and plants. See Fig. 13-8.

## ➤ A Clean & Neat Home

Do you feel proud of your home when it is clean and neat? Do you feel good knowing that your home is safe and secure? Keeping your home clean, neat, safe, and secure is worthwhile for many reasons. See Fig. 13-9.

● It saves time and energy. You waste time and energy when you have to search for items that you need. For example, have you ever wasted time looking for a missing notebook or shoe?

- Clothes and other possessions last longer. If you take care of your belongings, they last longer and do not need to be replaced as often.
- Family members stay healthier in a clean home. A clean home helps family members avoid disease-causing germs.
- Most home accidents can be prevented. By practicing safety, family members can prevent many home accidents and injuries.
- Security measures can keep a home safe. If a home has adequate locks, it will be more difficult for intruders to break into the home.

## ➤ Organizing Cleaning Tasks

Routine cleaning tasks are those that must be done every day or every week. These chores include washing dishes, making beds, keeping rooms picked up, and hanging up clothes. Routine tasks keep the home clean and neat so that heavy cleaning is needed less often.

**Fig. 13-9 When your home is clean, you are proud of your living space.**

A cleaning plan can help families manage their cleaning tasks. A cleaning plan is a list of daily, weekly, and occasional household jobs and of the family member responsible for each job. To make a cleaning plan, decide what jobs need to be done and who will perform each task.

### Cleaning Shared Space

When each person takes responsibility for keeping his or her personal space in order, much of the housekeeping gets done automatically. To get your share done with ease, you need to establish a routine. For example, hanging up your clothes or putting them in a hamper takes no more time than dropping the clothes on the floor.

Because the bathrooms and the kitchen are used by all family members, every person must help keep them in order. Rinse the bathtub and sink after each use. Hang towels neatly after each use. Return personal grooming items to their proper place. In the kitchen, wash and dry the dishes, or put them in the dishwasher.

## Cleaning Your Room

It will be easier to keep your room clean if you take time each day to put it in order. All the tasks do not have to be done at the same time. For instance, a good plan may be to hang up your clothes and straighten the dresser and desk at night. You can dust or empty the wastebasket in the afternoon after you finish your homework. Put away your belongings as soon as you finish using them. It doesn't take long to make your bed in the morning. See Fig. 13-10.

## ➤ Home Safety

Many of the accidents that happen in homes could be prevented or avoided with a little care. Don't let someone in your family get hurt by carelessness. Read the following guidelines and then take the time to make your home safe.

**Fire safety.** Protect your home from fire by following these safety rules.

- Have an exit route planned.
- Make sure that smoke alarms are installed in the home. Alarms should be installed near the kitchen, outside the bedrooms, and at the top of the stairs. Check smoke alarms once a month to be sure that they are working properly, and change the batteries routinely.
- Keep a fire extinguisher in the home, and learn how to use it properly. Keep the extinguisher properly serviced.
- Make sure that all electrical cords are in good condition. A damaged cord can cause surrounding material to catch fire.
- Do not let curtains, towels, or potholders get too close to the stove. If you are cooking, avoid wearing a shirt with loose sleeves that might easily catch fire.
- Keep the area around the stove free of grease. Grease burns easily and can spread a fire.
- If you have a fireplace in your home, make sure that it is used properly. Keep flammable objects away from the fireplace, and be sure to use a screen. See Fig. 13-11.

**Fig. 13-10 Straighten your room each day to make cleanup easier.**

Kitchen Fires. **According to the U.S. Fire Administration, cooking is the leading cause of home fires and home fire injuries. These fires often happen when people leave the stove on and walk away, leaving food cooking.**

**Fall safety.** Protect people from falls in your home by following these safety rules.

- If something is spilled, wipe it up immediately.
- Place nonskid pads under rugs so that they won't slide.
- Be sure to use nonskid strips or mats in bathtubs and showers.
- Make sure that stairs are in good repair, well lit, and free from clutter. Stairs should also have handrails.

**Internet safety.** Whether you use the Internet at home or school, you need to take these precautions for your personal safety.

- Never give out personal information, such as your address or phone number, over the Internet.
- Remember that people aren't always who they say they are on the Internet. Someone who tells you she is a 12-year-old girl may actually be an older man.
- Never respond to chat room or bulletin board messages that are suggestive, threatening, or make you feel uncomfortable. Tell your parents immediately when you feel uncomfortable.
- Never arrange a face-to-face meeting with someone you've met over the Internet.
- Get your parents' permission before entering a chat room.

**Fig. 13-11 Using a fire-place screen is one way to keep your home safe.** What else can you do to keep your home safe?

# Explore

## Planning an Escape Route

### State the Task

- Plan an escape route for your family.

### Develop a Plan

1. Sit down with all your family members.
2. Make sure everyone in the family knows ways to get out of every room in your home.
3. Teach younger children to crawl on their hands and knees and stay low under smoke.
4. Plan your escape routes. Choose a place that everyone will meet outside in the event of a fire. Make sure younger children know that they should never re-enter the building after leaving.
5. Teach younger children to shout their names out if they are trapped in a smoke-filled room.
6. Assign someone to call 9-1-1 or the fire department.
7. Assign an adult the responsibility for getting any pets out of the building.

### Implement the Plan

1. Make a drawing of the layout of each floor of your home. Indicate where the windows and doors are. Mark the escape routes from each room.
2. Hold fire drills once a month.
3. Use a buddy system to assure everyone gets out safely.

### Evaluate the Result

1. How did your family react to creating the escape plan?
2. After your family held a fire drill, did you find anything in the procedure that you wanted to change? If so, what? How will you change it?
3. What other types of disaster plans could you make?

## Other Safety Precautions

In addition to fires and falls, there are many other types of accidents that can happen in homes. If there are small children in the home, poisoning is a serious danger. Make sure that all cleaning products and chemicals are kept out of the reach of children. Read the label on every chemical or cleaning product before using it so that you will know how to handle it correctly. If anyone in your family accidentally swallows a poisonous substance, immediately call a poison control center or a hospital.

Power tools and sharp knives can also cause injuries if they are not used with care. Knives and other dangerous objects should be kept out of children's reach. See Fig. 13-12.

Improper use of electrical appliances is another common cause of accidents. Be sure to connect and disconnect an electrical appliance with dry hands. Do not use any appliance that has a damaged cord. Do not use a hair dryer while in the bathtub or while standing in water.

**Fig. 13-12 Properly store knives to prevent accidents.** What other knife safety rules should you follow?

## Community Safety

Have you ever been startled by a loud noise? Have you ever felt uneasy when you walked home from a friend's house at dusk?

Everyone wants to feel safe in his or her own neighborhood. There are steps you can take to protect yourself. Make sure your home is well lit on the outside. Keep a porch light or yard light on. Solar lights can be placed around the outside of the home and do not require electrical wiring. They absorb light during the day and then glow at night, providing light.

Your family can join or help set up a Neighborhood Watch group. Members of such groups are trained by the police to identify and report suspicious activities. When you walk down the street, keep alert—especially at night. Pay attention to the people around you and to what they are doing. Stay away from dangerous areas and poorly lighted streets. Avoid taking any unnecessary risks.

# Career CHOICES

## Interior Designer

Plans, designs, and furnishes interiors of residential, commercial, and industrial buildings. Talks with client to determine preferences, purpose, and function of living or working spaces. Advises client on space planning, furnishings and color schemes. Presents design ideas to client for approval.

## Architect

Plans and designs buildings for clients. Uses knowledge of design, construction, zoning and building codes, and building materials. Plans layout of project for client approval. Prepares scale drawings and contract documents.

## Carpet Layer

Lays carpet and rugs inside buildings. Measures and cuts carpeting to size. Sews sections of carpeting together by hand. Secures carpeting to floor.

## Upholstery Cleaner

Cleans upholstered furniture using vacuum cleaner or dry-cleaning fluids. Rubs leather or plastic surfaces with oil and buffs with cloth or hand buffer to restore softness and luster.

## Hotel Housekeeper

Moves and arranges furniture. Hangs draperies and dusts blinds. Prepares rooms. Arranges decorations and furniture for social functions. Collects soiled linens for laundering. Stores and distributes linens.

**AT** School

Select three of the careers listed. Research the education, training, and work experience required for each career. Compare the results to select a career to investigate further.

**IN THE** Workplace

Make a list of five ways you could use the elements and principles of design at work. Share the list with your classmates.

**Color is an important element for each of the careers on this page.** Consider job shadowing someone who holds one of these positions.

# Chapter 13 Review & Activities

## Chapter Summary

- Your home not only provides shelter but also reflects your personality.
- You can make your home appealing and functional by arranging your living space with care.
- Sharing living space with others requires respect for privacy.
- The elements of design are space, shape, line, texture, and color.
- Organize cleaning tasks by making a list of jobs and who is responsible for each task.
- Prevent accidents in the home by practicing safety every day.

## Words You Learned

1. What is a floor plan?
2. What is meant by the traffic pattern in a room?
3. Define design.
4. How do accessories complete a room?

## Check Your Facts

1. How can using a floor plan help you organize space?
2. Which colors are considered warm?
3. Which colors are considered cool?
4. List the six principles of design.
5. List five reasons to keep your home clean and neat.
6. Give two examples of ways to prevent falls in the home.

## Apply Your Learning

1. How could a teen who shares a bedroom with a brother or sister show respect for the other person's space?
2. What aspects of day-to-day living do you think an architect has to consider when designing a living space?
3. How could you use the elements of design to create a room that looks large, yet efficient?
4. **Great Gardening.** Create a window or patio planter by choosing a pretty pot or box. Fill it with potting soil and a variety of plants and flowers. Choose plants and flowers based on how much sunlight the container will receive. Remember to water your plants regularly.

# Chapter 14

## Your Environment

### You Will Discover . . .

- the natural resources that make up the environment.
- ways to conserve natural resources.
- ways to use energy wisely.
- what it means to reduce, reuse, and recycle waste.
- why personal safety is important.

### Key Words

- natural resources
- pollution
- conservation
- landfills
- decompose
- incineration
- biodegradable
- recycling

Do you like to spend time at the beach or in the mountains? Have you ever gone swimming or fishing in a lake or an ocean? Enjoying outdoor activities is one of the greatest pleasures of life. In addition, you could not survive without the elements that nature provides. Taking care of the environment is essential to our survival.

## ➤ Natural Resources

**Natural resources** are materials that are supplied by nature. You might not think about them very often, and you may even take them for granted. However, your health and well-being depend on several key natural resources. These include air, water, soil, and the energy derived from coal, oil, and gas. See Fig. 14-1.

At one time these resources seemed almost limitless. Some, however, are nonrenewable, and if they are used up or permanently damaged, they will no longer be available. This damage is often caused by pollution. **Pollution** is the changing of air, water, and land from clean and safe to dirty and unsafe.

**Fig. 14-1 Plants as well as animals and humans depend on natural resources for survival.**

### Air

Your body uses the oxygen in air to produce energy. Plants use the carbon dioxide in air to produce food and oxygen. Unfortunately, the air you breathe is not completely clean. It may contain dust, smoke, chemical particles, and smog. These substances, which are all forms of air pollution, can be harmful to your health. Some causes of air pollution are:

- the release of poisonous gases such as car exhaust fumes that combine with the atmosphere to create smog when fuels are burned to provide energy.
- smoke from sources such as fireplaces, barbecues, and burning leaves.
- chemicals, including those that kill insects and those used as cooling agents in air conditioners and refrigerators.

## Water

Water, like air, is necessary to all living things. In fact, water is your body's most essential nutrient. It is needed for every bodily function.

You may think that there is plenty of water. After all, about 70 percent of the earth's surface is covered by water. Most of it, however, is salt water. Many plants and animals cannot use salt water. They need clean, fresh water to survive.

Much of the earth's water is polluted by wastes. Common sources of water pollution are human wastes, detergents, and the chemicals used to kill insects or to fertilize crops. Polluted water can cause people to become sick or even die.

## Soil

The earth's land is made up of soil, the loose material in which plants can grow. Plants get the nutrients and water they need from the soil. People, in turn, need the nutrients that plants provide in order to live.

## Energy

What would happen if there weren't any gasoline left for cars, trucks, and buses? How would we heat homes, schools, and office buildings if we ran out of oil and other kinds of fuel? You may think that this could never happen. However, many sources of energy are in limited supply. When oil, natural gas, and coal are used up, they cannot be replaced.

Another form of energy is nuclear energy. Nuclear energy boils water, creates steam, and turns generators to create electricity. Nuclear energy uses uranium, a dense metal found in most rocks, as its base. Uranium is more plentiful than fossil fuels, such as coal.

**CHECK the Facts**

Lead Poisoning. According to the National Institute of Environmental Health Sciences, lead is the number one health hazard to children. Exposure to lead at high levels can cause muscle and abdominal pain, brain disease, and even death.

## Conserving Resources

You may feel that pollution and the shrinking supply of natural resources are beyond your control. There are many ways, however, that you can make a difference. One important way is to practice **conservation**, or the saving of resources. The best way to conserve a resource is to use less of it. Whenever possible, walk or use a bicycle instead of riding in a car. See Fig. 14-2.

Families can also work together to conserve natural resources. Some families have added more insulation to their homes to save fuel. Insulation is a material installed in a building to keep it cooler in summer and warmer in winter.

Fig. 14-2 These teens are conserving natural resources by riding bicycles. What can you do to conserve natural resources?

**Wise water use.** Here are some ways you can conserve water.

- Turn off the water when brushing your teeth.
- Take showers instead of baths.
- Ask your family to install water-saving showerheads and toilets.
- Repair leaky faucets.
- Run the washing machine only with a full load.

## Using Energy Wisely

An important way to conserve resources is to learn to use energy wisely. Look for appliances that are energy-efficient, or made to use less energy. By using energy efficiently, you not only conserve resources but also reduce pollution of the environment.

You can save energy at home in many ways. Most of the energy used at home is for heating and cooling. The rest of the energy used in homes is for heating water, running appliances, and lighting. See Fig. 14-3. When your family members buy new appliances, they can look for the most energy-efficient ones by comparing guides that list energy costs per year.

**Conserving energy.** Here are some ways to save energy around your home.

- Use hot water sparingly.
- Keep doors to closets and unused rooms closed. There is no need to heat or cool those spaces.
- Whenever possible, use the microwave oven.
- When you use the oven, cook several items at the same time and avoid opening the oven door while foods are cooking.
- Run the dishwasher only with a full load.
- Avoid leaving the refrigerator door open for an extended period of time.
- Keep the thermostat turned up during the summer.
- Keep the thermostat turned down to 68°F in winter.
- Use lined drapes to keep the cold out in the winter and the heat out in the summer.
- Seal and close up cracks around the doors and windows.

**Fig. 14-3** You can save energy by researching the performance of different light bulbs. What type of light bulb is most energy-efficient?

# Making Connections

**Science.** Natural resources can provide alternative sources of energy. Alternative energy sources must be renewable, nonpolluting, practical to obtain, and affordable. For example, some possible sources come from geothermal energy, hydropower, tidal power, wind, and solar power.

*Get Involved!*

- - - - - - - - - - - - - - - - - - - - - - - - - - - - - - - - - - - -

What other types of power sources can you think of that could be developed in the future?

## ➤ Protecting the Environment

You may think that as long as you don't litter, you are doing your part to keep your community clean. There is much more to it than that, however. Since about the middle of the 20th century we have lived in a "throwaway" society. Many items are used only once and then thrown away. As a result, we now have a serious problem because we have too much waste and not enough safe ways to get rid of it.

Protection of natural resources and the environment begins with people like you. There are plenty of ways for you to make a difference.

**Fig. 14-4 Recycling helps protect the environment. What else can you do?**

- You can use air, water, land, and energy wisely.
- You can make an effort to be energy-efficient at home.
- You can be a concerned citizen who cares about the environment and works with others to keep it clean. See Fig. 14-4.

## ➤ Removing Waste

Billions of tons of waste are disposed of every year in the United States. Where does it all go? Where should it all go? These questions are urgent because the mountains of waste continue to grow.

You can work to change the situation. Even though the waste problem is a national issue, the solution depends on individual actions. Your actions can help to make a difference.

## Landfills

About 80 percent of the waste in the United States is disposed of in landfills. **Landfills** are huge pits where waste is buried between layers of earth. Most large communities have landfills somewhere on their outskirts. These landfills are carefully designed to control the odors, germs, and other unhealthy situations that are created by piles of waste.

Landfills do cause problems, however. They take up huge amounts of space, and no one wants to live near a landfill. Waste buried in landfills is supposed to **decompose**, or break down, so that it becomes part of the soil. However, recent studies have shown that certain kinds of waste, such as plastic foam, do not break down for many years. See Fig. 14-5.

## Incineration

Another common way to dispose of waste in the United States is by incineration. **Incineration** means disposing of waste by burning. About 10 percent of the waste in the United States is incinerated. When poisonous waste is burned, its smoke is especially dangerous. The air pollution is so great that many communities do not allow waste to be burned.

Fig. 14-5 There are thousands of landfills around the country. Why can't we rely on landfills in the future?

# A CLOSER LOOK

## ...at American Waste

**Every day Americans throw away thousands of pounds of trash that ends up in land-fills. What can you do to help reduce the level of waste?**

**At home** you can recycle items such as plastic containers.

**The result** is your contribution to reusing plastic. Manufacturers can melt and reshape plastic containers for use as other packaging.

WE RECYCLE

## At school
you can recycle items such as paper plates.

## The result is your contribution to reusing paper. Recycled paper is used to make newspaper and other everyday paper products.

## In your community
you can contribute to a recycling program, such as aluminum cans.

## The result is your contribution to reusing aluminum cans. Recycled aluminum is used every day by manufacturers around the world.

## Limiting Waste

Burying waste in landfills and incinerating it both have serious drawbacks. What should be done about the problem? The key is to reduce the amount of waste we create. All Americans can do their part by following the "three Rs"—Reduce, Reuse, Recycle.

## Reduce

The first step is to reduce the amount of waste created. To start reducing the amount of waste you create, you can:

- reduce the amount of paper you throw away by using both sides of notebook and printer paper, using only washable cups and plates, and using cloth napkins.
- avoid buying disposable products.
- pre-cycle, or avoid buying products that use more packaging than necessary.
- plan meals carefully so there is little waste of food and energy for cooking.
- use cloth grocery bags instead of paper or plastic ones.
- buy products that are **biodegradable**, or broken down and absorbed by the environment.

## Reuse

The second of the "three Rs" is reuse. You can limit the amount of waste you create by reusing items you might otherwise throw away. If you use your imagination, you can probably think of many ways to reuse items. Here are a few ideas.

- Buy products packed in containers that can be refilled or used for something else.
- Keep boxes, bottles, and cans to use as storage containers.
- Save and use old towels and clothes as rags.
- Think twice before throwing something away. Ask yourself, "What else can I do with this?" See Fig. 14-6.

## Recycle

Many of the materials we throw away can be easily recycled. **Recycling** is turning waste items into products that can be used. Recycling can greatly reduce the amount of waste in our country. For example, newspapers can be turned into pulp to make new paper. Aluminum cans can be melted down and turned into new cans and other products. Plastic can also be recycled. Over half of the waste we create is recyclable.

Recycling also means donating clothes, books, and other items to charities. You also recycle when you give or receive secondhand clothes or exchange magazines with a friend after reading them. Can you see how holding a yard sale is also a way to recycle? These actions may seem small, but each one helps to limit the amount of waste. By applying the "three Rs" you will do your share to preserve the environment. See Fig. 14-7.

Fig. 14-6 Find clever ways to reuse items instead of throwing them away. What items do you reuse?

Fig. 14-7 You can repaint, refinish, or reupholster furniture instead of throwing it away.

# Explore

## Recycling

### Supplies

- Cardboard boxes or official recycling containers
- Plain labels
- Markers
- Notebook
- Pen or Pencil
- Telephone book

### State the Task

- Find out about your city's recycling program and how you can participate in it.

### Develop a Plan

1. Find out where the recycling center is in your area. Cans, bottles, and newspapers may be picked up at your home or school, or dropped off at the recycling center.
2. Call and ask the recycling center how to prepare items for recycling. For example, you may have to rinse out and flatten plastic containers, crush cans, or separate glass bottles by color.
3. Find out the days and times that recyclables are collected in your area.

### Implement the Plan

1. Set up a recycling system at home. Make separate, labeled containers for glass, cans, plastic, paper, and other recyclable items. Use cardboard boxes or containers provided by the recycling center.
2. Make a list in your notebook of the trash your family throws away every day for a week. Every time an item is thrown out, add it to the list. At the end of the week, look over your list. Put a circle around each item that could have been recycled.
3. Separate and save everything that the recycling center will take.
4. Make a list of how many different items your family recycles. Share the list with your classmates.

### Evaluate the Result

1. What part of the recycling process, if any, would you change? Why?
2. Describe what kind of an impact your family's recycling efforts will have on your community and the world.

## ➤ Personal Safety

In addition to protecting the environment, you need to be aware of your personal safety. Whether you travel on foot, on skates, on a bike, or in a car, the most important way to keep safe is to know and follow the rules of the road. As a pedestrian, or a person who travels on foot, you must stay aware of what drivers and other pedestrians are doing. Always cross at crosswalks or intersections, and look out for vehicles turning right after stopping for a red light. In a car, make sure that you wear a seat belt—both the lap belt and the shoulder harness—and never distract the driver.

Have you ever been sunburned from being outdoors without sunscreen or gotten blisters from walking too long in new shoes? Outdoor safety requires common sense—just like safety at home and on the road.

- When participating in water sports, the most important precaution is knowing how to swim. If you plan to swim, make sure that you go with a buddy and that there is a lifeguard on duty. If you go boating, wear a life jacket, and be sure that you know how to handle the boat properly.
- When hiking or camping, make sure that you wear the right clothing for the weather. You should also be careful to use marked trails and designated campsites. Tell someone where you are going and when you expect to return.
- Wearing appropriate clothing and dressing in layers are necessary precautions for enjoying the outdoors in winter. You also have to check to see that the conditions are safe.
- Know how much you are really capable of doing. Pushing yourself beyond your training and ability is taking unnecessary risk.
- Use the correct equipment for each activity.
- Know the safety rules and follow them.
- Remember to warm up before and cool down after an activity to avoid injury.

**Never feed the wild animals you encounter hiking or camping. They are not like zoo animals or the pets you have at home. Keep a safe distance from them.**

- Practice the buddy system. When people pair up during activities, they can look after each other and help each other in an emergency.
- Check the weather conditions where you plan to go. Avoid being out in extreme temperatures and electrical storms.
- Use sunscreen to protect your skin from ultraviolet rays. See Fig. 14-8.

Many activities involve some risk. If you stay within the limits of your abilities and take safety precautions, however, you will greatly reduce your risk of accident or injury.

**Fig. 14-8** Apply sunscreen to protect your skin from the sun.

## Internet ACTIVITIES

1. **Search the Internet for survival techniques to use in the event you are lost in the wilderness.**

   Key Search Words:
   - **wilderness survival**
   - **survival training**

2. **Search the Internet for information on the ozone layer. Write down some practices that contributed to the hole in the ozone layer.**

   Key Search Words:
   - **ozone layer**
   - **atmosphere**

# How To...

## Recognize Edible Plants

### State the Task

• Recognize edible plant life.

### Develop a Plan

1. Study resources to find out which plants are edible. Look for books at your library to begin the process. Call your local park district for information or search the Internet.
2. Make a list of edible plants. Add a description of each one to identify them.
3. Make a list of the most common poisonous plants. Add a description of each to identify them.

### Implement the Plan

1. Divide your notebook into the following sections: roots, leaves and stems, berries and nuts, and flowers.
2. Place each acceptable plant in the correct section of your notebook. Cross-reference if desired.
3. Sketch each plant next to its name and description.
4. Place the list of poisonous plants in the back of your notebook. Add a sketch to help you remember them.

### Evaluate the Result

1. What is the most important fact you learned about edible plants?
2. What is the most important fact you learned about poisonous plants?
3. How could this information help you if you got lost in the woods?

Create a bird feeder by rolling a medium-sized pine cone in peanut butter and then rolling it in birdseed. Use a piece of yarn or string to hang it from a tree.

# Career CHOICES

## Environmental Analyst

Conducts research studies to develop methods of controlling pollutants. Analyzes sources of pollution to determine their effects.

## Ecologist

Researches environmental concerns. Makes studies to determine in what conditions different varieties of plants grow. Studies light and soil requirements and how different species resist disease and insects. Investigates how different species adapt to environmental changes in soil type, climate, and altitude.

## Pollution Control Engineer

Plans and conducts engineering studies. Evaluates methods of pollution control to determine contaminants. Performs calculations to determine pollution emissions.

## Forester

Manages forests for economic and recreational purposes. Maps forest areas. Estimates the number of current trees and future growth. Plans cutting programs to assure continuous production of trees. Plans projects for flood control and soil erosion.

## Energy-Control Officer

Monitors energy use. Coordinates energy conservation programs. Compiles report on consumption of electricity, fuel, oil, coal, natural gas, and water. Sets up energy-monitoring devices.

### AT School

Select three of the careers listed. Research the education, training, and work experience required for each career. Compare the results to select a career to investigate further.

### IN THE Workplace

Make a list of five ways you could save resources in the workplace. Share your list with your classmates.

A forester spends almost all of his or her time outdoors. Research five other careers that require you to work outdoors.

# Chapter 14 Review & Activities

## Chapter Summary

- Some natural resources are in limited supply. If they are used up they will no longer be available.
- Ways to conserve natural resources include using less of them and using energy efficiently.
- Use energy wisely at all times.
- Waste goes to landfills or is incinerated after you throw it away.
- You can limit the amount of waste by reducing, reusing, and recycling.

## Words You Learned

1. What are natural resources?
2. List three causes of pollution.
3. Why should you practice conservation?

4. What are landfills?
5. Define the term decompose.
6. Explain incineration.
7. Why is it better to purchase products that are biodegradable?
8. How is recycling different from reusing?

## Check Your Facts

1. List 10 ways to use energy wisely.
2. Name the major causes of air pollution.
3. How is an energy-efficient appliance beneficial?
4. How can biodegradable products help the environment?
5. What can you do to practice outdoor safety?

## Apply Your Learning

1. List ways that you can contribute to solving the larger problems associated with pollution and waste disposal.
2. Think of something you threw away recently. Describe two ways that you could have reused it.
3. **Book Beauty.** Make a bookmark using pressed flowers. You'll need small blossoms, paper towels or tissue paper, a heavy book, and clear contact paper. Place the flowers between paper towels or tissue paper and set a heavy book on them overnight. Place the pressed flowers between two sheets of contact paper and gently push out any air bubbles. Cut the bookmarks in 1½"- to 2"-wide strips.

# UNIT **3**

# Exploring Fashion & Clothing

# Chapter 15

# Your Fashion Statement

## You Will Discover . . .

- the differences among fashions, fads, and classic styles.
- how the color, line, and texture of clothing affect your appearance.
- how to assess your wardrobe needs.
- how accessories can stretch your wardrobe.

*W*hat is your favorite outfit? Is it casual or dressy? Do you like to be comfortable or always get noticed? The clothes you wear are your fashion statement. They send a message about how you see yourself. Clothes and accessories can reflect your individuality. They can also identify you as part of a group.

## Key Words

- status
- style
- fashions
- fads
- classic styles
- hues
- tint
- shade
- intensity
- texture

# ➤ Clothing Choices

People first wore clothing to protect themselves against the wind, snow, rain, cold, and heat. That first clothing was made from animal skins. As time went on, people decorated their clothes with natural materials, such as earth and clay. Seeds, stones, and shell beads were sometimes added to clothing to show a person's **status**, or level of importance.

Today, clothing choices are much more varied, but the purpose of clothing has not changed. Here are some of the reasons people wear clothing:

- **Protection.** Clothes protect you from the weather and climate.
- **Decoration.** Clothes, such as scarves and vests, are used as decoration.
- **Identification.** Clothes tell as much about you as what you say. For example, uniforms may signify that you work at a particular restaurant, play in a school band, or are part of an athletic team.
- **Modesty.** The way you wear your clothes and the type of clothing you wear suggest your personal sense of modesty, or the way you feel is proper to cover your body. See Fig. 15-1.
- **Status.** Some clothes are worn to show a person's status. Designer labels, logos, and other recognized names and symbols can give a person a feeling of importance.

**Fig. 15-1 People wear clothes for many reasons. Why do you wear clothes?**

Learning what influences your clothing decisions will help you choose clothes that are best for you. Making good clothing choices will help you present a good image. Clothing can help you effectively present who you are and what is important to you.

## ➤ Making Clothing Decisions

The occasion or activity that you are dressing for helps to determine your clothing choices. For instance, you would wear different clothes to a basketball game than to a formal dance. Choosing the right outfit for the occasion is important to put your best "look" forward. When choosing clothes based on your *wants* instead of your needs, it is important to reflect your personality. For example, when Danielle and Brianna buy clothes, they choose different styles. A **style** is the design of a garment. A bomber jacket, a straight skirt, and baggy pants are all styles. What style reflects your personality?

Not all styles of clothing are considered fashions. **Fashions** are styles of clothing that are popular at a particular time. Fashions change frequently. Only a few changes in the style are made to give them a fresh, new look. Fashions may include changes in skirt length, jacket length, collar shape, or width of pant legs. At any one time, however, there will be some new fashions coming in, some going out, and other styles that remain popular season after season.

Many fashions become popular very quickly and then lose their appeal. Fashions that are very popular for a short time are called **fads**. Fad clothing is fun to wear. However, it is not a good idea to spend a lot of money on fad items. Instead, you can choose **classic styles**, which are styles that remain in fashion for a long time. Classics include a blazer, crew neck shirt, and cardigan sweater. You can alter styles and fashions with accessories such as belts, hats, and jewelry. *A Closer Look at Mixing and Matching* on pages 278-279 may give you some ideas about combining styles to create your "look."

# A CLOSER L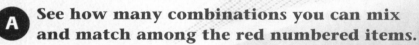K

## ...at Mixing & Matching

A good way to expand your wardrobe is by combining separates, or single pieces of clothing that can be mixed and matched. Lay out all of the pieces and try them together in different combinations to see what you like the best. You may be pleasantly surprised at how many items work together when you mix and match.

**A** See how many combinations you can mix and match among the red numbered items.

**B** Try mixing and matching the blue numbered items. How many outfits can you make?

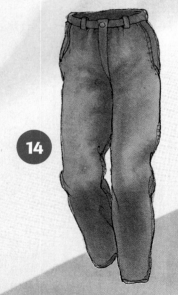

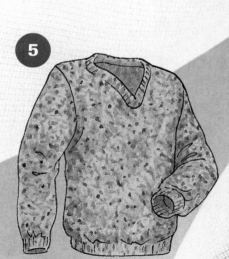

Fig. 15-2 You can express your personality through color. How do various colors of clothing affect your mood?

## ➤ Self-Expression

Your clothing tells others a lot about your personality. See Fig. 15-2. You may prefer bold colors and patterns, if you are an outgoing person. Your best friend, who is quiet, may prefer to wear clothes that are simple and subdued.

Your moods can also affect your clothing choices. When you are feeling happy, you may choose to wear bright colors. On days when you're feeling thoughtful and quiet, you may select pale or dark colors. You can use clothes to help change your mood. For example, Stephanie always wears a bright red shirt when she's feeling a little down, because it lifts her spirits.

# ➤ Color & Appearance

Why do some colors look better on you than others? If you become familiar with the relationships among colors, you will understand how colors affect your appearance and the way clothes look on you. See Fig. 15-3.

To understand the basic principles of color, you need to know the names of the colors, or **hues**. The three basic hues are red, yellow, and blue. They are called primary colors because all other colors can be made from them. Combining equal amounts of red and yellow makes orange. Equal amounts of blue and yellow make green, and combining red and blue makes violet. See Fig. 15-4.

**Fig. 15-3 When you shop for clothes, look for styles and colors that suit your skin tone and hair color.**

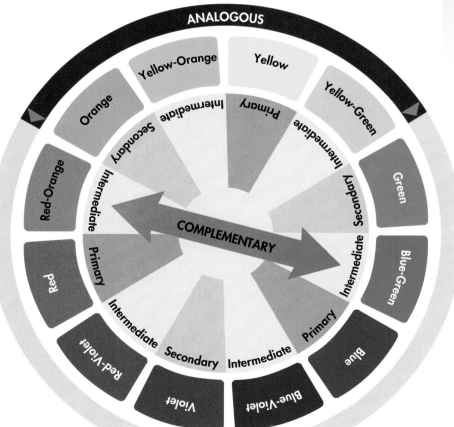

**Fig. 15-4 The color wheel shows how colors are related to one another.**

Another basic element to consider is the value, or the lightness and darkness of color. For instance, blue can vary in value from very light blue to navy blue. A light value of a hue is called a **tint**. A dark value of a hue is called a **shade**. The brightness or dullness of a color is called its **intensity**. Bright red is a high-intensity color. Pale pink is a low-intensity color.

Colors are considered either warm or cool. Red, yellow, and orange are warm colors. They are bright and cheerful. Blue, green, and violet are cool colors. They give a sense of calm.

When you put clothes together, you can create either single-color outfits or outfits that combine colors. You can learn to combine colors successfully using the color wheel. A color wheel shows the relationships of colors to each other. See Fig. 15-5.

- **Monochromatic color scheme.** A monochromatic color scheme is a one-color plan. This plan involves one hue and the tints and shades of that hue. Combining light blue and navy blue is an example of a monochromatic color scheme.
- **Complementary color scheme.** Complementary colors are those opposite each other on the color wheel. This type of color scheme gives great contrast. Orange and blue used together form a complementary color scheme.
- **Analogous color scheme.** An analogous color scheme is made up of hues found next to each other on the color wheel. The colors have one common hue. A combination of red-violet, violet, and blue-violet is an analogous color scheme.
- **Accented neutral color scheme.** Black, white, beige, and gray are considered neutral colors. An accented neutral color scheme uses one of the neutral colors plus another color as the accent, or focal point. A combination of black and red is an example of an accented neutral color scheme.

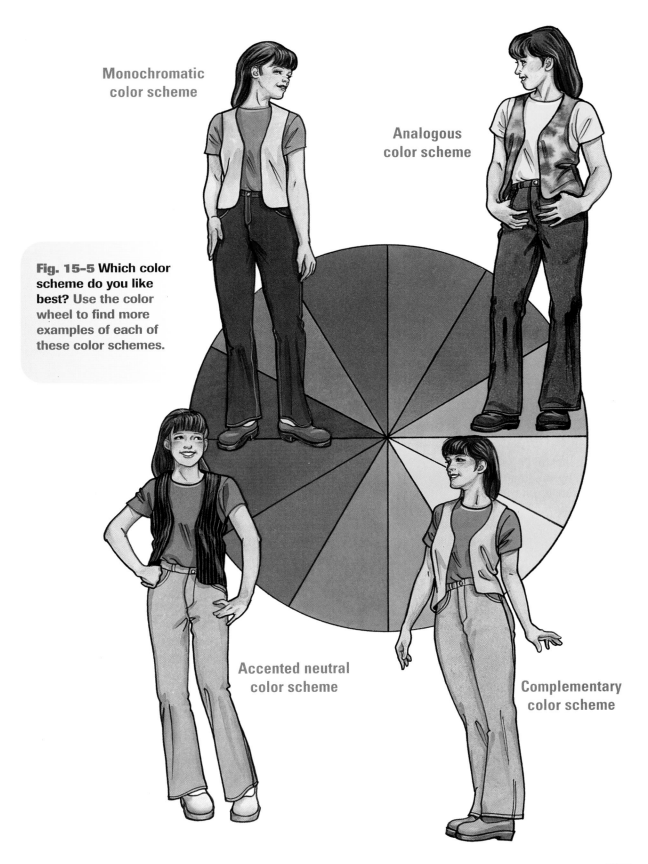

Monochromatic
color scheme

Analogous
color scheme

**Fig. 15-5** Which color
scheme do you like
best? Use the color
wheel to find more
examples of each of
these color schemes.

Accented neutral
color scheme

Complementary
color scheme

## Selecting Colors

When you try different color combinations, you will discover that some look better on you than others. Becoming colors make your complexion look healthy and show off your hair and eyes.

Colors affect your appearance in other ways too. They can highlight certain areas of your body. Light, warm, and bright colors can make you look larger. Dark, cool, and dull colors can make you look smaller. Carl wears one-color outfits so that he will look taller, whereas Judy selects contrasting colors so that she appears shorter.

**Fig. 15-6 The lines formed by these stripes affect how each of these boys looks. Describe the impact of each set of lines.**

## ➤ Lines & Appearance

The way a garment looks on you is also affected by its lines. Lines form the outer shape, or outline, of a garment. For example, compare straight-leg, tapered, and flared pants. Sometimes lines are formed by the seams and waistlines of a garment. Other lines can be part of the fabric's design, such as stripes or plaids. See Fig. 15-6.

---

## Making Connections

**Art & Design.** Tailored clothing follows body lines and fits snugly at the wrists and ankles to hold in body warmth. Draped clothes hang loosely, allowing air to flow around the body and cool it.

### Get Involved!

Look in magazines to find pictures that illustrate the tailored principle and the draped principle of clothing design. Discuss your pictures with your classmates.

---

Lines can be either straight or curved. Curved lines soften a garment's appearance. Straight lines look strong. When you shop for clothes, learn to look for lines. Try to see vertical lines instead of just a row of buttons or a zipper down the front. Look for horizontal lines instead of seeing only belts, waist-lines, or hemlines. See diagonal or curved lines instead of necklines and collars.

You can change the way you look by changing the lines of your clothes.

- Vertical lines make you look taller and thinner.
- Horizontal lines make you look shorter and wider.
- Diagonal lines can make you look taller and thinner or shorter and wider, depending on the length and angle of the lines. See Fig. 15-7.

Fig. 15-7 Lines are formed by the shape of clothes, by construction lines, and by fabric design. What types of lines do you see pictured here?

## Clothing Texture

When you choose clothing, you need to consider its **texture**, the way something feels or looks as if it would feel. Texture is created by using different yarns and weaves in making fabric. For instance, a wool sweater has a coarse texture that is created in the knitting process. A fabric may be dull or shiny, nubby or smooth.

| | |
|---|---|
| 1. **Search the Internet for examples of past clothing styles. Make a list of the old styles you find that are currently popular again. Compare the list with your classmates' lists.** | **Key Search Words:** <br> • **retro clothing styles** <br> • **historical clothing** |
| 2. **Search the Internet for information on fashion designers. Find out how they got started in fashion and what types of clothing they design.** | **Key Search Words:** <br> • **fashion designers** <br> • **fashion trends** |

You can use textures to change the way you look. Dull textures make you look smaller. Nubby or shiny textures add bulk. A tall person can wear a coarse texture, but the same fabric may overpower a small person. To see which textures look best on you, try on clothing with different types of textures. See Fig. 15-8.

## ➤ Your Clothing Needs

The first step in deciding what kind of clothes you need is to think about what kind of clothes you wear. See Fig. 15-9. Think about your various activities: you need clothes for school, casual clothes for spending time with friends, dressier clothes for special occasions, and clothes for activities such as sports or dance class.

Fig. 15-8 Texture affects your appearance. This nubby sweater makes Tammy appear larger.

Fig. 15-9 Before you go shopping for new clothes, look in your closet to see what you don't wear.

# Explore

| Wardrobe Inventory | Wear Often | Can't Wear | Never Wear | Needs Repair |
|---|---|---|---|---|
| Slacks | | | | |
| Shirts/Blouses | | | | |
| Skirts | | | | |
| Dresses | | | | |
| Jackets | | | | |
| Accessories | | | | |

## A Wardrobe Inventory

### State the Task

• Take a wardrobe inventory.

### Develop a Plan

1. Create a chart with four categories: wear often; can't wear; never wear; needs repair.
2. Make a list of items missing from your wardrobe, or items that could make a "new" outfit.

### Implement the Plan

1. To take your inventory, sort your clothing into the following four categories and log each item on your chart.

   • **Clothes that you wear often.** Use these clothes to help you evaluate your personal clothing style. What do you like about these clothes—style, color, texture?

   • **Clothes that you can't wear.** These might be clothes that no longer fit. There is no point in keeping these clothes in your closet. Before you set them aside, however, think about how they might still be used. If the sleeves on a shirt are too short, could they be cut off and hemmed to make a short-sleeved shirt instead? Clothes that you're sure you don't want can be donated to charity.

   • **Clothes that you never wear.** You may be able to add items to your wardrobe that will make these clothes more useful.

   • **Clothes in need of repair.** Set these to one side and see if they can be fixed.

2. Give away the items you no longer wear.

3. Repair the items you like and add these to the correct column on your inventory chart.

### Evaluate the Result

1. Look at your inventory chart to see what items you need to fill out your wardrobe. For example, do you have a lot of casual clothes, but nothing for special events? Make a list of these needed items.

2. Decide what specific items you need before you shop. Look for basics such as black pants or a white shirt that would allow for more clothing combinations.

3. Before you buy anything new, think about what is in style. Study clothing combinations and ways to change the look of an outfit by adding accessories.

**Fig. 15-10 Accessories can add a lot to an outfit.** What types of accessories do you like to wear?

## DID YOU know?

**Scarves & Ties.** Scarves and neckties can be used to add color or emphasis. Here are a few tips:

- Scarves can be wrapped around the head, around the waist, or around the strap of a purse.
- Wrap two scarves together to create interest. Two patterned scarves in the same color family or one patterned scarf wrapped with a solid scarf creates a good look.
- Ties are cut on the bias and will eventually pull out of shape.
- Some scarves and ties are made of silk and must be dry-cleaned.

You also need to evaluate your personal style, the kind of clothes you like best. For example, do you wear a lot of tailored, buttoned shirts, or do you feel more comfortable in T-shirts? The best planning involves thinking about all of your clothes, not just about individual outfits. Keep in mind that accessories, such as shoes, belts, scarves, hats, socks, and jewelry, are part of your clothing wardrobe.

## Adding Accessories

Well-chosen accessories can stretch your wardrobe by giving the same outfit an entirely different look. You can also use accessories to draw attention to your best features and away from less attractive ones. For instance, a wide belt can emphasize a slim waistline. A watchband or bracelet can draw attention to graceful hands. See Fig. 15-10.

When using accessories, it is best to choose one center of interest, or focal point. Choose a wide belt with a big buckle, for example. Any other accessories should be less noticeable and blend in with the outfit. Too many accessories will create a cluttered look.

# How To...

## Tie Scarves & Neckties

### State the Task

- Knot a woman's scarf or a man's necktie.

### Develop a Plan

1. Team up with a partner. It is easier to learn to tie scarves and neckties on someone else. If a partner is not available, work in front of a mirror.
2. Choose either a scarf or a tie.

### Implement the Plan

1. For a woman's scarf, choose one of the examples shown.
2. For a man's tie, follow the steps shown below.

### Evaluate the Result

1. What problems, if any did you encounter?
2. How could a scarf or tie make an outfit look different?
3. Make a list of places you might wear a necktie or scarf. Why did you make these choices?

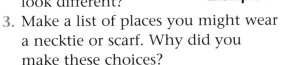

**Example 1**

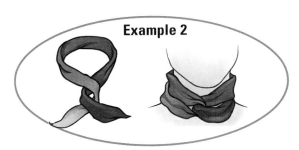

**Example 2**

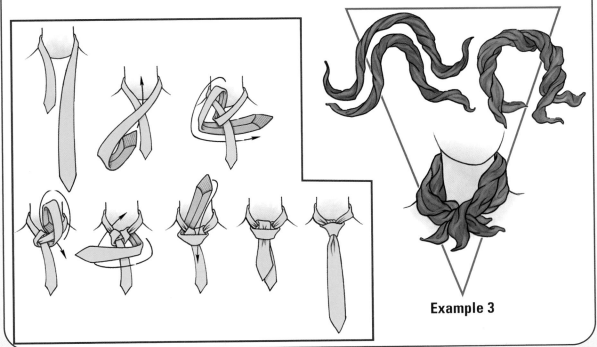

**Example 3**

# areer CHOICES

## Fashion Coordinator

Selects garments and accessories to be shown at fashion shows. Provides information on current fashions, style trends, and use of accessories. Travels to garment districts, fashion shows, and merchandise markets to obtain information on new fashion trends.

## Fashion Designer

Designs men's, women's, and children's clothing and accessories. Analyzes fashion trends. Uses knowledge to create new styles for clothing, shoes, and handbags and other accessories. Sketches drawings of garments and writes specifications describing color schemes, construction, and type of fabric to be used.

## Fabric Designer

Specifies weave patterns, colors, and threads to make new fabrics. Sketches designs and writes instructions to specify details, such as finish, color, and construction of fabric.

## Knitting Machine Operator

Manages one or more machines that knit fabrics, garment parts, or other articles from yarn. Watches knitting to detect yarn breaks, empty yarn packages, and knitting defects.

**Fashion designers use the elements and principles of design every day. Investigate fashion careers on the Internet.**

## Costume Historian

Researches documents and archives of museums, libraries, and historical societies. Describes what people wore and how the garments reflect a period of history.

### AT School

Select three of the careers listed. Research the education, training, and work experience required for each career. Compare the results to select a career to investigate further.

### IN THE Workplace

Make a list of at least 15 different clothing styles people could wear on the job. Compare lists with your classmates.

# Chapter 15 Review & Activities

## Chapter Summary

- Clothing is worn for protection, decoration, identification, modesty, and status.
- People choose among fashions, fads, and classic styles.
- Your clothing choices tell others a lot about your personality.
- Color, line, and texture affect your appearance by making you look taller, shorter, larger, or smaller.
- Choose clothing that suits the activity.
- Accessories can give the same outfit a different look.

## Words You Learned

1. What types of clothing do people wear to show their status?
2. What is style?
3. Describe fashions.
4. How long do fads usually last?

5. How can buying classic styles of clothing save you money?
6. Name the three basic hues.
7. What is a tint?
8. What is a shade?
9. What is color intensity?
10. How can you use texture to change the way you look?

## Check Your Facts

1. Explain why it is best not to spend a lot of money on fad clothing.
2. Name the three main directions of lines in fashions.
3. How can garment shape affect the way you look?
4. Describe how texture is created.
5. How can accessories be used to change the look of an outfit?

## Apply Your Learning

1. Make a list of clothing that is currently popular. Share your list of fad clothing with your classmates.
2. Analyze three favorite outfits to determine what looks best on you in terms of style, color, line, and texture.
3. Analyze how your current clothing choices help make you an effective individual. Explain your answer.
4. **Bead-Dazzled.** Create your own bracelet or key chain. Choose a variety of plastic, glass, or wood beads and thread them onto a plastic string or piece of very thin elastic. Knot the ends to secure.

SALE

clear
SA

SALE
SALE
15⁹⁹
LADIES' ROUTE 66
FASHION JEANS
Reg. 19.99

ROUTE
66

BACK-BU

CARPENTER

# Chapter 16

# Clothing Basics

## You Will Discover . . .

- how to recognize quality in clothing.
- how to develop a shopping plan.
- what clothing labels tell you.
- how to remove stains from clothing.
- guidelines for washing, drying, and ironing clothes.
- how to store clothes properly.

## Key Words

- fibers
- woven fabrics
- knit fabrics
- grain
- shopping plan

How do you feel about shopping for clothes? Maybe you love to shop, but your best friend would rather do almost anything than look for new clothes. No matter how you feel about shopping, you can save both time and money by looking for the best value, following care label directions, and storing your clothes properly.

# ➤ Recognizing Quality Fabrics

The best way to learn about fabrics is to make a trip to a fabric store. Check the label on the end of the fabric bolt to see the fiber content. Compare fabrics in different price ranges. Feel various fabrics to see how they handle when stretched or crushed. Quality fabric will spring back. A basic understanding of fabrics can help you make better clothing choices. See Fig. 16-1.

## Fibers & Fabrics

Most fabrics are made from tiny strands called **fibers**. Fibers can be made from natural or synthetic (sihn-THET-ik) materials. The natural fibers commonly used in clothing are cotton, linen, silk, and wool.

- Cotton comes from the seedpod of the cotton plant.
- Linen comes from the flax plant.
- Silk comes from silkworms.
- Wool comes from the hair of sheep.

Fabrics made of natural fibers absorb perspiration and generally feel cooler than fabrics made of synthetic fibers. Synthetic fibers are made partially or entirely from chemicals. Polyester and nylon are two types of synthetic fibers.

Fabrics can be made all of one fiber or by combining two or more fibers. The clothing label must tell you what percentage of each type of fiber makes up the fabric. For example, a shirt might be 100 percent cotton, or it might be a blend of 65 percent cotton and 35 percent polyester.

Fibers are made into fabrics by two main methods: weaving and knitting. The way a fabric is made affects its appearance and performance.

- **Woven fabrics** are made on a loom by interlacing lengthwise and crosswise threads at right angles. The most durable weaves are plain and twill. The fabrics used in bed sheets and men's dress shirts are examples of a plain weave. Denim used for jeans is one example of a twill weave.

**Fig. 16-1** All clothing items list the fiber content and care instructions.

- **Knit fabrics** are fabrics made by looping threads together. Depending on the knitting method, different fabrics can be made. Not all knits are heavy like sweaters. Cotton T-shirts are also made of knit fabric.

## Fabric Grain

**Grain** is the direction the threads run in a fabric. Both knit and woven fabrics have a grain. Well-constructed clothes are cut on grain, with the threads running straight up and down and straight across.

Threads may sometimes be pulled off grain when the fabric goes through the finishing process. This makes the grain slant. If the fabric is off-grain, the garment will appear to pull to one side, especially after a few washings.

You can test the fabric grain of a shirt by making sure that the grain runs straight across the back from one underarm seam to the other. Test pants and skirts at the back of the hipline. The grain should be the same on both sides. See Fig. 16-2.

**Fig. 16-2** Grain should run straight up and down and straight across. Check the grain before purchasing garments.

## Fabric Finishes

Manufacturers often add various finishes to improve the durability of fabrics. Some finishes add body or bulk. Some hold the threads in place so that the fabric will wear well and will not pull out at the seams. Other finishes add softness, luster, strength, crispness, or shrinkage control. Finishes can also make caring for fabrics easier.

Clothing labels often tell you what finishes have been added. For instance, a fabric may be treated to be stain- or water-resistant. Washable clothes may have a drip-dry or permanent-press finish, which means that the garment requires little or no ironing.

# Explore

## Natural Dyes

### Supplies

- Undyed fabric such as muslin
- Natural dyes, such as blackberries, blueberries, raspberries, tea, coffee, or carrot juice
- Stainless steel bowls

### State the Task

- Experiment with natural dyes.

### Develop a Plan

1. Choose three natural dyes.
2. Gather the supplies listed above.

### Implement the Plan

1. Take an undyed fabric, such as muslin, and cut it into 8-inch squares.
2. Place a fabric square in each stainless steel bowl.
3. Rub one natural dye on each fabric square. If working with coffee or tea, mix with water and completely submerse the fabric for a few minutes.
4. Make notes of how the fabric reacted to each dye. Did the dye go on evenly? What did it look like when it dried?
5. Rinse the fabric samples to find out which dye types retained their color.

### Evaluate the Result

1. Compare which dye samples looked the best after being submersed in water and drying.
2. Make a list of items you could dye naturally.
3. Write a paragraph on how using natural dyes could help the environment.

## ➤ Clothing Fit

To enjoy wearing your clothes, you must be comfortable in them. First, the clothes need to fit correctly. The fabric that a garment is made from and the style of the garment also affect comfort. Knowing how to evaluate these factors will help you select clothes that you will feel comfortable wearing. See Fig. 16-3.

Female clothing is sold in girls', juniors', misses', women's, and plus sizes. Girls' sizes go up to 14 and are roughly equivalent to the age of the wearer. Juniors' sizes are designed for a developing figure, but are smaller and shorter-waisted than misses' sizes. Petite sizes are shorter in length, while tall sizes are longer.

For males there are three basic size groups: boys', teen boys', and men's. Boys' sizes are designed for small, undeveloped bodies. Teen boys' sizes are for slim teens and young men. Men's sizes are designed for adult figures.

**Fig. 16-3** Choose clothing that is comfortable to wear and allows you room to move.

Men's pants are sized by the waist measurement and the inside leg measurement, or inseam. For example, jeans with a 28-inch waist and a 30-inch inseam would be labeled "size 28/30." Dress shirts also list two measurements, the collar size and the sleeve length, such as 15/34. Jackets are sold by chest measurement and length, such as 38 short or 38 long.

For both females and males, some clothing may be sized simply as small, medium, large, or extra-large. Examples of this type of clothing include sweatshirts, T-shirts, and sweaters. Try on and compare the fit of various styles until you find one that feels comfortable to you. Check the fit by looking at yourself in a full-length mirror. Be sure to also test the fit by sitting, bending, walking, and reaching. See Fig. 16-4.

**Fig. 16-4 Check these features for a comfortable fit.**

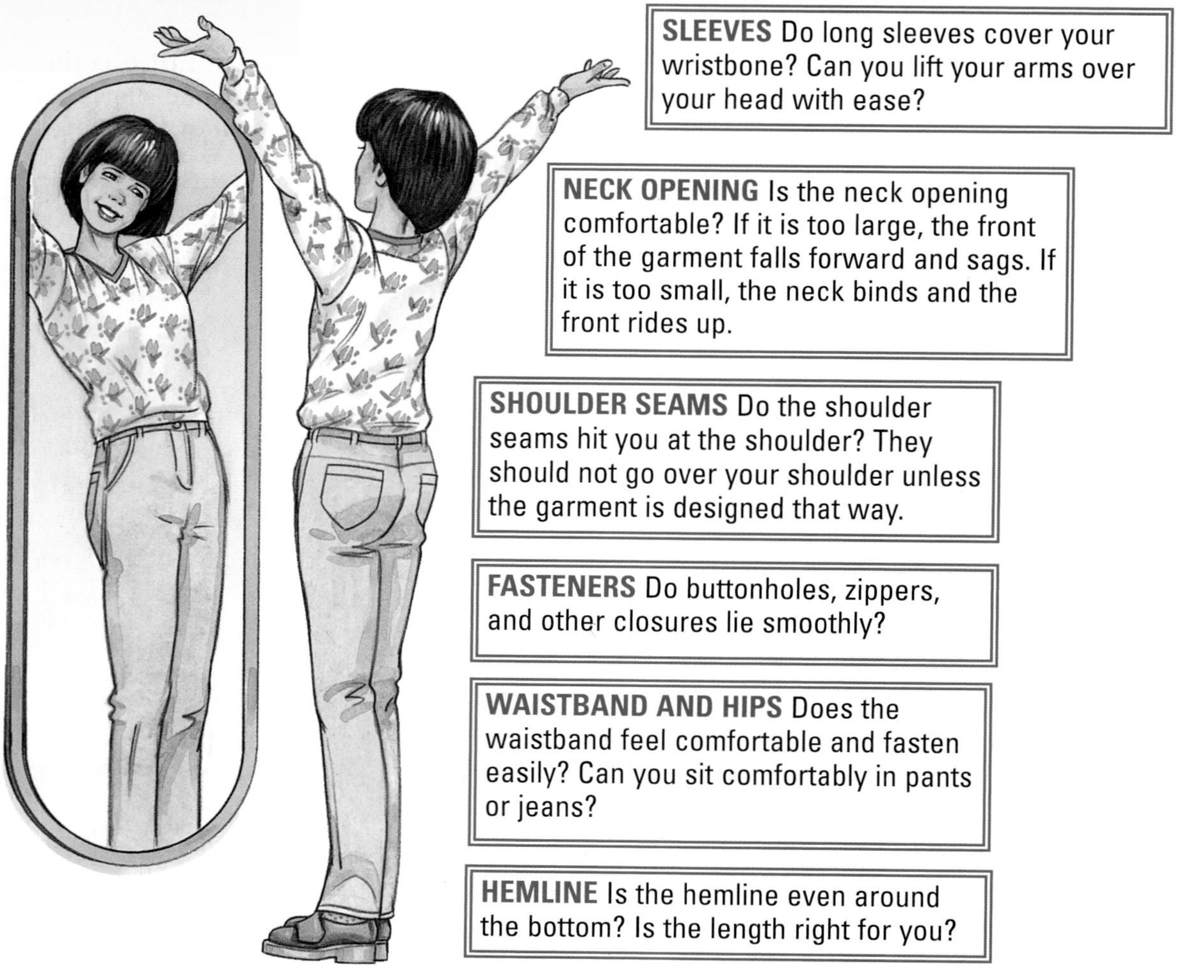

**SLEEVES** Do long sleeves cover your wristbone? Can you lift your arms over your head with ease?

**NECK OPENING** Is the neck opening comfortable? If it is too large, the front of the garment falls forward and sags. If it is too small, the neck binds and the front rides up.

**SHOULDER SEAMS** Do the shoulder seams hit you at the shoulder? They should not go over your shoulder unless the garment is designed that way.

**FASTENERS** Do buttonholes, zippers, and other closures lie smoothly?

**WAISTBAND AND HIPS** Does the waistband feel comfortable and fasten easily? Can you sit comfortably in pants or jeans?

**HEMLINE** Is the hemline even around the bottom? Is the length right for you?

## Comfort & Style

The fabric that a garment is made from can affect its comfort in many ways. Which fabrics do you think feel pleasant to the touch? Some people dislike the feel of slippery or clingy fabrics. Others find woolen knits rough and scratchy. You will want to buy clothes that suit your own preferences. When you buy clothes, be sure to check the feel of the fabric carefully.

Clothing style also affects its comfort. For example, a full skirt or pants with pleats may provide more room for you to move freely. A scoop neckline or an open collar may feel less restrictive than a turtleneck sweater.

Some styles may also suit your body shape better than others. Trying on a garment is the best way to decide whether a particular style is comfortable and looks good on you. See Fig. 16-5.

DID YOU **know?**

**Shoe Shopping.** Comfortable, durable shoes will complete your wardrobe. Use these buying tips:

- Shop early in the day to get a more accurate fit.
- Try on shoes with the type of socks or hosiery that you would normally wear.
- Look for shoes that are not too tight or too loose. Be sure that you have room to wiggle your toes.
- Try on both left and right shoes, and walk around in them.
- When shopping for shoes to match a certain outfit, wear the outfit or take a sample of the fabric with you.

**Fig. 16-5 Learning how to evaluate fit will help you make wise clothing choices.**

# A CLOSER LOOK

## ...at Quality Construction

No matter what type of fabric your clothing is made from, a quality garment requires quality construction. Poor construction can ruin the appearance or durability of an otherwise attractive style. Look for these details when judging the quality of a garment.

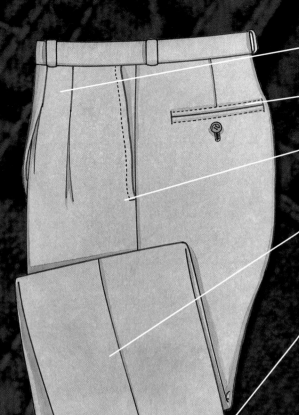

Darts taper to a sharp point.

Pockets are secure, smooth, and flat.

The seams are securely finished.

The seams on the outside of the garment are smooth. They should not be puckered or crooked.

Cuffs and sleeve plackets are neatly finished.

The seams are straight and made with short, evenly spaced stitches.

Seams on collars and facings are flat, not bulky.

Sleeves are evenly gathered or eased and smooth along the seams.

All the top stitching is evenly spaced and straight.

Buttonholes have enough stitches to hold the edges securely.

# Internet ACTIVITIES

1. **Search the Internet for information on how fabrics react to fire. Make a list of fire-resistant fabrics. Share your findings with your classmates.**

   **Key Search Words:**
   - **fire-resistant fabrics**
   - **fire-retardant fabrics**

2. **Search the Internet for information on new types of fabrics being developed, such as solar-reactive and vitamin-enhanced. Write a paragraph about three new types of fabric.**

   **Key Search Words:**
   - **fabric innovations**
   - **fabric technology**

## ➤ Shopping for Clothes

A **shopping plan** is a strategy for spending the money you have available to purchase the clothing you need or want. Before you develop a shopping plan, you should talk over your ideas with your parents. They can help you determine how much money should be used to buy the clothes you need, as well as how much money you can spend for items you want.

In addition to your list of clothing needs, your shopping plan should consider these three factors:

- **Clothing budget.** It is a good idea to set up a monthly spending plan. Go over your spending plan with your parents to decide how to make your money go further. For example, can you wait until that jacket goes on sale? Can you replace the missing buttons on your shirt instead of buying a new one?

- **Purchase plan.** You learned about several payment methods, including cash, check, credit card, and debit card, in Chapter 11. Can you recall some of the advantages and disadvantages of each payment method? For major purchases, such as a formal dress or a winter coat, you may need to save your money. Another alternative for more expensive items is to use a layaway plan. Unlike buying on credit, layaway means that you can't take the item home until it is paid for in full.
- **Shopping options.** In most areas, there are several stores to choose from. Specialty stores, discount stores, and department stores are some options. Another choice is to shop for clothes by mail order or on the Internet. Although you can't try on the clothes before you order them, you may prefer the convenience of shopping in your own home. Clothes that do not fit can usually be returned, but you must pay the return shipping costs.

## ➤ Reading Care Labels

You can find a great deal of helpful information by reading clothing labels. Taking time to check the care label before you buy can help you determine the quality, durability, and care of garments. See Fig. 16-6.

Every item of clothing must carry a label describing its fiber content and how to care for it. This information may be on the same label or on two different labels. Look for these labels inside the collar or waist. Sometimes you will find the care label sewn into a side seam instead.

- The fiber content is listed on the care label. It also gives the name of the manufacturer and tells where the garment was made.
- The care label will tell you the correct way to wash the garment.
- A "no bleach" warning on the label means all types of bleach will damage the fabric.
- If the label tells you not to iron the garment, it is because the fabric might be harmed.

**Fig. 16-6 Reading care labels before you buy clothing can save you time and money. How do you decide if a "dry-clean only" clothing item is worth the expense?**

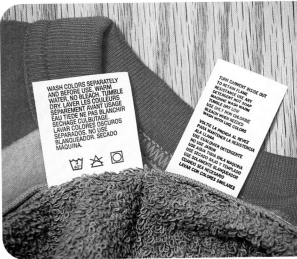

## CHECK the Facts

**Stains.** Water-based stains include those from some foods, perspiration, grass, and washable inks. Oil-based stains include makeup, ballpoint ink, and oil-based paints. Treat common stains as follows:

- **Catsup.** Apply a spot remover, wash as usual with detergent
- **Chewing gum.** Rub with an ice cube to harden the gum. Use a dull knife to scrape it off.
- **Grass.** Rub detergent into the stain and machine wash.
- **Blood.** Soak in cold water and detergent. Use bleach if it is safe for the fabric.
- **Paint.** Rub detergent into the stain and wash. If the stain remains, sponge with mineral spirits or turpentine and rinse.

- If the fabric is colorfast, that fact may be included on the hangtag. A colorfast fabric will keep its original color through many washings.
- Checking care labels before you buy clothing can save you time and money. Not following care labels can cause clothing items to shrink, fade, or lose shape.

## Brand Name Clothing

A brand name is a trademark used by a manufacturer to identify its products. Sometimes stores have their own brand names. In addition, clothing labels may identify the designer, which is another kind of brand name. Some people use brand names as a guide in selecting clothing. Through experience, you will discover which brands fit you well and are well-made. Brand name items are often more expensive than those with less well-known names. Brand names and designer labels are not always signs of quality, however. You will have to decide if brand name clothing is worth the extra cost.

## Making Connections

**Math.** Cost per wearing is the amount of money spent for each time you wear an article of clothing. To determine cost per wearing, first estimate how many times you will wear a particular garment. Then add up the cost of the garment and the cost of cleaning it. Divide the total cost by the number of times you will wear the garment. This will give you an estimated cost per wearing.

### Get Involved!

Determine the cost per wearing for a jacket that cost $50. It must be dry-cleaned. You will likely wear it 80 times. Each dry-cleaning bill will be $12. You plan to wear it twice between cleanings.

**304** **Unit 3** Exploring Fashion & Clothing

# ➤ Your Clothing Budget

When you made your shopping plan, you had to calculate your clothing budget, or how much money you had to spend. You can make that money go further by understanding and following some simple guidelines. See Fig. 16-7.

- **Start with two or three basic outfits.** Add coordinated pieces to build your wardrobe around a few basic colors. You can create many different clothing combinations that way.
- **Make the best use of what you have.** Try different combinations and accessories with clothes you already own.
- **Take good care of your clothes.** By following the directions on the care label, you can make clothes last longer. Hang or fold up clothes when they are not being worn. Treat stains and wash clothes before putting them away.
- **Compare cost and quality.** Keep in mind that it may not always be smart to buy the best quality. Why pay more for a fad item that won't be in fashion next year?

**Fig. 16-7 Learn to shop wisely. If a more expensive item is made better than a less expensive one, it will last longer.** How do you decide which is the best buy?

- **Take advantage of sales.** Plan ahead and shop during seasonal sales to get more for your money.
- **Learn to sew.** Making simple clothing items yourself can be a way to save money and express your personality. Making simple repairs will make your clothes last longer.

### Clothing Care

Keeping your clothes in good condition will save you money. See Fig. 16-8. Follow these simple guidelines to take proper care of your clothes:

- Wear appropriate clothing for the activity. When doing yard work or cleaning out the garage, for example, wear old clothes so that it doesn't matter if they get dirty.
- Dress and undress carefully to avoid snagging, ripping, or stretching garments.
- Inspect your clothes carefully after each wearing. Repair any tears or holes before they get bigger. If you find stains, treat them immediately and wash the garment as soon as possible.

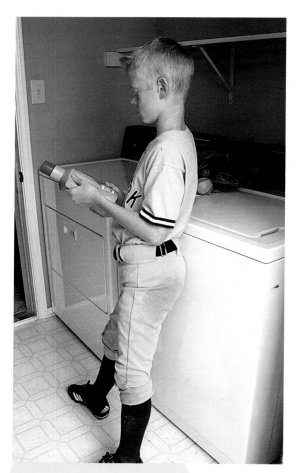

Fig. 16–8 Learn how to take care of special clothing, such as team uniforms. Do you know how to get grass stains out of clothes?

## ➤ Cleaning Clothes

Cleaning clothes properly requires a basic knowledge of fabrics and simple cleaning techniques. Doing laundry isn't hard if you follow the instructions on clothing care labels and on laundry products and appliances.

Learning the right way to launder clothes will help you keep your clothes looking newer longer. See Fig. 16-9. Follow these guidelines when washing your clothes:

- **Pre-treat stains.** Pre-treat means to apply a stain remover before laundering. Besides stains, sleeve cuffs and the fold line on collars often need to be pretreated.
- **Sort clothes.** Check care labels on clothes carefully. Then separate each pile by color: light-colored fabrics, medium-colored fabrics, and dark fabrics.

- **Select the correct water temperature.** Wash your clothes in the water temperature recommended on the care label. Unless otherwise specified, most clothing can be washed in warm water and rinsed in cold.
- **Choose the correct load size.** If you are washing only a few clothes, choose a small-load setting to save water and energy. Never overload the washing machine. Clothes won't get clean if they are packed in too tightly.
- **Add detergent.** Check the detergent label for the correct amount to use. Remember to adjust for the load setting you selected.
- **Use a fabric softener.** If static is a problem, liquid fabric softeners can be added in the washer or dryer sheets can be used in the dryer. Read product labels carefully to determine which type you are using and how and when it should be added.

Fig. 16–9 Doing laundry can be a simple task if you follow the directions on clothing care labels, laundry products, and appliances.

Clothes can generally be either line-dried or machine-dried. Line-drying saves energy and money but takes longer. Machine-drying is quick and convenient, but it uses energy and therefore costs more.

As soon as your clothes are dry, remove them from the dryer. This will help prevent wrinkling. Hang up items such as shirts, pants, and dresses as soon as you take them out of the dryer. Fold and sort the other items.

Some fabrics require ironing after each wash. Other items may require some light pressing with a steam iron. The care label gives the proper temperature setting for the fabric. Always match the temperature setting on the iron with the fiber listed on the label. Synthetic fabrics may melt if the iron is too hot.

Start by ironing or pressing small areas of the garment, such as the collar, yoke, and sleeves. Then press the larger areas. This way, you avoid wrinkling areas you have already ironed.

# How To...

## Remove Stains

### Supplies

- Old white T-shirt
- Scissors
- Chocolate
- Grease
- Ink
- Dark-color soft drink
- Pre-wash stain remover
- Detergent
- Hair spray
- Rubbing alcohol
- Stainless steel bowls
- Water

### State the Task

- Recognize stains and learn how to treat them.

### Develop a Plan

1. Gather your supplies.
2. Stain different sections of the T-shirt.
3. Use various methods to remove the stains.
4. Record the results.

### Implement the Plan

1. Cut the T-shirt into four sections.
2. Rub one section of cloth with chocolate. Rub the stain with a pre-wash stain remover. Then rub the stain with detergent and rinse.
3. Rub one section of cloth with grease. Use a pre-wash stain remover, then wash out the cloth. If the stain is still visible on the fabric, treat it again. Rinse the cloth.
4. Apply ink to the third section of cloth. Spray with hair spray. Then rub the stain with detergent and rinse.
5. Apply the soft drink to the last piece of cloth. Wet the stain with cold water. Wash the fabric with detergent, then rinse.

### Evaluate the Result

1. Write down how each stain reacted to the cleaning solution used. Make a note of any stains that were not completely removed.
2. How could treating stains help you get more life out of your clothes?

## Storing Clothes

An important, but sometimes overlooked, part of caring for clothes is storing them properly. When you hang up your clothes, take the time to close zippers and fasten buttons so that the garment will hang straight. Do not overcrowd closets and drawers, or your clothes may wrinkle. See Fig. 16-10.

Seasonal clothes, that are worn only for a few months each year, and clothes that are worn only for special occasions should be given extra attention. Check to be sure that pockets are empty and that garments are clean and repaired before putting them away.

**Fig. 16-10** Store your clothes properly so they will last longer.

# Career CHOICES

## Shopping Investigator

Shops in commercial and retail stores to test the integrity of sales and service personnel. Evaluates sales techniques and services. Reviews store policies and standards.

## Merchandise Distributor

Writes reports of stock on hand, plus the type and amount sold. Provides inventory data to units of retail chain. Routes merchandise from one branch store to another on the basis of sales. Usually specializes in one type of merchandise.

## Fabric Inspector

Inspects narrow woven fabrics, such as labels, ribbon, and trims. Finds defective weaving, color variations, and damaged or dirty fabrics. Pulls defective fabrics off the line. Writes quality control reports. Suggests changes that will help prevent defects from occurring.

## Dry Cleaner

Operates various dry-cleaning machines to clean garments, draperies and other items as specified by customer.

## Silk Spreader

Tends machines that fluff and combine silk fibers. Weighs cleaned, raw silk. Separates silk into small bunches of specified weights.

**AT** School

Select three of the careers listed. Research the education, training, and work experience required for each career. Compare the results to select a career to investigate further.

**IN THE** Workplace

Name several types of stains you might get while on the job and how you could best treat those stains.

**Working in dry cleaning demands that you focus on customer needs and wants.** Interview someone who works in the dry-cleaning industry.

## Chapter Summary

- Recognize quality clothing by handling and comparing different fabrics.
- Your shopping plan should include a list of clothing needs, your budget, method of payment, and stores.
- Clothing labels inform you of the garment's quality, durability, and care requirements.
- Stains can be either water-based or oil-based. Most stains can be removed if they are treated immediately.
- Wash and dry your clothes using the correct detergent and water temperature.
- Iron or press your clothes according to care label instructions.
- Properly store clothes by carefully hanging or folding them. Store seasonal items only after they are cleaned.

## Words You Learned

1. What are fibers?
2. Describe how woven fabrics are made.
3. Describe how knit fabrics are made.
4. What is meant by grain in fabric?
5. What is a shopping plan?

## Check Your Facts

1. Name four natural fibers and identify the source of each.
2. Describe synthetic fibers.
3. Why should you check the fabric grain when purchasing clothing?
4. How can you reduce your clothing costs?
5. Explain how to pre-treat a stain.

## Apply Your Learning

1. Suppose that a friend wants to buy an expensive outfit for a special party. What advice would you give him or her about making that purchase?
2. Explain the difference between style and fit.
3. Imagine that you are a clothing designer. Describe one garment that you would design and the fabric you would use to make it. Explain how the characteristics of this fabric would enhance the garment's design.
4. **Clothing Collage.** Look through magazines and cut out pictures of clothing and accessories that you like. Make a collage on poster board. Write down how the pieces could fit into your wardrobe.

# Chapter 17

# Preparing to Sew

## You Will Discover . . .

- how to operate a sewing machine.
- what to look for when choosing a sewing project.
- how to determine your correct pattern size.
- how to select the best fabric for your sewing project.

## Key Words

- pattern
- darts
- alteration
- nap
- notions

Amelia likes sewing because it gives her a chance to be creative. Sewing is a way to show her individuality in the styles, fabrics, and finishing touches she chooses. You, too, can personalize your garments or create your own designs. You'll need several types of equipment, plus fabric, patterns, and notions for your sewing project.

# The Sewing Lab

School is a great place to learn and practice basic sewing skills, including how to cut out a pattern and how to use a sewing machine. You will also need to work cooperatively with others and manage your time wisely. See Fig. 17-1. The keys to making the most of your time are organization, preparation, and consideration.

- **Organization.** Put your supplies in a small container with your name on it. Keep your supplies neat and organized and they will be ready to use when you need them.
- **Preparation.** Bring in the required supplies. Before you start to sew, read the instructions carefully.
- **Consideration.** When you finish using an item, return it to where it belongs.

## The Sewing Machine

Most sewing machines have the same basic parts. See Fig. 17-2. Sewing machines all operate in the same way. A needle moves up and down through the fabric, and two sets of threads interlock to form stitches. However, sewing machines vary greatly in what they can do and how much they cost.

Before using any sewing machine, be sure to read the instruction manual. You can use it to find the parts on your sewing machine, and learn how to use its special features.

**Fig. 17-1 You can learn basic sewing skills at school.** What do you want to make as your first sewing project?

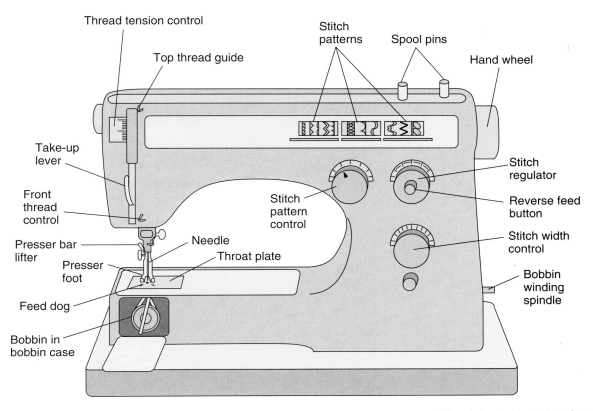

Thread tension control

Top thread guide

Stitch patterns

Spool pins

Hand wheel

Take-up lever

Front thread control

Presser bar lifter

Presser foot

Feed dog

Bobbin in bobbin case

Needle

Throat plate

Stitch pattern control

Stitch regulator

Reverse feed button

Stitch width control

Bobbin winding spindle

**Fig. 17-2 The parts of a standard sewing machine.**

# Making Connections

**Math.** Caitlin is making dolls for an upcoming craft fair. Her cost for materials is $75 per doll. Each doll takes three hours to make, and Caitlin hopes to earn at least $15 per hour making dolls.

## Get Involved!

How much should Caitlin charge per doll if she makes 10 dolls at a rate of $15 per hour? She plans to show the dolls at two craft fairs, each with a $10 entry fee.

# How To...

## Use a Sewing Machine

**State the Task**

- Learn to use a sewing machine.

**Develop a Plan**

1. Wind the bobbin.
2. Thread the machine.
3. Practice making four basic stitches.

**Implement the Plan**

1. Wind the thread you will be using from your spool onto the bobbin, a small spool that holds the thread inside the machine. (*Note:* Check your machine's manual to see how to wind the bobbin.)
2. After you have threaded the bobbin, insert it in the bobbin case.
3. Thread the machine. (*Note:* There is a diagram in the machine manual that shows you how to thread the machine.)
4. Use a separate fabric scrap to make each of the four basic stitches:
   - **Regular stitch**—a medium-length stitch used for sewing most projects.

     **Regular**

   - **Basting stitch**—a very long stitch used for holding layers of fabric together temporarily.

     **Basting**

- **Reinforcement stitch**—a short stitch used to strengthen a corner or a point.

  **Reinforcement**

- **Zigzag stitch**—a sideways stitch used to make button-holes, finish seam edges, and sew special seams.

**Evaluate the Result**

1. Write down what caused you problems. Consult your sewing machine manual to find out what you can do to correct these problems.
2. Compare your stitch samples with your classmates. How are they the same or different?

Walter Hunt. **Inventor Walter Hunt built America's first sewing machine in 1834. He also invented the safety pin.**

# ➤ Pattern Selection

Most sewing projects call for a pattern. A **pattern** is a plan for making a garment or project. It contains paper shapes of the various pieces and gives the instructions for sewing. Your success in completing your project depends in part on the pattern you choose. See Fig. 17-3.

When you choose a pattern, you will want one that matches your abilities and the time you have to complete the project. Before you choose a pattern, consider the following:

- **Purpose.** Do you want to make clothing for yourself, something for your room, or a specialty item, such as a backpack?
- **Sewing skills and experience.** If you have never worked on a project before, choose a simple pattern.
- **Time.** Do you have enough time to complete the project? This is especially important if you are sewing at school and are sharing a sewing machine.
- **Cost.** How much money are you willing to spend?

These factors will help you choose the best pattern for your needs. When you find a pattern that you like, make a note of the brand name and pattern number. Then you can read the pattern envelope for more information.

**Fig. 17-3** Choose a pattern that matches your skill level, time frame, and budget.

## The Pattern Envelope

The pattern envelope provides you with the information you need to plan a sewing project. The front of the envelope shows a picture of the completed project. Sometimes more than one view is shown. For example, a shirt pattern may show one view with short sleeves and another with long sleeves.

On the back of the envelope, you will find the following:

- A drawing showing the pattern pieces and construction features, such as darts. **Darts** are tapered, V-shaped seams used to give shape.

- A chart that tells you how much fabric to buy for the view and size pattern you are using.
- Recommendations on the types of fabrics that can be used.
- Additional materials you will need, such as thread and buttons. These are called notions.

## Choosing Patterns

How can you find an appropriate pattern for your first project? Pattern books indicate which patterns are simple to sew and even have special sections for quick-and-easy projects.

In addition, look for these features to help you choose an easy-to-make pattern:

- **Number of pattern pieces.** Fewer pattern pieces mean fewer pieces of fabric to cut out and stitch.
- **Number of seams.** Seams join two pieces of fabric together. The fewer seams involved, the easier it will be to complete the pattern.
- **Garment fit.** Loose-fitting styles are easier to sew than close-fitting styles.
- **Closures.** Elastic waists require less advanced sewing skills than do zippers and buttonholes.

# Internet ACTIVITIES

1. **Search the Internet for articles that can help you learn sewing techniques. Choose an article and make a list of sewing tips.**

   Key Search Words:
   - **sewing fashion**
   - **sewing techniques**

2. **Search the Internet for information on the latest sewing machines. Write a paragraph on how technology has changed sewing.**

   Key Search Words:
   - **sewing machines**
   - **sewing advances**

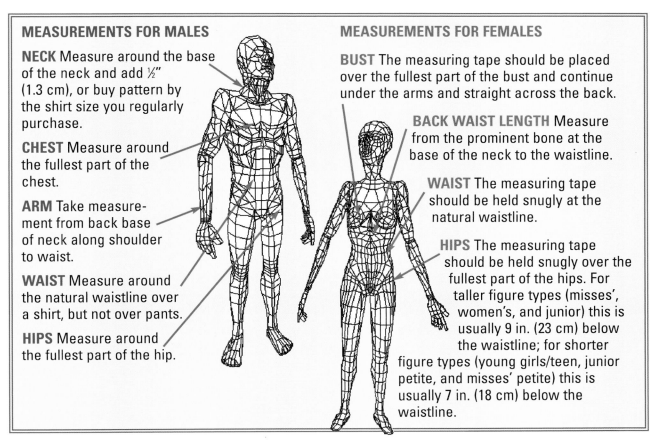

**MEASUREMENTS FOR MALES**

**NECK** Measure around the base of the neck and add ½" (1.3 cm), or buy pattern by the shirt size you regularly purchase.

**CHEST** Measure around the fullest part of the chest.

**ARM** Take measurement from back base of neck along shoulder to waist.

**WAIST** Measure around the natural waistline over a shirt, but not over pants.

**HIPS** Measure around the fullest part of the hip.

**MEASUREMENTS FOR FEMALES**

**BUST** The measuring tape should be placed over the fullest part of the bust and continue under the arms and straight across the back.

**BACK WAIST LENGTH** Measure from the prominent bone at the base of the neck to the waistline.

**WAIST** The measuring tape should be held snugly at the natural waistline.

**HIPS** The measuring tape should be held snugly over the fullest part of the hips. For taller figure types (misses', women's, and junior) this is usually 9 in. (23 cm) below the waistline; for shorter figure types (young girls/teen, junior petite, and misses' petite) this is usually 7 in. (18 cm) below the waistline.

## Pattern Size

Patterns, like ready-to-wear clothing, come in different sizes. They are grouped by figure types. Pattern sizes for female clothing are based on four measurements: bust, waist, hip, and back waist length. Patterns for male clothing are based on five measurements: chest, waist, hip or seat, neck, and sleeve length. See Fig. 17-4. When taking measurements, be sure that the measuring tape is held parallel to the floor. Never stretch the measuring tape.

You want to select a size that does not require **alteration**, or change to make a certain size fit. Compare your measurements to the measurements on the pattern envelope. Choose the size that has the closest measurements. Use the following guidelines to decide which measurement is most important for a particular type of garment:

- For blouses and tops, fit the bust measurement.
- For shirts, fit the chest and neck measurements.
- For full skirts, fit the waist measurement.
- For pants and semi-fitted skirts, fit the hip measurement.

**Fig. 17-4** This chart explains how to take your measurements.

# A CLOSER LOOK

## ...at Small Sewing Tools

**To complete any sewing project successfully, you have to know which tools to use and how to use them. Small sewing tools are important to any project's success.**

### Shears, Scissors & Pinking Shears

Shears are large scissors that often have a raised handle for easier cutting. Scissors are used for trimming, clipping, and cutting threads. Pinking shears are scissors that have a zigzag edge.

## Sewing Gauge

A sewing gauge is a 6-inch (16-cm) ruler with an adjustable pointer. It is used to measure short spaces, such as hems and seam widths.

## Needles & Thread

Needles are used for hand sewing. Select thread color that matches your fabric.

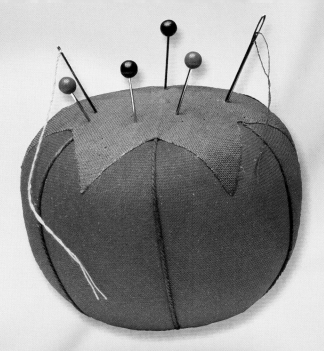

## Pins & Pincushion

Dressmaker pins are slender, sharp-pointed, and rust proof. The pincushion is a convenient holder for pins and needles.

## Seam Ripper

This pen-shaped tool has a small, hook-like blade at one end for removing stitches.

## Thimble

A thimble protects your finger while you're hand sewing. It makes it easier to push the needle through the fabric.

## Tape Measure

A flexible tape is used to take body measurements.

## ➤ Choosing Fabrics

Fabrics come in many different colors, textures, designs, and finishes. How do you know which fabric to buy? You will want to evaluate the fiber content, how the fabric is made, and any finishes that have been added. You should also check the fabric grain for quality.

When selecting fabric, you can use the information on your pattern envelope. The back of the envelope provides a list of suggested fabrics and how much fabric you will need. The pattern envelope provides special instructions for fabrics with **nap**, or a one-way texture, such as corduroy.

**Fig. 17-5** When choosing fabrics, check the fiber content and care instructions listed on the end of the fabric bolt.

### Recognizing Quality Fabrics

When you shop for fabrics, you will notice that they come in many price categories. How can you tell which ones are high quality? Keep in mind that you don't have to buy the most expensive one to get a good fabric. When judging quality in fabrics, examine the following:

- **Crosswise threads.** They should be straight and at right angles to the lengthwise threads. This means the fabric is on grain.
- **Pattern.** Make sure that a printed pattern runs straight with the grain. If the fabric is not printed properly, the garment will look off-grain.
- **Weave.** The weave should be firm and durable.
- **Color.** All colors should be consistent.
- **Finish.** The finish should feel comfortable and pleasing to the touch.
- **Label.** Read the label on the end of the bolt of fabric. It gives facts about fabric width, fiber content, finishes, shrinkage, and care instructions. See Fig. 17-5.

When choosing a fabric, think about your project requirements. You should consider the following factors:

- **Your sewing experience.** Select fabrics that are easy to sew for your first few projects.
- **Who will use the item.** When making something for yourself, look for colors that can be mixed and matched with other clothes you own.
- **When the item will be used.** The time of day and the season of the year the item will be used may affect the type of fabric you choose.
- **How the item will be used.** For instance, when making a non-clothing item, such as a tote bag, a dark-colored fabric that doesn't show dirt is a good choice.
- **Type of care needed.** Look for fabrics that are machine washable and that require little or no ironing.

Some fabrics are difficult to sew. For example, lightweight and extremely soft fabrics can be slippery and hard to sew. Loosely woven fabrics may not be a good choice because they tend to ravel, or have threads pull out of the cut edge. Plaids, stripes, and large prints need to be matched at the seams and may require extra fabric.

## Pressing Fabrics

Whenever you sew, you will need to use an iron to press seams and other details. See Fig. 17-6. Follow these safety tips:

- Use distilled water in the iron to reduce stains caused by the minerals in tap water.
- Always rest the iron on its heel.
- To see if the iron is hot, try it on a scrap of fabric, not on your fingers. Always point the steam vents away from your hands.
- Turn off and unplug the iron when you finish.
- Coil the cord so that no one trips over it or pulls the iron off the ironing board.

**Fig. 17-6** Always set the iron on the correct temperature for the fabric you are pressing.

## ➤ Selecting Notions

After you have chosen a fabric, refer to the back of the pattern envelope for a list of the type of notions you will need. **Notions** are the items you need to complete the project. Commonly used notions include the following:

- Thread.
- Fasteners such as zippers, buttons, snaps, hook and loop tape.
- Elastic.
- **Interfacing** is placed between two pieces of fabric to give more shape to the garment. It is often used in waistbands, cuffs, and collars.

When you buy notions, use your fabric to match colors. Thread should be the same color as the fabric or slightly darker because it will appear lighter when stitched. See Fig. 17-7.

**Fig. 17-7 Choose thread that is the same color or a shade darker than your fabric. How do you know what type of thread to purchase?**

# Explore

## Making a Sewing Kit

### State the Task

- Create a travel-size sewing kit.

### Develop a Plan

1. Gather the supplies listed.
2. Choose several thread colors that match most items in your clothes closet. In addition, add black, white, and beige thread.
3. Assemble the kit.

### Implement the Plan

1. Cut the cardboard into a 1½" x 3½" rectangle.
2. Cut small, V-shaped notches in each side of the cardboard. The notches should be directly across from each other.
3. Wrap different colors of thread around the cardboard, using the notches to hold the thread in place.
4. Insert the needles carefully into the cardboard.
5. Tape the safety pins and buttons to the cardboard so that the tips of the needles are covered.

### Evaluate the Result

1. What other items could you add to your travel-size sewing kit?
2. Who else could use a sewing kit? How could it help that person?

> **Supplies**
> - Several spools of thread in different colors
> - Hand-sewing needles
> - Needle threader
> - Two safety pins
> - Two small shirt buttons
> - Small piece of cardboard
> - Clear tape

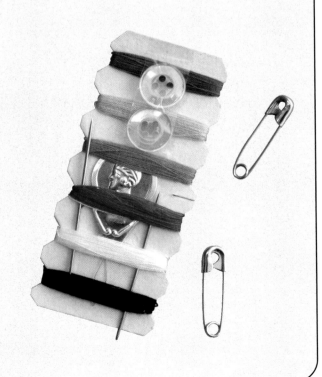

# Career CHOICES

## Alterations Specialist

Alters clothing to fit individual customers. Repairs garments as requested by customers. Remakes old garments into new styles.

## Machine Operator

Creates fibers, yarns, and fabrics by spinning, weaving, knitting, printing, and dyeing. Oversees multiple machines that treat tanks, dye jigs, and vats. Prepares a specific set of machines for production and corrects or reports any problems during a run.

## Patternmaker

Translates sample garments into paper patterns. Increases and decreases the size of all pattern pieces to correspond to garment sizes. Works in the sample room of a fashion house or in a clothing manufacturer's product engineering department.

## Apparel Stylist

Creates adaptations of expensive designer originals. Produces clothes that are fashionable, yet affordable. Makes garments that fit the image of a certain company or an overall clothing line.

## Textile Converter

Applies designs, textures, and other finishes to fabrics. Buys unfinished fabric from textile mills and turns it into fabrics for apparel manufacturers.

### AT School

Select three of the careers listed. Research the education, training, and work experience required for each career. Compare the results to select a career to investigate further.

### IN THE Workplace

Write down five examples of how fabrics are used in a workplace. Compare lists with your classmates.

**Working in the fiber and fabrics industry is physically demanding. However, think how exciting it would be to create so many different colors, patterns, and textures.**

## Chapter Summary

- Operate a sewing machine according to its instruction manual.
- Choose a sewing project based on its purpose, your sewing skills, the amount of time you have, and the cost.
- Determine your correct pattern size by taking your measurements.
- Select the best fabric for your sewing project based on the recommendations on the back of the pattern envelope.

## Words You Learned

1. What is a sewing pattern?
2. Why would a garment be designed with darts?
3. Describe an alteration that could make a garment fit better.
4. Define the term nap as it relates to fabric.
5. Name the basic notions.

## Check Your Facts

1. Describe the basic procedure for threading a sewing machine.
2. Name four basic types of stitches and the purpose of each.
3. What do you use to control the speed on a sewing machine?
4. Name three pieces of information that you can find on the back of the pattern envelope.
5. What can help you choose an easy-to-make pattern?

## Apply Your Learning

1. Estimate the cost of a sewing project you are interested in making. How does the total cost compare with that of a similar item you could buy ready-made? What other factors should you consider when deciding whether to make or buy this item?
2. Identify the most important measurement for each of the following types of garments: blouses and tops, shirts, full skirts, pants, and semi-fitted skirts.
3. **Fabric Guide.** Cut out small samples of different types of fabrics. Arrange the fabric samples in a scrapbook or photo album. Add samples as you discover new fabrics you like to use when sewing.

# Chapter 18

## Sewing & Serging Basics

### You Will Discover . . .

- how to prepare your fabric and use a pattern guide sheet.
- how to check pattern pieces and measurements.
- the basics of machine sewing.
- hand-sewing techniques.
- how a serger works.
- how to make basic repairs and alterations.

### Key Words

- selvage
- bias
- guide sheet
- layouts
- markings
- ease
- staystitching
- casings
- cones
- loopers

*E*van bought a pattern, some fabric, and notions. He plans to start sewing immediately. Is he leaving out a step? Take the time to prepare your fabric and pattern *before* you start sewing. Your sewing projects will be more successful if you carefully complete each step— from laying out the pattern pieces to finishing the hem.

## ➤ Fabric Preparation

You can run into problems if you don't prepare your fabric before you begin sewing. Just imagine how you would feel if, after you spent hours sewing a shirt, it shrank when you washed it. To avoid such problems, take the time to preshrink your fabric. Some fabrics will not "shrink," while others may. Launder the fabric as directed. You can find cleaning instructions on the end of the bolt of fabric.

### Checking the Grain

After you have preshrunk the fabric, you need to check the grain by looking at the fabric and locating the two selvages along the lengthwise edges. See Fig. 18-1. The **selvage** is the tightly woven edge of the fabric that has no visible loose threads. Raw edges are the unfinished edges of the fabric.

To test the grain, fold the fabric lengthwise so that the selvages are on top of one another. If the raw edges of the fabric do not line up, do the following:

Fig. 18-1 Always check the fabric grain before beginning to sew.

- For woven fabrics, clip the selvage and pull a crosswise thread. Cut along the line made by the pulled thread. Preshrink the fabric by following the cleaning instructions given on the bolt.
- For knitted fabrics, cut along one crosswise row of loops to straighten the edges.

Test the grain again by folding your fabric and matching selvages. If the crosswise ends match exactly and are at right angles to the selvage, the fabric is straight. The fold will be smooth and unwrinkled. If the edges do not match, the fabric is not straight.

You can straighten the fabric by pulling it on the true **bias**, or diagonal. To do that, open up the fabric and pull the two short corners.

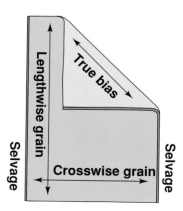

# Internet ACTIVITIES

## ➤ Pattern Preparation

Study the guide sheet inside your pattern envelope before you begin sewing. A **guide sheet** is a set of step-by-step instructions for sewing a pattern. See Fig. 18-2. The guide sheet contains general information on how to use the pattern, a diagram of the pattern pieces, an explanation of the pattern markings, and layouts. **Layouts** are diagrams of how the pattern pieces should be placed on the fabric.

If you use the pattern guide sheet, you will be able to sew more quickly and efficiently. For best results, follow these steps:

- Study the diagram of the pattern pieces.
- Circle the letters of the pieces needed for the view that you plan to make.
- Circle the layout diagram that you will use for your size and style.
- Read through all of the pattern directions before you start to work.
- As you make your project, put a check mark next to each step after you complete it.

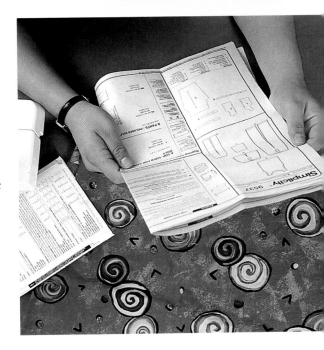

**Fig. 18-2** Read the entire pattern guide sheet before you begin to sew.

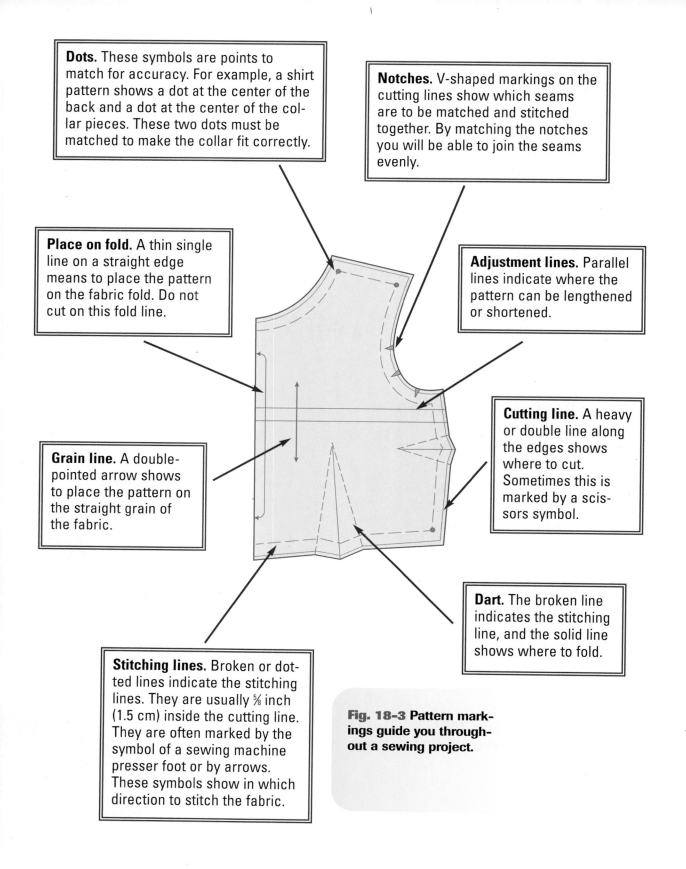

**Dots.** These symbols are points to match for accuracy. For example, a shirt pattern shows a dot at the center of the back and a dot at the center of the collar pieces. These two dots must be matched to make the collar fit correctly.

**Notches.** V-shaped markings on the cutting lines show which seams are to be matched and stitched together. By matching the notches you will be able to join the seams evenly.

**Place on fold.** A thin single line on a straight edge means to place the pattern on the fabric fold. Do not cut on this fold line.

**Adjustment lines.** Parallel lines indicate where the pattern can be lengthened or shortened.

**Grain line.** A double-pointed arrow shows to place the pattern on the straight grain of the fabric.

**Cutting line.** A heavy or double line along the edges shows where to cut. Sometimes this is marked by a scissors symbol.

**Dart.** The broken line indicates the stitching line, and the solid line shows where to fold.

**Stitching lines.** Broken or dotted lines indicate the stitching lines. They are usually ⅝ inch (1.5 cm) inside the cutting line. They are often marked by the symbol of a sewing machine presser foot or by arrows. These symbols show in which direction to stitch the fabric.

**Fig. 18-3 Pattern markings guide you throughout a sewing project.**

After you have read through the guide sheet, you are ready to prepare the pattern pieces. Follow these steps:

1. Cut apart the pieces you will use, but do not trim them. You will cut off the margins later, when you cut the fabric. Put the pattern pieces that you will not use back in the envelope.
2. Study each pattern piece, and refer to the guide sheet to find out what each marking means. **Markings** are guides on the pattern pieces. See Fig. 18-3.
3. If the pattern pieces are wrinkled, press them with a warm, dry iron.

## Checking Pattern Measurements

Before you place the pattern pieces on the fabric, you need to make sure that the pattern you selected fits your body. To do that, compare your measurements with the body measurements listed on the pattern envelope. If you need to make any alterations to the pattern, now is the time to do so—before you cut the fabric.

- **Length adjustments.** Use the two parallel lines labeled lengthen or shorten. Your teacher can show you how to do this. Be sure that you make the same changes on both the front and back pieces of the pattern.
- **Width adjustments.** Determine how much actual ease is included in the pattern. **Ease** is the amount of fullness added for movement and comfort. The amount of ease depends on the stress that will be put on that part of the garment when it is worn. Your teacher can show you how to adjust the amount of ease.

## Pinning the Pattern

Look at the layout you circled on the guide sheet to see how to fold your fabric. Most layouts show the right sides folded together. Lay the pattern pieces on top of the fabric. The lengthwise grain markings must be parallel to the selvage. Check them with a ruler or seam gauge as you pin. Don't cut out any pieces until they have all been pinned in place.

Here are some pinning guidelines:

1. Pin the large pattern pieces that belong on the fold.
2. Pin the pattern pieces that have a grain-line arrow. To check the grain line, place a pin at one end of the grain-line arrow. Measure from the arrow to the selvage of fabric edge. Position the pattern so that the other end of the arrow is exactly the same distance from the edge. Then pin the piece in place.
3. Place the pins diagonally inside the cutting line. This keeps the fabric flat and makes it easier to cut.
4. Place pins about 2 inches (5 cm) apart.
5. Double-check your pinned layout against the layout on the pattern guide sheet.

## Cutting Out the Pattern

Before you cut out your project, practice cutting on fabric scraps. It will be easier to sew straight seams, if you cut the edges of the fabric evenly. See Fig. 18-4. Follow these guidelines:

**Fig. 18-4 Carefully cut out all the pattern pieces.**

- Place the fabric flat on the table. Use one hand to hold the fabric in place and the other hand to cut.
- Cut with long, even strokes.
- Cut in the direction of the arrows printed on the pattern's seamline. In this way, you will be cutting with the fabric grain, and you will not stretch the fabric.
- Cut around the outside of each notch. Cut double and triple notches together with one long edge across the top.
- Leave the pattern pieces pinned to the fabric until you are ready to stitch that piece.

## Transferring Markings

After you cut out your pattern, transfer markings from the pattern to the fabric. Markings include darts, dots, fold lines, and buttonholes. You'll find many marking devices available today: tailor's chalk, water-soluble marking pens, air-soluble pens, and the traditional tracing wheel and tracing paper.

When transferring markings:

- Always test your marking device on a fabric scrap to make sure the marks come out of the fabric completely.
- When using a tracing wheel and paper, choose a color of tracing paper that will show up on the fabric.
- Mark dots with an X.
- Mark the ends of darts with a short line.
- Mark each seamline so that you will know exactly where to stitch.

## ➤ Beginning to Sew

When you make a garment, the first step is to staystitch the seams. **Staystitching** is a row of stitching made on or very near the seamline within the seam allowance. Staystitching prevents stretching and helps in turning under edges of hems and bands. See Fig. 18-5.

### Making Darts

Darts are used to help shape fabric to the curves of the body. They are usually found at the bustline, waistline, elbow, or back of the shoulder. For darts to create the right effect, they must have the correct width and shape. Make sure that they are accurately marked, folded, and pinned before you stitch them. When you are ready to stitch, follow these steps:

- Fold the darts so that the right sides of the fabric are together. Match the stitching lines and pin.
- Stitch from the wide end of the dart to the point.
- Stitch the last two or three stitches as close to the fold line as possible. This will make a sharp point without a bubble at the end. Do not backstitch.
- Tie the thread ends securely, and cut about ½ inch (1.3 cm) from the knot.
- Press vertical darts toward the center and horizontal darts downward.

**Fig. 18-5** Staystitching seams prevents stretching.

## Stitching Straight Seams

You will sew most projects together by stitching straight seams. To sew a seam, place two pieces of fabric right sides together. Line up the edges so that they are even. Match all markings and notches, and pin the two pieces together. The heads of the pins should be near the outside edges of the fabric. For most sewing, pins should be placed about 2 inches (5 cm) apart.

Now look at the throat plate on your sewing machine. The line markings show how far the needle is from the seam edge. Most seams are ⅝ inch (1.5 cm) wide. Find the line on the machine that is ⅝ inch (1.5 cm) from the needle. Keep the fabric edge against this mark as you sew and your seam will be straight. See Fig. 18-6. As you stitch, guide the fabric with both hands, but do not push it. The feed dog will move the fabric as you sew. Operate the machine at a slow, even speed. Backstitch 2-3 stitches at the beginning and end of the seam.

## Stitching Curved Seams

With curved seams, you must guide the fabric with your hands so that the curves are smooth. You also need to keep the stitching an even distance from the edge of the fabric. The best way to learn how to sew curved seams is to practice. Start by stitching curves on a piece of paper. Then practice on scraps of fabric.

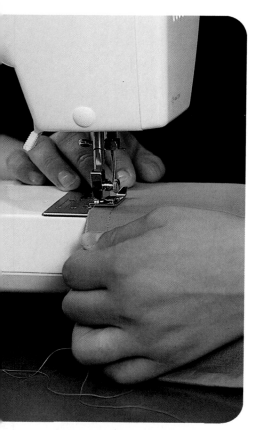

Fig. 18-6 Keep the fabric edge against the mark on the needle plate as you stitch. Practice stitching on fabric scraps before sewing your project.

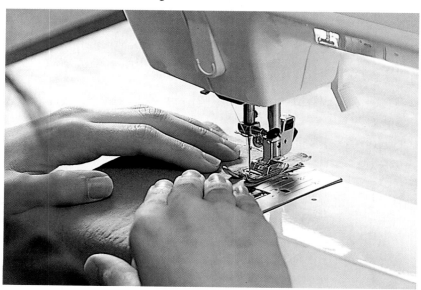

Fig. 18-7 Turning corners takes practice. Remember to leave the needle in the fabric before lifting the presser foot.

## Turning Corners

Learning how to turn corners, or pivot, when you sew is another skill that takes practice. Follow these steps:

- When you come to a corner, slow down the sewing machine. The last stitch should position the needle exactly in the corner. See Fig. 18-7.
- Lift the presser foot. Turn the fabric, with the needle still in it. Put the presser foot back down again and stitch the next side.

## Adding Seam Finishes

After stitching your project, you may need to add a seam finish. Seam finishes are treatments used on the seam edges to prevent fabric from raveling. The most effective seam finish depends on the type of fabric being used. If the fabric ravels only slightly, pink the edges with pinking shears. For greater protection against raveling, stitch ¼ inch (6 mm) from each edge before pinking. If your fabric ravels easily, use a zigzag finish. Some fabrics do not ravel and, therefore, do not need seam finishes.

## ➤ Gathering Fabric

When you need to fit a longer piece to a shorter one, you gather fabric. For example, you might use gathering at the tops of sleeves or at the waist of a full skirt. Gathering gives a soft, full effect. See Fig. 18-8. Follow these guidelines when gathering fabric:

1. Set the sewing machine for a long stitch of six to eight stitches per inch. Loosen the upper tension.
2. Sew two rows of stitches. Stitch one row on the seamline. Stitch the second row ¼ inch (6 mm) closer to the fabric edge. Leave long thread ends. Do not backstitch or tie knots.
3. Pin the right side of the piece to be gathered to the right side of the other fabric piece. Match the notches, seams, and other markings.

Betsy Ross. **Betsy Ross was an upholsterer who sewed the first American flag in 1776. George Washington and two other representatives of the Continental Congress asked her to make the flag.**

**Fig. 18-8 You will often gather fabric at the waistline or on the sleeves of a garment.**

4. Pull up both bobbin threads from one end. Gently slide the fabric along the threads to gather half of the section. Repeat at the other end until the gathered section is the proper length.
5. Distribute gathers evenly, pinning about every ½ inch (1.3 cm). Gathers should not bunch up or thin out in any area.
6. Stitch with a regular stitch length along the seamline, gathered side up. Make sure that the gathering stitches do not show on the right side of the garment.
7. Press the seam allowances flat.

### Easing Fabric

When one piece of fabric is only slightly longer than the piece that it will join, easing is used. Easing creates a slight fullness. To ease fabric, you need to pin it before you stitch the seam. Place the fabric right sides together, matching the notches and ends. Pin every ½ inch (1.3 cm). When you stitch, place the longer piece of fabric on top and gently ease in the extra fullness. An eased seam should look smooth, without puckering.

**Fig. 18-9**
**(A) Fold-down casing.**
**(B) Applied casing.**

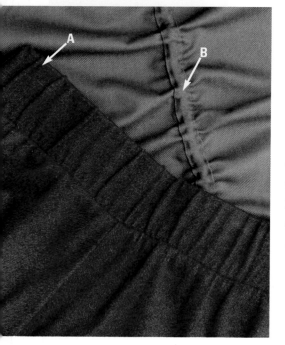

## ➤ Making Casings

You may need to sew casings if your garment has a pull-on waistband or sleeve band. **Casings** are fabric tunnels made to enclose elastic or drawstrings. When you draw up the elastic or drawstring, a gathered appearance is created.

When you sew a casing, make sure that it is ¼ to ½ inch (6 mm–1.3 cm) wider than the elastic or drawstring it will enclose. This will allow the elastic or drawstring to move freely through the fabric tunnel. The two types of casings are fold-down and applied. See Fig. 18-9.

- **Fold-down casing.** A fold-down casing is often used for pull-on pants and skirts. To make a fold-down casing, fold the garment edge ¼ inch (6 mm) to the inside and then again, ¼ to ½ inch (6 mm–1.3 cm) wider than the elastic. Pin it in place.

Stitch close to the inner-pinned edge of the casing. Leave a 2-inch (5-cm) opening for inserting the elastic.

- **Applied casing.** An applied casing is often used at the waistline. To make an applied casing, you need to stitch a separate strip of fabric or bias tape to the garment.

If you are inserting elastic into a casing, attach a safety pin to one end of the elastic. Pull the pin through the casing. Be careful not to twist the elastic. Leave the ends of the elastic extending several inches at the opening. Overlap the ends ½ inch (1.3 cm), and pin them securely. Then try on the garment to make sure that it fits, and make any necessary adjustments. Next, use the sewing machine to stitch the overlapped ends of the elastic securely. Complete the stitching needed to finish the casing opening.

When using a drawstring, make an opening for pulling the ends through to either the outside or the inside of the garment. Refer to your pattern guide sheet for directions.

## ➤ Making Facings

Facings are used to finish the raw edges of a garment. Facings are sewn around the edges of necklines, armholes, and some waistlines. You stitch facings to the right side of the garment and then turn them to the inside as follows:

1. Staystitch the notched edge of each facing piece.
2. Stitch the facing pieces together. Trim the seams, and press them open.
3. Unless you are using a knitted fabric, finish the outside edge of the facing. Knitted fabrics do not require a finish.
4. Pin the facing to the garment edge, with the right sides together and the notches and ends matching.
5. Stitch the seam. Then trim and grade the seam allowances, and clip the curved areas. See Fig. 18-10 on page 340.
6. Turn the facing to the inside. Press it along the seam-line, rolling the seams toward the facing side.
7. Understitch the facing to help hold it in place. To understitch, open the facing with the seam allowances

toward the facing. Stitch close to the seamline from the right side of the facing through all of the seam allowances. Turn the facing back to the inside, and press it.

8. To achieve a smooth appearance, you need to trim and grade the seam allowance to reduce bulk. See Fig. 18-10. You may also need to clip or notch the seam allowance so that the facing can be pressed flat.

9. Use several hand stitches to fasten the edge of the facing at each seam.

**Fig. 18-10 Four ways to reduce bulk in seams.**

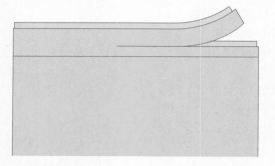

**Trimming.** A seam is trimmed by cutting the seam allowance to ⅜ or ¼ inch (9 or 6 mm). This reduces the bulk of the seam. This is usually done when the seam is enclosed in a collar, cuff, facing, waistband, or set-in sleeve.

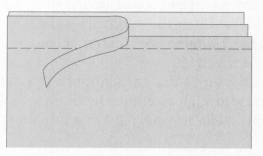

**Grading.** A seam is graded by trimming the seam allowances to different widths. Trim the seam allowance toward the inside of the garment narrower than the outside one. This further reduces the bulk. Grading is often done on seams for facings.

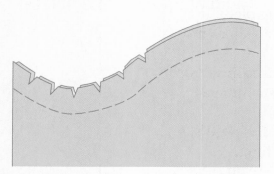

**Notching.** Some curved seams that have too much fabric in the seam allowance may need to be notched. Little Vs or triangles are cut out of the trimmed seam allowance.

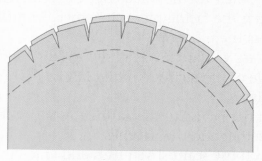

**Clipping.** Curved seams are clipped so that they will lie flat. Slits are cut into the trimmed seam allowance about every ¼ inch to ½ inch (6 mm–1.3 cm). Clip only to within ⅛ inch (3 mm) of the seam line, being careful not to cut through the stitching.

# How To...

## Make a T-Shirt

### Supplies
- T-shirt pattern of your choice
- Cotton-knit fabric
- Cotton-knit ribbing
- Thread

### State the Task
- Make a basic T-shirt on a sewing machine.

### Develop a Plan

1. Choose a basic T-shirt pattern in your size.
2. Acquire the amount of fabric yardage and thread needed.
3. Gather the notions you will need to construct the T-shirt, including scissors, pins, and tape measure.
4. Read through the pattern guide sheet to become familiar with the instructions.
5. Cut out the pattern pieces from your fabric.
6. Transfer markings onto your fabric from the pattern pieces.
7. Wind the bobbin and insert it in the sewing machine. Thread your machine needle.
8. Follow the instructions on the pattern guide sheet to sew your T-shirt.

### Implement the Plan

1. Pre-wash and dry your cotton-knit fabric and ribbing.
2. Circle the correct pattern layout on the pattern guide sheet.
3. Cut out the pattern pieces for your size.
4. Pin the pattern pieces to your fabric according to the pattern layout.

### Evaluate the Result

1. What did you learn about pattern layout?
2. Is there anything you would change the next time you make a T-shirt? Explain your answer.

# A CLOSER LOOK

## ...at Hand-Sewing Techniques

**S**ome sewing must be done by hand. Hand sewing gives you more control than you have using a sewing machine or serger. Try these basic stitches.

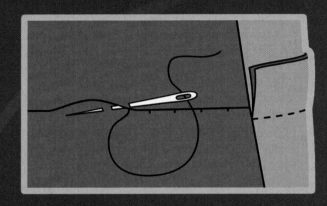

### Slipstitch

The slipstitch provides an almost invisible finish. Slide the needle in one folded edge and out, picking up a thread of the under layer.

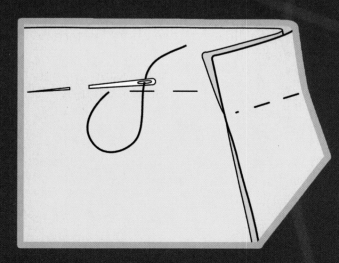

### Basting Stitch

The basting stitch is a temporary stitch used to hold fabrics together for fittings, and for matching plaids and seams. To baste, pin fabric layers together and use even stitches.

# Blanket Stitch

The blanket stitch can be used as a decorative edge finish. Stick the threaded needle through the right side of the fabric and pull it out at the edge. Keep the thread from the previous stitch under the needle point, pulling the needle and thread through and over the edge.

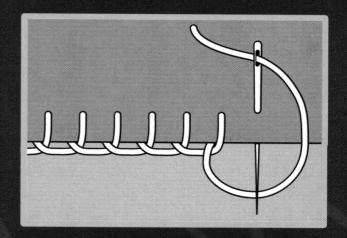

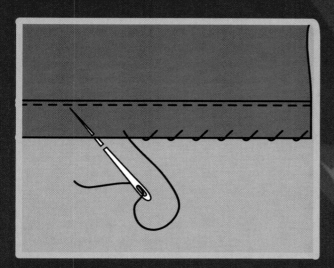

# Hem Stitch

A hem stitch is made by taking a tiny stitch in the garment, then bringing the needle diagonally through the hem edge.

# Backstitch

The backstitch is made by carrying the thread back half the length of the preceding stitch. Bring the needle through to the underside of the fabric. Insert the needle back at the beginning of the first stitch, and bring it out again one stitch length in front of the thread.

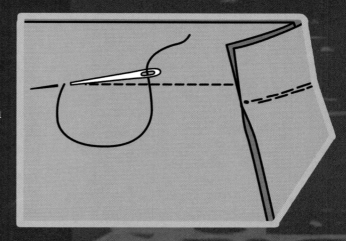

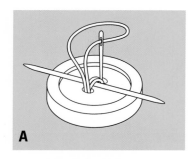

**A**

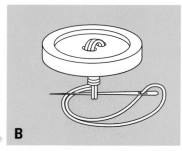

**B**

Fig. 18-11 Learning to sew on buttons is an essential repair skill. (A) Sew-through button. (B) Shank button.

## Sewing on Buttons

There are two types of buttons: sew-through and shank. A sew-through button has two or four holes through it and no loop on the back. A shank button has a stem on the back. When you attach a sew-through button, you will need to add a thread shank. See Fig. 18-11.

To attach sew-through buttons, follow these steps:

1. Start on the underside of the fabric, and bring the needle and thread to the right side.
2. Stick the needle and thread through one hole in the button. Place a toothpick across the top of or underneath the button to allow for a thread shank. Stitch in and out several times through the fabric and button-holes and over the toothpick or pin. Finish stitching so that your needle and thread are under the button.
3. Remove the pin or toothpick. Pull the button to the top of the thread loop. Wind the thread several times around the stitches under the button to make a shank.
4. Bring the needle back to the wrong side of the fabric.
5. Secure the thread by taking several small stitches in the fabric and knot it.

Sew a shank button in place using five or six small stitches through the shank and into the fabric; fasten the thread securely. When sewing a metal shank button, insert an eye fastener and sew the eye in place first.

## Sewing on Snaps

Snaps are used to hold together overlapping edges, such as those at a neckline. There are two parts of a snap—the ball half and the socket half. Follow these guidelines when replacing a snap:

• Place the ball half of the snap on the underside of the overlap, far enough from the edge so that it will not show. Sew five or six stitches in each hole. Carry the thread under the snap from hole to hole.
• Mark the position of the socket half. Stitch it in place. Secure the thread and knot it.

## ➤ Sewing on Hooks & Eyes

Hooks and eyes are often used on waistbands or above zippers, where they are not visible. Attach hooks and eyes by sewing small stitches around each loop. Finish by sewing three or four stitches across the end of the hook to make it lie flat. Secure the thread and knot it.

## ➤ Serging Basics

A serger is a high-speed machine that sews, trims, and finishes a seam in one step. A serger is a very useful piece of sewing equipment because it can save time and handle a variety of fabrics, from slippery silks to stretchy knits.

A serger feeds several strands of thread through guides that are placed above the machine to prevent tangling. **Cones** are the large cylinders used to hold thread. Sergers use cones instead of spools because sergers use more thread than sewing machines do. A cone can hold up to five times more thread. See Fig. 18-12.

Sergers are known as two-thread, three-thread, four-thread, or five-thread, depending on the number of threads used to make the stitch. Each thread passes through its own tension dial. Sergers do not have bobbins. Instead, they have **loopers**, which are rounded parts that hold the thread inside a serger. The looper threads loop around each other and are interlocked with the needle thread or threads. Depending on the model, sergers may have one or two needles. The remaining threads are wrapped by the loopers. See Fig. 18-13 on page 346.

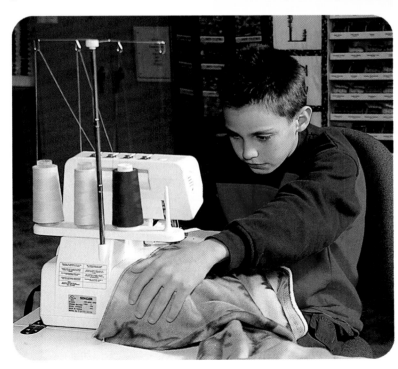

**Fig. 18-12** A serger sews, trims, and finishes a seam in one step.

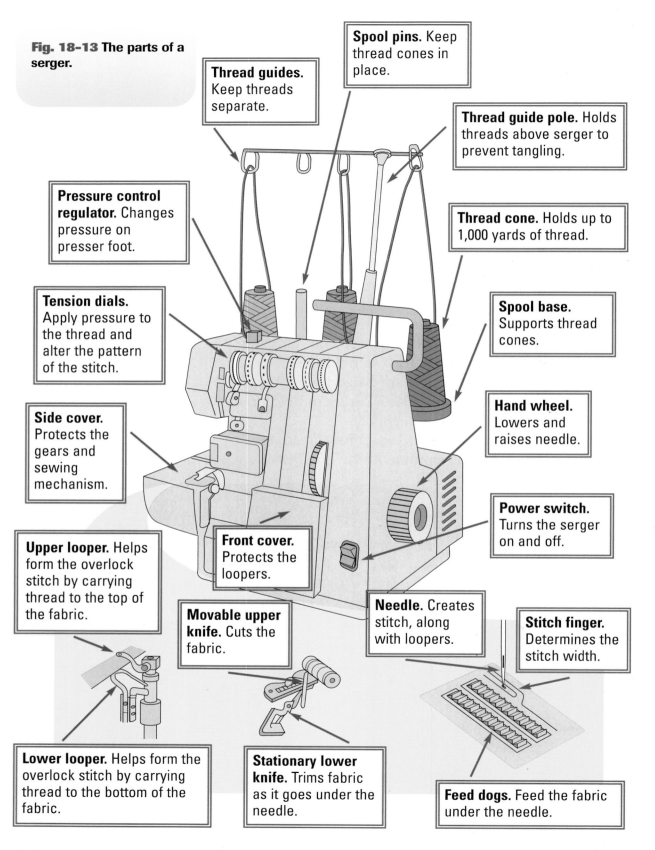

**Fig. 18-13** The parts of a serger.

**Spool pins.** Keep thread cones in place.

**Thread guides.** Keep threads separate.

**Thread guide pole.** Holds threads above serger to prevent tangling.

**Pressure control regulator.** Changes pressure on presser foot.

**Thread cone.** Holds up to 1,000 yards of thread.

**Tension dials.** Apply pressure to the thread and alter the pattern of the stitch.

**Spool base.** Supports thread cones.

**Side cover.** Protects the gears and sewing mechanism.

**Hand wheel.** Lowers and raises needle.

**Power switch.** Turns the serger on and off.

**Upper looper.** Helps form the overlock stitch by carrying thread to the top of the fabric.

**Front cover.** Protects the loopers.

**Movable upper knife.** Cuts the fabric.

**Needle.** Creates stitch, along with loopers.

**Stitch finger.** Determines the stitch width.

**Lower looper.** Helps form the overlock stitch by carrying thread to the bottom of the fabric.

**Stationary lower knife.** Trims fabric as it goes under the needle.

**Feed dogs.** Feed the fabric under the needle.

Small knife blades are located inside the serger. These knives, which are positioned like the blades of scissors, trim the fabric as it passes through the machine. The result is a seam allowance that is exactly the width of the serger's stitch. As you serge, the entire seam allowance is wrapped inside the stitch.

A serger does not replace a sewing machine because it cannot sew a single line of locked stitches. It does, however, allow you to use a greater variety of fabrics, including stretchy knits and sheers. See Fig. 18-14. It also allows you to take many shortcuts without reducing the quality of your sewing project.

Sergers are most commonly used to sew knits. With a serger, you can easily stitch on stretch fabrics. Sergers can also be used to sew conventional skirt or pant hems or narrow, rolled hems, such as those on scarves. You can also use a serger to produce decorative stitching and reversible seams.

**Fig. 18-14 Hard-to-handle fabrics, such as stretchy knits, are easier to handle on a serger than a sewing machine.** Check some of your knit garments for "serged" seams.

## Using a Serger

When you are ready to begin a project, set the stitch-length and tension dials on the serger to the desired settings. For your test, make sure that you use fabric scraps. Serge as you will on the final product—either with or against the grain. Keep adjusting the stitch length and tension until you achieve the result that you want.

When you have tested the stitch and basted your fabric, you are ready to serge. Position the fabric for feeding through the machine. Unless the fabric is unusually thick, you should not need to lift the presser foot. The fabric is moved along by the feed dogs. The feed dogs are the parts of the machine that position the fabric for the next stitch.

You should begin and end each seam with a tail chain, a length of thread shaped like a chain. A tail chain is made without placing fabric under the needle. It keeps the fabric from raveling and eliminates the need to tie off the threads of the seam.

**DID YOU know?**

**Serging Without Pins.** Instead of pinning the fabric into position, baste the fabric, or tack it with glue. Pins can seriously damage the serger's knife blades.

# Explore

## Serging Stitches

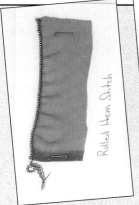

Rolled Hem Stitch

Wide Three Thread Overlock Stitch

### Supplies

- Serger and thread
- Fabric scraps
- 8½" x 11" cardstock
- Three-ring binder

### State the Task

- Create six serger stitch samples.

### Develop a Plan

1. Create six serger stitch samples.
2. Place them in a binder for reference.

### Implement the Plan

1. Stitch on fabric scraps until you have made a good sample of each stitch. <u>Do</u> <u>not</u> throw away your bad samples.
2. Attach each sample to a piece of 8½" x 11" cardstock. Write the name of the stitch on the cardstock.
3. File it in a three-ring binder.
4. Label the "bad" stitch samples with the problem and how you corrected it. File these samples in your binder for reference.

### Evaluate the Result

1. What types of thread gave you the best-stitched samples? Why?
2. How will a reference book of stitch samples help you on future projects?

### Common serger stitches:

- **Chain Stitch**—uses two threads to baste fabric.
- **Flatlock Stitch**—works well for flat, stretch seams and for decorative stitches.
- **Overedge Stitch**—uses two threads to secure the edges of fabric and prevent raveling. On some sergers, the overedge stitch wraps around the fabric to produce a decorative finish. This stitch is sometimes used for lightweight seams.
- **Overlock Stitch**—combines three threads and is most often used on stretch seams and fabrics of moderate to heavy weight. It is also used to finish seams on knits and woven fabrics.
- **Rolled Hem Stitch**—creates narrow hems and seams and is also used for decorative stitching on knit or woven lightweight fabrics.
- **Safety Stitch**—uses four threads to create a stable seam on lightweight woven fabrics. The extra threads help to limit how much the fabric will stretch.

## ➤ Basic Repairs & Alterations

You can get more use out of your clothes if you learn how to make basic repairs and alterations. It is best to repair tears and holes while they are still small.

- To repair small tears, stitch back and forth across the tear to hold the torn edges together. Be sure to begin and end your stitches about ¼ inch (6 mm) above and below the tear.
- To cover up a hole, apply a fusible patch, or sew on a patch or appliqué.
- To fix a split seam, line up the pieces of fabric and pin them in place. Then sew the seam.

A common alteration is hemming. To hem:

1. Use a seam ripper to remove the thread in the old hem. Press out the hem crease.
2. Put on the garment to determine the new hem length. Wear the shoes that you plan to wear with the garment. If possible, have someone mark the hem for you. Place pins every 2 to 4 inches (5–10 cm) around the hemline.
3. Fold the hem to the new length, and pin it in place. Double-check the length to make sure that it is even.
4. Take off the garment, and place it on a table or an ironing board with the hem facing you. Using a sewing gauge or a ruler, mark the proper length of the finished hem with pins or chalk.
5. Trim away the excess fabric along the markings. Lightly press the fold of the hem.
6. For most woven fabrics, you will need to use some type of hem finish to prevent raveling. The raw edge can be pinked, zigzag stitched, edge stitched, or overlapped with hem tape.
7. Stitch the edge of the hem, making sure that the stitches do not show on the outside. Keep the stitches loose so that the hemline doesn't pucker.
8. Carefully press the hem.

**Hem Facing. If you are lengthening a garment and you don't have enough fabric to form a hem allowance, you can use wide-bias hem facing. Stitch one edge of the facing to the fabric edge. Then turn the facing to the inside of the garment, and stitch it in place.**

# Career CHOICES

## Inspector

Checks finished garments for stitching, colors, and sizes. Corrects errors in a partially completed garment or returns it for repairs. Works in teams to prevent and spot errors on an assembly line.

## Wardrobe Consultant

Analyzes a person's style and body type. Helps assemble a wardrobe to project the desired image. Teaches basic clothes-buying strategies, such as mixing and matching and accessorizing. Gives seminars on the messages clothing sends to others.

## FCS Teacher

Teaches Family & Consumer Sciences courses in fashion and clothing construction. Prepares lessons and maintains records. Manages demonstrations and group work in the classroom.

## Pattern Preparer

Determines style and size of patterns. Also creates patterns to be used for custom-made clothing. Prepares work orders providing customer's measurements and style and fabric preferences.

## Clothier

A dressmaker or tailor who designs original garments. Uses existing patterns. Does repairs and alterations. Some clothiers are self-employed and develop their own computer-aided design (CAD) software.

**Needles and thread are used in most textile careers.** What other common tools would people working in this career field use?

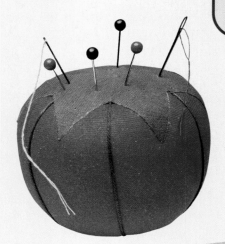

### AT School

Select three of the careers listed. Research the education, training, and work experience required for each career. Compare the results to select a career to investigate further.

### IN THE Workplace

Make a list of 10 items in the workplace that are inspected. Share your list with your classmates and discuss your choices.

# Chapter 18 Review & Activities

## Chapter Summary

- To prepare your fabric, preshrink it and check the grain.
- Begin your sewing project by reading the pattern guide sheet.
- Check the pattern pieces and compare your measurements to the body measurements on the pattern envelope.
- Hand-sewing techniques are used to repair small tears, sew on missing buttons, and change hemlines.
- A serger sews, trims, and finishes a seam in one step.
- Common alterations can help you get more use out of your clothes.

## Words You Learned

1. What is a selvage?
2. How can you tell if a garment was cut on the bias?

3. Explain what you can learn from a pattern guide sheet.
4. Explain the purpose of pattern layouts.
5. Why are pattern markings important?
6. What is ease?
7. What is the purpose of staystitching?
8. Why are casings used?
9. What is used to hold serging thread?
10. What are loopers?

## Check Your Facts

1. Why should you preshrink fabric?
2. Describe two ways to reduce bulk in seams.
3. Name two types of seam finishes.
4. What is the difference between a seam stitched on a sewing machine and one stitched on a serger?
5. List the six types of stitches produced by a serger.

## Apply Your Learning

1. Outline the steps that you would take to prepare a pattern before beginning to sew.
2. Explain why you should test your marking device before using it on a project.
3. **Sweet Dreams.** Make a personalized pillowcase. Cut a rectangle of fabric 42½ inches x 35½ inches. Serge around the edges of the rectangle. Fold the fabric right sides together and stitch along one long and one short edge. Turn up a 3-inch hem along the remaining short end, facing the wrong side. Stitch in place. Turn the pillowcase right side out and insert a piece of cardboard. Decorate the case with fabric markers or paint. Remove the cardboard.

# Chapter 19

# Expressing Creativity

## You Will Discover . . .

- how art allows you to express yourself.
- ways to create wearable art.
- how to use creativity to decorate.

## Key Words

- outlet
- gusset

$\mathcal{S}$ ewing is one way Alexa likes to express her creativity. She's a whiz at recycling her old clothes into new wearable pieces. Alexa loves to use her sewing skills to create wearable art, too. Creativity can be expressed with sewing, but it doesn't end there. You can express your creativity in a variety of art forms, from painting to writing to crafting.

**Walt Disney.**
The founder of
Disneyland and
Walt Disney World
made his first ani-
mated cartoon in
1920. He created
Mickey Mouse in
1928.

## ➤ Art as Expression

Art can provide a wonderful outlet for your energy,
emotions, and thoughts. You can even express negative
emotions such as fear, anger, and sadness in healthy, constructive ways. Writing a poem or making something with
your hands gives you a way to express yourself in a positive manner. Art also helps you relieve stress. See Fig. 19-1.

Perhaps you think that you don't have any artistic
ability, but everyone possesses creativity. You just have to
find the **outlet**, or means of release, that is most satisfying to you. If you want to enjoy art with a group of people, you can join many organizations that include art in
their programs. Here are a few suggestions for artistic
outlets:

- Learn to play a musical instrument.
- Write poetry.
- Draw or paint pictures.
- Take up woodworking.
- Make crafts for friends and family members.
- Work in the garden.

**Fig. 19-1 You can create
art in a group setting
or by yourself.** What
types of art do you
enjoy creating?

## ➤ Wearable Art

Wearable art, such as jewelry or clothing, not only allows for creative expression, but is also practical. You can create new accessories or clothing pieces to extend your wardrobe. See Fig. 19-2. Add artistic flair with paints, dyes, stamps, beads, buttons, trims, and other media. You can also create wearable art by cutting, tearing, folding, dyeing, or otherwise changing the original look or texture of a fabric.

**Fig. 19-2 Creating wearable art is fun and practical.** Try making a design on an old shirt to give it a new look.

### Accessories

You've already learned that you can change and expand your wardrobe with key accessories. Add a personal touch by creating your own. Here are a few suggestions:

- Use safety pins to string small beads in colorful patterns for lapel pins. String shank buttons or safety pins and then lace elastic through the pins to make bracelets.
- String beads to create bracelets and earrings.
- Decorate plain scarves with fabric paint and dyes.
- Decorate plain baseball caps with paint, buttons, or appliqués.
- Sew beads and trims on ankle socks.
- Make a new tote bag by sewing together pieces of old jeans.
- Find one decorative button and glue a pin on the back.

## ➤ Clothing

You can decorate or alter clothing to make a unique statement about your style. Here are a few ideas:

- Add braid or beaded trim to the hem of your jeans.
- Paint a design on the back of a shirt.
- Replace the buttons on a shirt with decorative buttons.
- Open the sides of jeans from the knee to the hem and add a gusset of patterned fabric to widen the legs. A **gusset** is a triangle- or diamond-shaped piece of fabric cut on the bias.

# How To...

## Personalize a T-Shirt

### State the Task

• Personalize a plain T-shirt.

### Develop a Plan

1. Draw a design for your T-shirt on white paper. Indicate where you will incorporate paint, buttons, ribbons, trims, or beads into the design.
2. Gather your supplies.

### Implement the Plan

1. Pre-wash the T-shirt. After drying, iron the T-shirt if necessary.
2. Working on a flat surface, place a piece of cardboard inside the T-shirt so paint, ink, and glue will not bleed through to the back.
3. Use a chalk marker to draw your design on the front of the T-shirt.
4. Place a small amount of paint on a paper plate. Dip your brush or stamp in the paint. (*Note*: Do not allow the paint to drip. Blot off any extra paint with a paper towel.)
5. Apply the paint to your shirt as desired. Allow the paint to dry completely before adding any other decorations.
6. Sew on buttons, ribbons, trims, or beads as desired.
7. Apply liquid seam sealant to the ends of ribbons and trims so they won't ravel.

### Evaluate the Result

1. How does this technique allow you to show your individuality?
2. How could you recycle old clothing using this technique?

### Supplies

• Plain T-shirt
• Fabric paints, buttons, ribbon, trims, or beads
• Fabric stamps
• White paper
• Pencil or pen
• Chalk marker
• Cardboard to fit inside shirt
• Paper plate
• Paper towels
• Needle and thread
• Liquid seam sealant

You can also use many of the hand-sewing skills you have learned to recycle garments. If a garment is truly beyond repair, you can cut it into scraps and pieces to be used for other projects, such as a patchwork pillow. See Fig. 19-3. You can also save the fabric pieces to use as cleaning rags. Just be sure to remove any buttons or zippers that might scratch surfaces. Recycle the buttons for other projects.

Fig. 19-3 Recycle old garments into new items like this patchwork pillow.

For stained or torn garments that you still like, try using a decorative technique such as appliqué or embroidery to allow you to continue wearing the garment. Sewing machines with embroidery capability use computerized design disks or cards. You can stitch directly on ready-to-wear clothing or you can create appliqués by stitching on fabric, cutting around the design and then sewing it to clothing. Designs of every type are available, from sports to flowers. See Fig. 19-4.

Fig. 19-4 Embroidery can dress up plain clothing items and accessories.

1. **Search the Internet for information about another country's traditional clothing. Compare it to your style of dress. Share your findings with your classmates.**

Key Search Words:
- **clothing customs**
- **clothing traditions**

2. **Search the Internet for ideas on recycling clothes. Write down five ideas and share them with your classmates.**

Key Search Words:
- **recycled clothing**
- **recycled fashions**

# A CLOSER LOOK

## ...at Decorative Storage

**W**ho couldn't use more storage space? Oftentimes, the most useful storage comes from containers that can be left out in the open. A little creativity goes a long way in making practical, attractive storage units.

### Basket Case

Any size basket can be decorative when you add a pretty liner. Buy a ready-made liner or make your own. Embroider or paint the edges of the liner for a special look. Store papers, magazines, or clothes in the basket.

## Hats Off

Cover a hatbox with fabric to match your room. Cut the fabric to fit the box. Spray the back of the fabric lightly with adhesive and stick it on the box. Store photos, keepsakes, or clothes inside the box.

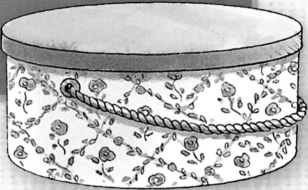

## Pillow Wrap

Store pajamas, sweats, or jeans inside an envelope pillow. Look for a pattern at your local fabric store to make simple envelope pillows.

## Hang-Ups

Create a pocketed hanger for your closet or the back of a door. Small pockets can hold jewelry or hand-sewing tools. Larger pockets can hold yarn or shoes. Look for a pocketed hanger pattern at your local fabric store.

## Decorating Your Room

Decorating your room or a personal space in your home is a great use of your creativity. See Fig. 19-5. Get your parents' permission first before putting your creativity to work. Here are some ideas:

- **Walls.** Paint can quickly change the look of a room. Draw and paint a scene or a geometric pattern on a wall. You can also use an accent color to draw attention to one wall.
- **Ceilings.** Use glow-in-the-dark thread to embroider stars and stick them to the ceiling with adhesive and contact paper. When the lights go out you'll have your own indoor view of the evening sky.
- **Furniture.** Choose a fabric and cut out shapes. Spray the back with adhesive then stick the fabric to clear contact paper. Peel the contact paper and stick the shapes to furniture, walls, or even the ceiling. Contact paper won't hurt furniture and you can change it when you're tired of it.
- **Lampshades.** Jazz up an old lampshade. Use hot glue to attach trim or fringe to the upper and lower edges. Add an appliqué as a focal point to the center of the shade front.
- **Pillows.** Make toss pillows for your bed. Choose fabrics to complement your room colors and stitch them using a pattern that you can find at your local fabric store.
- **Picture frames.** Decorate plain, inexpensive picture frames. Use hot glue to attach buttons, bows, shells, small polished rocks, team pins, appliqués, or felt or foam shapes in a random pattern around the frame. Showcase your favorite photos inside.

**Fig. 19-5 Rooms are fun to decorate. How could you use your creativity to improve your room?**

# Explore

## Faux Finishes

Rag

Sponge

### State the Task

- Experiment with paint to create faux finishes. The word faux (FOH) is French for "fake." Faux finishes create the illusion of texture.

### Develop a Plan

1. Choose two or three colors of paint to combine for a layered effect.
2. Use brushes, sponges, and rags to create faux finishes.

### Implement the Plan

1. Cut a piece of foam-core board into two, equal halves.
2. Use a light color of paint for the undercoat of your finishes. Paint each half of the foam-core board. Let the boards dry for at least 24 hours.
3. **To create a sponged effect:**
   a. Choose two contrasting shades of paint to go over your base coat.
   b. Dip the sea sponge into one color. Blot off the extra paint.
   c. Randomly press the sea sponge onto a board that you previously painted with a base coat.
   d. Let the paint dry thoroughly.
   e. Repeat with the contrasting color. (*Note:* It is OK to overlap colors. This will enhance the effect.)

> **Supplies**
> - Latex paint in light color
> - Glaze paint in darker colors
> - Paintbrush
> - Sea sponge
> - Cotton-knit rags. (*Note:* A T-shirt works well.)
> - A large piece of foam-core board
> - Paper towels
> - Pan of water

4. **To create the ragged effect:**
   a. Cut a T-shirt into hand-size pieces.
   b. Use a darker glaze color to paint over your base coat. (*Note:* Use a shade in the same color family.)
   c. Twist the rag and roll it over the wet paint in a random pattern.

### Evaluate the Result

1. Which faux finish did you like the best? Why?
2. What did you learn about choosing colors?

# Career CHOICES

## Fashion Writer

Writes columns and articles for fashion magazines, newspapers, and Web sites. Does research and conducts interviews. Must meet deadlines and adjust copy as directed. Works from home or in an office.

## Art Therapist

Plans art therapy program to fulfill physical and psychological needs. Conducts art therapy programs. Instructs individuals and groups in use of art materials, such as paint, clay, fabric, crayons, and yarn.

## Computer Animator

Uses knowledge of computer graphics to produce animation for software products. Animates 3-D models. Works for commercial clients in the media, entertainment, manufacturing, engineering, and education fields.

## Embroidery Digitizer

Uses software to program stitches from artistic drawings into computerized designs that an embroidery machine can read. Has an art and sewing background. May instruct clients in the use of embroidery software.

## Art Director

Creates basic layout design concepts. Supervises workers who lay out designs for artwork to be presented by magazines, books, newspapers, television, posters, and the Internet.

### AT School

Select three of the careers listed. Research the education, training, and work experience required for each career. Compare the results to select a career to investigate further.

### IN THE Workplace

Make a list of ways you could use your creativity on the job. Share your list with your classmates.

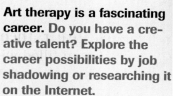

**Art therapy is a fascinating career.** Do you have a creative talent? Explore the career possibilities by job shadowing or researching it on the Internet.

# Chapter 19 Review & Activities

## Chapter Summary

- Express your creativity through music, drawing, writing, poetry, sewing, crafts, or another form of art.
- Create wearable art by cutting up clothing and piecing it together in another form, painting it, or embroidering it.
- Creativity can be functional when you make everyday objects more interesting, such as decorating baskets and boxes for storage.

## Words You Learned

1. How can art be an outlet for your emotions?
2. Describe the function of a gusset.

## Check Your Facts

1. Describe one way you could use art to express your creativity.
2. Describe two ways to decorate your clothing.
3. Describe two ways to decorate your room.
4. Describe how you could decorate a storage container for your room.

## Apply Your Learning

1. Use creativity to make or adapt a clothing accessory.
2. Find one garment that you own but no longer wear. Either repair, update, or change it. Share your changed garment with your classmates.
3. Create added storage space for your room. Share your project or a photo of it with the class.
4. **Out of the Garden.** Decorate clay pots of different sizes. Simply paint the outside of a pot in simple geometric shapes. Spray over the paint with an acrylic sealer. Then use the pots on a window sill or in a bathroom filled with soaps and folded hand towels. You could also fill several pots with your art supplies.

# Investigating Food & Nutrition

# Chapter 20

# Nutrition & Wellness

## You Will Discover . . .

- the difference between hunger and appetite.
- the functions of proteins, carbohydrates, and fats in the human body.
- the functions of vitamins, minerals, and water in the human body.
- how the Dietary Guidelines promote health.
- the importance of limiting fat, sugar, and salt in the diet.

## Key Words

- nutrients
- wellness
- calorie
- digestion
- proteins
- amino acids
- carbohydrates
- fiber
- cholesterol
- vitamins
- minerals
- osteoporosis

Carl's favorite foods are pizza and yogurt. Carl knows that he needs to eat a variety of foods to supply his body with the nutrients it needs. **Nutrients** (NOO-tree-uhnts) are substances that are important for the body's growth and care. Carl eats his favorite foods, but balances his diet by including other foods.

## ➤ Looking & Feeling Good

Your diet affects the way you look and feel. Eating healthful foods can help you look your best. Reaching for your best level of health is called **wellness**. Exercise, adequate rest, and personal hygiene also contribute to your personal health and wellness. See Fig. 20-1.

Feeling good and being healthy go hand in hand. Along with exercise and rest, food affects how you feel, no matter what your age. Food is your source of energy for physical and mental activities. You need energy to perform well in school and in all your activities. Without adequate nutrients, you may tire easily and feel less alert. Proper nutrition has a direct effect on achievement. By eating right you will have the energy needed to perform mental and physical activities well. You will be able to look, feel, think, and act your best.

A healthful diet protects you from illness. By getting the nutrients you need, your body is better able to fight infections, heal wounds, and recover quickly when you do get sick.

**Fig. 20-1 Healthful foods help you look your best.**

## Satisfying Your Hunger

When your stomach growls, you are experiencing signs of hunger. Hunger is the physical need to eat. Hunger tells you that your body needs food, but it does not tell you what to eat. You must learn to select healthful foods. You must also learn how much to eat.

Appetite is different from hunger. Appetite is the desire to eat. When you smell fresh strawberries or a chocolate cake, you might develop an appetite without really being hungry.

When your hunger is satisfied, it is time to stop eating. Some people still have an appetite, however, so they continue to eat. If they eat too much food, or food that is too high in calories, they may gain weight. A **calorie** is a unit used to measure the energy used by the body and the energy that food supplies to the body. However, that energy is stored as fat if you eat food that has more calories than your body uses.

## ➤ Nutrients for Health

Nutrients in food keep you healthy, help you grow, and give you energy. See Fig. 20-2. Nutrition is the study of nutrients and how the body uses them. Nutrients are released from food during digestion. **Digestion** is the process of breaking down food into a form the body can use. Nutrients are absorbed into the bloodstream and carried to cells to do their work.

Nutrients affect body processes such as your heartbeat, blood flow, and breathing. These processes, in turn, affect the way you feel and how much energy you have. They also affect the quality of your skin, hair, and nails. To keep your body functioning properly, you must choose foods that supply enough of each nutrient. Lack of nutrients can cause health problems.

Fig. 20-2 Eating nutritious foods is essential to your health.

There are six kinds of nutrients: proteins, carbohydrates, fats, vitamins, minerals, and water. Each one has an important function.

- Proteins help build, repair, and maintain body cells and tissues.
- Carbohydrates provide energy and fiber.
- Fats provide energy and supply essential fatty acids for normal growth and healthy skin.
- Vitamins, minerals, and water help regulate the work of the body's systems.

## Proteins

**Proteins** are nutrients that are needed to build, repair, and maintain body cells and tissues. Your skin, hair, blood, muscles, and vital organs are made of proteins. During the teen years, you need proteins to help your body grow and develop to its adult size. Even after you stop growing, you still need proteins to help your body repair itself. Billions of worn-out body cells are replaced every day, and proteins are used to make those new cells.

Each protein is a different combination of amino acids. **Amino** (UH-mee-noh) **acids** are the building blocks that make up proteins. Your body can manufacture some amino acids. Others, called essential amino acids, can't be made by your body. They must come from the food you eat.

Some foods contain all the essential amino acids. These foods are called complete proteins. Meat, fish, poultry, milk, cheese, and eggs are examples of complete proteins. Other foods are good sources of protein, but they lack one or more of the essential amino acids. These foods, called incomplete proteins, come from plants. Dry beans, nuts, and grains are examples of incomplete proteins.

You can combine incomplete protein sources to make complete proteins. By combining proteins from grains with proteins from dry beans or nuts, you can get all the essential amino acids that your body needs. See Fig. 20-3.

Fig. 20-3 Combining proteins will provide the essential amino acids your body needs.

## Carbohydrates

**Carbohydrates** are the starches and sugars that give the body most of its energy. Starches and sugars are excellent energy sources. Starches are found in grains, such as oats, rice, and wheat. Foods made from grain, including bread, tortillas, pasta, and cereals, also provide starch. Potatoes, corn, dry beans, and nuts are additional sources of starch.

Natural sugars are found in fruits and milk. These foods are good sugar sources because they are also high in other nutrients. Foods such as candy, cake, and soft drinks also contain sugar, but they are high in calories but low in other nutrients. They should be eaten less often than fruits and milk.

Almost all carbohydrates come from plant sources, which also provide fiber. **Fiber** is plant material that your body cannot digest. Although fiber is not a nutrient, eating the right amount of fiber-rich foods helps the body function normally. Fiber provides bulk, which helps move food through your digestive system. It also helps your body eliminate waste. A diet rich in high-fiber foods can reduce the risk for certain diseases, such as colon cancer.

Good sources of fiber include foods made from whole grains. Whole grains are foods that contain all of the edible grain, including the bran and the germ. Whole-wheat breads, whole-wheat cereals, and popcorn are whole-grain foods. Fruits and vegetables, especially those with edible skins, stems, and seeds also contain fiber. See Fig. 20-4.

## Fats

Like carbohydrates, fats are an important source of energy. Fats contain twice as many calories as carbohydrates. Your body relies on fat cells to store energy and to help regulate body temperature. Your skin needs fats to stay smooth, and your nervous system needs them to work properly. Fats also carry several vitamins needed by the body, such as vitamin A and vitamin E.

**Fig. 20-4** Fruits and vegetables are good sources of fiber.

# Internet ACTIVITIES

1. **Search the Internet for information about bio-engineered foods. Write a paragraph about one bio-engineered food and share what you learned with your classmates.**

   Key Search Words:
   - **bio-engineered foods**
   - **genetically engineered foods**

2. **Search the Internet to find nutrition information on your favorite fast-food menu items. Share your findings with the class.**

   Key Search Words:
   - **fast-food facts**
   - **nutrition facts**

Fats come from both animal and plant sources of food. Saturated fats are fats found in food from animal sources. Meats, egg yolks, cheese, and butter contain saturated fats. Eating too much saturated fat can cause an increased risk of heart disease. Unsaturated fats are fats that come from plants. They are generally liquid at room temperature and are found mainly in vegetable oils, such as olive, corn, or canola oil. No more than 30 percent of the calories you consume should come from fat, preferably unsaturated fats.

Saturated animal fats contain a waxy substance called **cholesterol** (kuh-LES-tuh-rahl). Because your body produces all the cholesterol it needs, you don't need to add cholesterol to your diet. In fact, diets high in cholesterol have been linked to an increased risk of heart disease.

## Vitamins

**Vitamins** are substances needed in small quantities to help regulate body functions. They help your body use other nutrients, store and use energy, and fight infection. See Fig. 20-5A on page 374.

## CHECK the Facts

**Cholesterol.** Cholesterol is carried through your bloodstream by lipoproteins. Two of the main kinds are high-density lipoprotein (HDL) and low-density lipoprotein (LDL). The cholesterol carried by HDL is sometimes called "good" cholesterol. That's because HDL helps remove cholesterol from the blood and may reduce the risk of heart disease. The "bad" LDL cholesterol builds up in the arteries and may increase the risk of heart disease.

**Fig. 20-5A**

# Vitamins

### Benefits

### Food Sources

**Vitamin A**
- helps eyes adjust to darkness.
- helps keep skin healthy.
- protects linings of nose, mouth, throat, and other organs from infection.

Dark green vegetables, deep yellow vegetables and fruits, eggs, whole milk, fortified low-fat milk

**B-Complex Vitamins***
- help carbohydrates, fats, and proteins produce energy.

Whole-grain and enriched breads and cereals, pork, organ meats, dry beans, peas

**Thiamine**
- promotes growth, appetite, and digestion.
- helps keep nervous system healthy.

Whole-grain and enriched breads and cereals, pork, organ meats, dry beans, peas

**Riboflavin**
- helps keep eyes and skin healthy.

Milk, cheese, yogurt, eggs, organ meats, poultry, fish, enriched breads and cereals

**Niacin**
- keeps digestive tract working normally.
- helps keep nervous system and skin healthy.

Whole-grain and enriched breads and cereals, liver, meat, fish, poultry, nuts

*Other B complex vitamins—vitamin $B_6$, folic acid, vitamin $B_{12}$, pantothenic acid, and biotin—also help the body use carbohydrates, fats, and proteins.

**Vitamin C** (also called ascorbic acid)
- helps the body fight infection.
- helps wounds heal.
- helps keep gums healthy.

Oranges, grapefruit, other citrus fruits, berries, melon, broccoli, spinach, potatoes, tomatoes, green pepper, cabbage

**Vitamin D**
- works with calcium to build strong bones and teeth.

Fortified milk, fish-liver oil

**Vitamin E**
- keeps oxygen from destroying other nutrients and cell membranes.

Vegetable oil, salad dressing, margarine, grains, fruits, some vegetables

**Vitamin K**
- helps blood clot.

Green leafy vegetables, egg yolks

**Fig. 20-5B**

# Minerals

**Benefits**                                          **Food Sources**

**Calcium**
- helps build strong, healthy teeth and bones.
- helps the heart beat properly.
- helps muscles move.
- helps keep soft tissue and nerves healthy.
- helps blood clot.

Milk, cheese, yogurt, green leafy vegetables, fish with edible bones

**Fluoride**
- helps make teeth strong.

Drinking water

**Iodine**
- helps the thyroid gland work properly.

Saltwater fish, iodized salt

**Iron**
- helps blood carry oxygen.
- helps cells use oxygen.

Meat, liver, eggs, dry beans, dried fruits, whole-grain and enriched breads and cereals, spinach

**Magnesium**
- helps muscles contract.
- helps produce energy.
- helps regulate many body functions.

Nuts, peanut butter, edible seeds, dry beans and peas, whole-grain breads and cereals, milk, fish, green leafy vegetables, bananas

**Phosphorous**
- helps calcium and vitamin D keep bones and teeth strong and healthy.
- helps the body produce energy.

Milk, yogurt, cheese, egg yolk, meat, fish, poultry

**Potassium**
- helps regulate body fluids.
- helps muscles, including the heart, function properly.

Orange juice, bananas, meat, nuts, dried fruits

**Sodium**
- helps reguate body fluids.
- helps muscles work properly.

Table salt, cured meats, pickles, many processed foods

**Zinc**
- speeds healing of wounds.
- affects growth, taste, appetite, and smell.

Meat, organ meats, eggs, poultry, seafood, cheese, milk

The essential vitamins include A, B-complex, C, D, and E. Because your body cannot make most vitamins, you must get them from the foods you eat. These nutrients can easily be obtained from a variety of delicious foods.

**Fig. 20-6 Dark green, leafy vegetables contain vitamin A.** Do you eat dark green, leafy vegetables every day?

- **Vitamin A.** Have you ever walked into a dark room after being in the bright sunlight? Did you notice that your eyes had to adjust to less light before you could see again? Vitamin A enables your eyes to adjust to the dark. It also helps keep your skin healthy and helps your body resist infection. Dark green, leafy vegetables, deep yellow vegetables, and dairy products are good sources of vitamin A. See Fig. 20-6.

- **B-Complex Vitamins.** Thiamine, niacin, and riboflavin are B-complex vitamins. They give you energy by helping your body use calories from carbohydrates, fats, and proteins. Riboflavin also helps keep your eyes and skin healthy. Thiamine and niacin promote a healthy nervous system. B-complex vitamins come from many different foods. Dairy products contain riboflavin. Thiamine and niacin are found in meat, dry beans, and some grain products. When selecting grain products, such as flour and bread, choose whole-grain or enriched foods.

- **Vitamin C.** Vitamin C helps keep you well. When you cut or bruise yourself, for example, vitamin C helps the wound heal. It keeps your gums healthy and helps your body fight infection. Good sources of vitamin C include such fruits as oranges, melons, and berries. Some dark green, leafy vegetables, such as spinach and broccoli, also contain vitamin C.

- **Vitamin D.** Vitamin D helps your body use minerals, such as calcium and phosphorus. It is essential for normal bone and tooth development. Your body makes its own vitamin D when your skin is exposed to sunlight. Foods that provide vitamin D include fortified milk, fish oils, beef, butter, and egg yolks. See Fig. 20-7.

- **Vitamin E.** To keep red blood cells healthy, your body needs vitamin E. You can find it in vegetable oils, yellow vegetables, grains, nuts, and green leafy vegetables.

## Minerals

Food also contains **minerals**, which are elements needed in small amounts for sturdy bones and teeth, healthy blood, and regular elimination of body wastes. Like vitamins, minerals are essential to good health.

Every day your body uses small amounts of minerals. Trace elements, such as iron, zinc, and iodine, are needed only in tiny amounts. Calcium, phosphorus, and magnesium are needed in greater amounts. The minerals your body needs can be found in various types of food. See Fig. 20-5B on page 375.

**Fig. 20-7** Milk is a good source of vitamin D and calcium.

- **Calcium.** You need calcium to grow and to stay healthy. Calcium is a mineral that helps build bones and teeth and ensures normal growth. Young people need calcium to develop strong teeth and bones. Calcium is also necessary throughout life to reduce the risk of **osteoporosis**, a condition in which bones gradually lose their mineral content and become weak and brittle. Calcium also has other functions, including helping your muscles move and your heart beat. When you bleed, calcium aids vitamin K in helping your blood clot. Calcium also helps keep your nerves and soft tissues healthy. The best sources of calcium are dairy products and dark green, leafy vegetables.
- **Iron.** Like calcium, iron is one of the most important nutrients. Iron is an essential component of blood. Females need about twice as much iron as males. It helps carry oxygen to your brain, your muscles, and all of your body's cells. Oxygen helps your body produce energy for physical activity. The best sources of iron are meat, poultry, dry beans, dried fruits, and dark green, leafy vegetables.

## Water

Although you may not think of water as a nutrient, you can't live without it. Water helps regulate your body functions and carries nutrients to body cells. It aids in digestion, removes wastes, and helps control your body temperature.

Because water is lost through perspiration and urine, you must replace it. You should drink at least eight glasses of water each day. When you play basketball, tennis, or other active sports, your body perspires a great deal, and you need even more water.

## ➤ MyPyramid

Figure 20-8 MyPyramid is a colorful reminder to make healthful food choices and increase physical activity. Each color band represents a food group. The width of each band is a guide to portion size. The smallest band is yellow for oils and not a food group.

**Fig. 20-8 MyPyramid.**

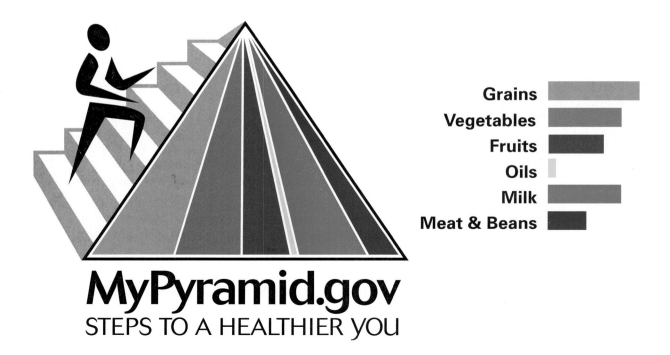

MyPyramid.gov
STEPS TO A HEALTHIER YOU

Grains
Vegetables
Fruits
Oils
Milk
Meat & Beans

The person climbing the side of MyPyramid represents the physical fitness component. Your level of physical activity varies depending on your age. People who are physically active, for example, need to eat more than less active people. The important point to remember is that you need to eat foods from all the food groups to get the nutrients you need. Fig. 20-9 charts special nutrition requirements across the life span.

**Fig. 20-9**

| Nutrition Requirements Across the Life Span | |
|---|---|
| **Life Span Period** | **Nutrition Requirements** |
| **Pregnancy** (includes nursing mothers) | Approximately 300 additional calories are required each day for increased energy needs. |
| **Infancy** (Birth—1 yr.) | Most of the infant's nutritional needs during the first year are met through human milk or infant formula. |
| **Early childhood** (2—5 years) | Breakfast is especially important, and nutritious snacks help meet the child's daily nutrient needs. |
| **Middle childhood** (6—11 years) | Snack foods may need to be monitored because consumption of sugary foods and empty calorie foods increases during this stage. |
| **Adolescence** (12—19 years) | An increased need for calcium occurs due to rapid bone growth. Teens need to increase their intake of foods from the milk group. |
| **Young Adulthood** (20—39 years) | Eating a well-balanced diet and exercising on a regular basis are good beginnings for young adults. Iron and calcium intakes are very important. |
| **Middle Adulthood** (40—65 years) | Eat a variety of foods, maintain desirable weight, avoid too much fat and cholesterol, increase fiber intake, avoid too much sugar and sodium, exercise regularly, refrain from smoking, and limit stress. |
| **Older Adulthood** (over 65 years) | A healthy diet can help reduce some of the effects of aging. Vitamins $B_6$, $B_{12}$, thiamin, C, D, E, and calcium, iron, and zinc are important. Regular exercise is needed. |

# A CLOSER LOOK

## ...at Portion Sizes

**Actual portion sizes can be deceiving. When you fill your bowl with ice cream or cereal you may actually be eating several helpings. Here are some examples of portion sizes. The photos shown here are about 70% of the actual sizes of the objects.**

### An Ounce
An ounce of cheese is about the size of a walnut. Cheese is healthy but can pack on the pounds if you unknowingly eat too much.

### A Tablespoon
One tablespoon is about the size of your thumb to the first knuckle. Measure carefully so you don't add too much butter or oil to your food.

## One-half Cup

One-half cup of rice or pasta is about the size of a tennis ball. If you are used to filling your whole plate with pasta, stop and think about how many helpings you are actually eating.

## One Cup

A cup of fruit or a medium-sized piece of whole fruit is about the size of your fist, or a tennis ball if you have large hands. Whole fresh fruits provide fiber as well as vitamin C.

## 3 oz. Serving

A 3 oz. serving of meat, fish, or poultry is about the size of a deck of cards. One egg, two tablespoons of peanut butter, or one-half cup of dry beans is equal to one ounce of meat.

# ➤ The Dietary Guidelines

How can you make sure that your diet contributes to your wellness? The Dietary Guidelines take into account the important effect diet has on your health. These guidelines were developed by the U.S. Government using recommendations by nutrition authorities.

By following the Dietary Guidelines, you can ensure that you are eating the right types of foods. You can also reduce your chances of developing certain health problems. Of course, food alone can't make you healthy. Good health also depends on your heredity and environment. Your exercise habits also play an important role in your health. Following the Dietary Guidelines can help keep you healthy, and perhaps even help improve your health.

- **Get enough nutrients.** Choose a variety of nutritious foods and beverages from the basic food groups.
- **Manage your weight.** To maintain body weight in a healthy range, balance your intake of calories from food and beverages with the calories you burn in physical activities.
- **Be physically active.** Regular physical activity promotes health, well-being, and a healthy body weight. Teens should be physically active for at least 60 minutes every day.
- **Eat key foods.** Choose a healthy eating plan that emphasizes fruits, vegetables, whole grains, and fat-free or low-fat milk and milk products.
- **Limit fats.** For teens a total fat intake should only be 25 to 35 percent of the total calories. Most fats should come from sources such as fish, nuts, and vegetable oils.
- **Be choosy about carbohydrates.** Choose fiber-rich fruits, vegetables, and whole grains often. Look for foods and beverages low in added sugars.
- **Reduce sodium (salt) and increase potassium.** Choose and prepare foods with less salt. Eat plenty of potassium-rich foods, such as fruits and vegetables.
- **Play it safe with food.** Know how to prepare, handle, and store food safely to keep you and your family safe.

**Fig. 20-10 Different body types have different healthy weights.** Have you asked a doctor about your healthy weight?

## ➤ Maintain a Healthy Weight

A person who is at a healthy weight is not overweight or too thin. Being overweight is linked with illnesses such as high blood pressure, heart disease, stroke, diabetes, cancer, and others. Although being too thin is less common, it is also linked with disease and a greater risk of early death.

How can you know if your weight is "healthy"? You can't compare your weight with that of your friends. There are differences among people of the same age. For example, people with a large body frame usually weigh more than people of the same height with a smaller body frame. At this time in your life, growing and gaining weight are normal. See Fig. 20-10.

To determine if your weight is right for you, consult your doctor. He or she can consider all the factors that contribute to a healthy weight for you.

**CHECK the Facts**

Healthful Foods. **Not all foods labeled low fat or sugar-free are healthful. For instance, cereals made with whole grains may also be high in fat. Compare several brands of an item to see which one is really most healthful.**

## ➤ Eating Right

Eating the right foods can help you live a long and happy life. Keep the following suggestions in mind.

- **Fats and cholesterol.** Fat is an important nutrient that provides energy. However, health experts recommend a diet that is low in fat and cholesterol. A diet high in fat leads to such health problems as obesity and an increased risk of heart disease. The amount of fat in your diet depends on what you eat over several days, not on one meal or type of food. Foods that contain fats and cholesterol such as meats, milk, cheese, and eggs also contain high-quality protein and important vitamins and minerals. To reduce fat and cholesterol, choose low-fat versions of these foods such as nonfat milk and cheese.

- **Vegetables, fruits, and grains.** These products are an essential part of a varied and healthful diet. They contain complex carbohydrates, fiber, and other nutrients that contribute to good health. In addition, these foods are usually low in fats. If you eat the suggested amounts of them, you are also likely to decrease the fat in your diet and get more fiber. Fiber is found naturally in whole-grain breads and cereals, dry beans and peas, vegetables, and fruits.

- **Sugars.** Sugar is a type of carbohydrate that is found in many foods. Sugar provides calories, and most people like the way it tastes. Eating too much sugar is not healthful, but it isn't necessary to avoid sugar entirely. Fruit contains natural sugar. Many processed foods, such as cookies and soft drinks, contain refined sugar.

- **Salt and sodium.** Salt contains sodium, a mineral that helps regulate the amount of fluid in our bodies. You need some sodium to stay healthy. However, most Americans eat more sodium than they need. Too much sodium can lead to high blood pressure.

# Explore

## Healthful Snacks

### State the Task

- Choose healthful snacks.

### Develop a Plan

1. List five of your favorite "healthful" snacks.
2. Explain why you think each snack is healthful.
3. Find out which snack choices are actually healthful.

### Implement the Plan

1. Make a list of five healthful snacks that you like to eat.
2. Write down why you think each snack is healthful.
3. Consult the list of vitamins and minerals on pages 374-375 to see whether each snack is healthful.
4. Try making one of the healthful snacks listed under *Just For Fun*.

### Evaluate the Result

1. Why are healthful snacks a better choice than empty-calorie snacks?
2. How can learning good snack habits now be of benefit to you later in life?

**Just For Fun**

Try making these healthful snacks:

- Blend orange juice with nonfat yogurt and ice cubes to make a healthful fruit smoothie.
- Cut pita bread into triangles and bake on a cookie sheet for five minutes at 450°F (230°C). The pita crisps are a healthful snack.
- Mix nuts, raisins, pretzels, and dry cereal to form a healthful grab-and-go snack.
- Microwave some popcorn.

- **Snacks.** Consume empty-calorie snacks in very limited amounts. Empty-calorie foods are foods that are high in calories but low in nutrients. Potato chips, candy, and soft drinks are empty-calorie foods. They often contain large amounts of sugar, salt, and fat, but little nutrition. Select whole-grain items from the bread group. A wide variety of nutrient-dense snacks can be found in the fruit and vegetable groups.

## ➤ Eating Out

Do you enjoy eating out? Maybe you like getting together with friends over a meal. Perhaps your family enjoys eating at a restaurant to try new foods. When you eat out, remember to choose your meals with the same eye on nutrition as when you eat at home.

As you look at a menu, the most important point to remember is to choose foods from all five food groups. Here are some tips for ordering when you eat out.

- Eat only until you feel satisfied.
- Most portion sizes are larger than a serving. Bring leftovers home.
- Select dishes that are low in fat, sugar, salt, and calories. For example, baked potatoes have much less fat than French fries.
- Choose nutrient-dense dishes. For example, order whole-wheat or vegetable pasta. Instead of soft drinks or milk shakes, order juice or milk.
- Remember that sauces and salad dressings add calories. When eating Italian foods, choose sauces made with tomatoes, rather than sauces made with butter and cream.
- Limit the number of treats you allow yourself. For example, if you can't resist fried ice cream at a Mexican restaurant, have simmered beans instead of refried beans, and avoid the tortilla chips.

# How To...

## Plan a Balanced Meal

### State the Task

- Plan a balanced meal.

### Develop a Plan

1. Plan a balanced meal based on the foods you like.
2. Compare your chosen foods to the Food Guide Pyramid.
3. Discover what vitamins and minerals are included in the foods you chose.
4. Discover what foods you need to eat a balanced diet.

### Implement the Plan

1. Write down your favorite meal.
2. Compare your meal to the Food Guide Pyramid. Add any food groups to your meal that are missing.
3. Make a list of the basic vitamins and minerals that can be found in your menu.

4. Be creative with your meal plan. Some foods can be combined, such as a casserole with vegetables, pasta, and cheese.

### Evaluate the Result

1. What types of food were missing from your favorite meal?
2. What foods did you add to complete a balanced meal?
3. How can eating balanced meals help you be healthy?

# Career CHOICES

## Nutritionist

Develops nutrition education materials and classes. Teaches nutrition education courses. Counsels pregnant women on proper nutrition.

## Dietician

Plans therapeutic diets. Oversees preparation and service of meals. Consults with health care personnel to determine nutritional needs and diet restrictions. Creates menus based on medical and physical condition of patients.

## Chef

Oversees food preparation. Trains and supervises kitchen staff. Uses safe food-handling procedures. Develops menus and purchases supplies. Works long hours in a fast-paced environment.

## Food & Drug Inspector

Inspects establishments where foods, drugs, and cosmetics are manufactured. Investigates handling of consumer products. Enforces legal standards of sanitation.

## Dietary Manager

Oversees food service planning for institutions. Plans and directs operation of the dietary department. Ensures that quality food service and nutrition are provided at all times.

### AT School

Select three of the careers listed. Research the education, training, and work experience required for each career. Compare the results to select a career to investigate further.

### IN THE Workplace

Name five ways you can practice good nutrition and wellness in the workplace. Share your findings with your classmates.

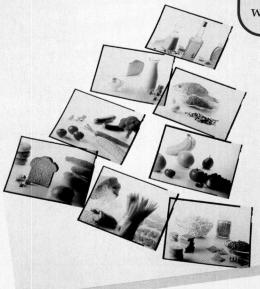

**People who work in the food industry use the Food Guide Pyramid and the Dietary Guidelines.** Research career opportunities in nutrition and wellness.

# Chapter 20 Review & Activities

## Chapter Summary

- You can have an appetite without being hungry.
- Proteins are needed to build, maintain, and repair your body.
- Carbohydrates provide energy.
- Fats provide energy, keep skin smooth, and help your nervous system work.
- Vitamins, minerals, and water help regulate your body functions.
- The Dietary Guidelines promote a balanced diet.

## Words You Learned

1. What is a nutrient?
2. Describe wellness.
3. What is a calorie?
4. Explain digestion.
5. What is protein?
6. What are amino acids?

7. Name three carbohydrates.
8. What is fiber?
9. Why can eating too much cholesterol be bad for your heart?
10. Name three vitamins.
11. Name three minerals.
12. What can you do to prevent osteoporosis?

## Check Your Facts

1. How does diet affect your energy level?
2. List the six nutrients and their functions.
3. Name a complete protein.
4. Why is it important for you to get enough calcium in your diet?
5. What happens if you eat more calories than your body needs?

## Apply Your Learning

1. Write a paragraph describing your eating habits. Are you a picky eater? Do you need to make changes in your diet?
2. Write down the number of servings of fruits and vegetables you eat every day for one week. At the end of the week, create a graph showing the varieties and total servings.
3. **State of Nutrition.** Draw a large map of the United States. For each state, find out what foods are produced there. For example, Wisconsin is known for its cheese products. Cut out a picture of one of the food products and glue it on the state. Show one product for each state.

# Chapter 21

# Health & Fitness

## You Will Discover . . .

- why health and fitness are important.
- how exercise can help you stay healthy and fit.
- what you can do to maintain a healthy body weight.
- how eating disorders can destroy your health.

## Key Words

- fitness
- stamina
- obesity
- eating disorders
- anorexia nervosa
- bulimia nervosa
- binge eating
- fad diet

Schoolwork takes up much of Aaron's time. He has chores to do at home, and he delivers fliers for some local restaurants. Aaron spends time with friends too. Even though Aaron is busy, he still finds time to exercise and to eat well. He stays fit by riding his bike, skating, and swimming at the community pool. What do you do to stay healthy and fit?

## ➤ Staying Healthy & Fit

When you are physically fit, you look and feel your best. A healthy, fit body means you take care of yourself. See Fig. 21-1. **Fitness** is the ability to handle daily events in a healthy way. Fitness means that you:

- have enough energy to do your schoolwork and chores, and have fun too.
- are confident about your abilities.
- make exercise and activity a part of your life every day.
- can keep your weight at the right level for you.
- can deal with stress and the ups and downs of life.

**Fig. 21-1 Exercise is a way to have fun while staying healthy and fit. What types of outdoor exercise do you enjoy?**

You cannot be fit unless you exercise. By exercising regularly you will enjoy all the benefits of fitness.

- You will feel positively about yourself. Knowing you're taking care of your body is good for your self-esteem.
- You will look your best. Exercise helps control weight and gives you a healthy glow.
- Day-to-day tasks will seem easy because you will have the energy you need.
- You will be able to relax and sleep easily.
- You will have physical and mental stamina. **Stamina** is the ability to focus on a single activity for a long time. For example, you will be able to dance without getting very tired, and you can pay attention in class and learn easily.
- You will be able to deal with stress.

There are plenty of enjoyable, inexpensive ways to exercise. What's important is that you make exercise a regular part of your life. For example, Jennifer walks to school instead of taking the bus. Her friend Nick plays on a softball team and enjoys getting together with friends to play volleyball on weekends.

## ➤ Your Body Weight

Are you happy with your weight? Do you think that you're too heavy or too thin? People who maintain a healthy body weight are neither overweight nor underweight. See Fig. 21-2.

Being overweight can lead to obesity. **Obesity** is a condition in which a person's weight is 20 percent or more above his or her healthy weight. Obese people are at greater risk for such illnesses as diabetes and heart disease.

Being underweight is unhealthy too. People who are underweight often aren't eating enough or properly. This means that they aren't getting the nutrients they need.

**Fig. 21-2** Your healthy body weight depends on your height and body type.

# A CLOSER LOOK

## ...at Exercise

Choose an exercise routine that suits you. From walking to in-line skating to team sports, the options are endless. Here are a few suggestions to get you on a fitness path.

**Organized Exercise**
Volleyball, baseball, basketball, and soccer are just a few types of organized exercise. Exercising in groups allows you to meet new friends.

## Indoor Exercise

You can lift small hand-weights or work out on larger machines to build muscle and bone density. Indoor exercise can be fun with a partner, or alone.

## Exercise Anywhere

Sit-ups, push-ups, jumping rope, and yoga are exercises you can do indoors or outdoors. These routine exercises are always fun to do in groups or as a class.

## Outdoor Exercise

Walking, swimming, biking, and skating are activities you can enjoy outdoors. Exercising outdoors can be fun with a friend, or alone.

# ➤ Eating Disorders

Some people develop **eating disorders**, or extreme eating behaviors that can lead to depression, anxiety, and even death. Eating disorders are psychological problems that are related to food. Both boys and girls can have an eating disorder. Teens with eating disorders often try to hide them. If left untreated, eating disorders will damage your body. Following are three common eating disorders.

- **Anorexia nervosa** (an-uh-REK-see-yuh ner-VOH-suh). This eating disorder involves an extreme urge to lose weight by starving oneself. The person fears becoming fat. No matter how thin this person becomes, he or she still feels overweight. Dieting turns into self-starvation. The person cuts food into tiny pieces, chews food for a long time, or constantly rearranges food. An anorexic person also may exercise for long periods of time. He or she will also spend less time with friends. Anorexia can cause heart disease, stunted growth, and brain damage.

- **Bulimia nervosa** (byoo-LIM-ee-yuh ner-VOH-suh). This eating disorder involves extreme overeating followed by vomiting or the use of laxatives to get rid of the eaten food. Bulimia patients often suffer from depression and are likely to become dependent on drugs. Because bulimia is a secret ritual, it is hard to recognize. Bulimics usually weigh within 15 pounds of a healthy weight. A bulimic person often has stained teeth and swollen cheeks due to damage to the teeth, gums, and esophagus. Eventually, kidney problems and heart failure can result.

**Fig. 21-3 You can still eat favorite foods, such as ice cream, if you balance exercise and calories.**

- **Binge eating.** This eating disorder involves eating large quantities of food at one time. This person has a lack of control over his or her eating habits and cannot stop eating. Bingers do not exercise excessively. These people may be overweight or they may gain and lose weight frequently. Binging often results in weight gain, high blood pressure, heart disease, and diabetes.

Eating disorders can be caused by low self-esteem, depression, troubled relationships, poor body image, or chemical imbalances in the brain. Most people with eating disorders need professional help. If you think you or someone you know has an eating disorder, talk to a parent, teacher, school nurse, doctor, or counselor. The sooner treatment begins, the better the chances of recovery. It often takes medical, nutritional, and psychological counseling to defeat an eating disorder.

Remember that you are unique. Don't compare your body type to a celebrity. Be the very best "you" by following a healthy diet and exercising. Also remember to:

- Keep a positive attitude about yourself.
- Resist media images of body types.
- Discuss concerns about your body with a trusted adult.

## ➤ Managing Your Weight

Think of controlling your weight as a balancing act. You have to balance the calories you get from the foods you eat with the calories you use for energy. You gain weight when you consume more calories than your body uses. You lose weight when your body uses more calories than you consume. To maintain your weight, you must make sure that the calories you eat equal those you burn as energy.

Many teens think that they need to lose or gain weight. They believe that they have to eat or avoid certain foods or skip meals. See Fig. 21-3. You need to eat a balanced diet. Include foods you enjoy, but limit the amount of fats, oils, and sweets. The most healthful way to lose excess weight is to take in fewer calories and exercise more. That helps you burn the calories you take in while also burning excess body fat.

**CHECK the Facts**

**Burning Fat. You cannot burn fat in a specific area of the body. Exercise burns calories and fat from all parts of the body. That's why a variety of exercises helps your overall appearance.**

# Explore

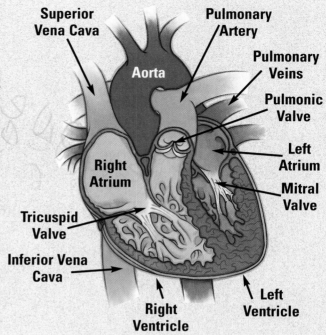

Superior Vena Cava · Pulmonary Artery · Aorta · Pulmonary Veins · Pulmonic Valve · Right Atrium · Left Atrium · Mitral Valve · Tricuspid Valve · Inferior Vena Cava · Right Ventricle · Left Ventricle

## Heart-Healthy Menus

### State the Task

• Create a heart-healthy menu.

### Develop a Plan

1. Draw the heart and name the parts.
2. Create a heart-healthy menu, low in fat and cholesterol.
3. List activities that benefit heart health.

### Implement the Plan

1. Using the drawing above as a guide, draw the human heart on poster board.
2. Label each part of the heart.
3. Using the Internet, cookbooks, and magazines, research a diet low in fat and cholesterol.
4. Create a one-week menu that includes breakfast, lunch, dinner, and snacks for each day.
5. Write your menu below your drawing on the left side.
6. Make a list of five activities that benefit the heart. Explain why you chose each activity. Write your list below your drawing on the right side.

### Evaluate the Result

1. What did you learn about the anatomy of the heart?
2. How can you keep your heart healthy through diet and exercise?

**Your Heart.** The human heart is an amazing organ.

• The heart has two upper and two lower chambers, consisting of two atriums and two ventricles.
• Blood that has flowed through the body has been used and is low in oxygen. It returns to the heart in the right atrium, empties into the right ventricle, and is moved to the lungs for fresh oxygen. From the lungs it returns to the left atrium and empties into the left ventricle. From there it moves back out through the aorta to circulate through the body. This cycle continues with every beat.

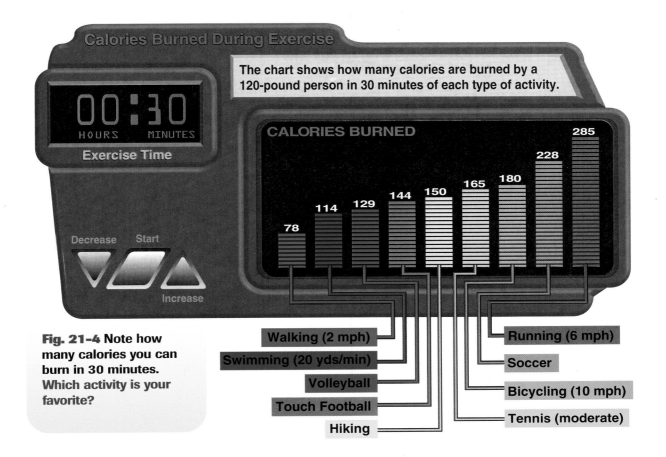

Calories Burned During Exercise

**00:30**
HOURS : MINUTES
Exercise Time

The chart shows how many calories are burned by a 120-pound person in 30 minutes of each type of activity.

CALORIES BURNED

78  114  129  144  150  165  180  228  285

Decrease    Start
                Increase

**Fig. 21-4** Note how many calories you can burn in 30 minutes. Which activity is your favorite?

Walking (2 mph)
Swimming (20 yds/min)
Volleyball
Touch Football
Hiking
Running (6 mph)
Soccer
Bicycling (10 mph)
Tennis (moderate)

## Exercise Regularly

Exercise is necessary if you want to reach and maintain a healthy body weight. Whether you want to lose weight, gain weight, or maintain your weight, exercise has many benefits. See Fig. 21-4.

- Exercise burns calories.
- Exercise helps your heart and lungs work better.
- Exercise tones your muscles and skin.
- Exercise helps you control your appetite.
- Exercise relieves tension that could lead to overeating or loss of appetite.

## Avoid Fad Diets

Achieving a healthy body weight through exercise and a well-balanced diet takes time. If you are overweight or obese, you might be tempted to lose weight quickly by going on a fad diet. A **fad diet** promises quick weight loss through unusual means.

Fad diets are rarely successful in controlling weight. Most people who lose weight on a fad diet gain the weight back and sometimes more. Fad diets are often unbalanced, as they don't provide all of the nutrients you need. Some may even cause physical harm. See Fig. 21-5.

A more sensible approach to controlling your weight is to combine a good diet with exercise. In the long run, you will be more likely to maintain a healthy weight.

**Fig. 21-5** Fad diets always promise quick results, but only a balanced diet is healthy. **Name three fad diets that are popular today.**

# Internet ACTIVITIES

1. **Search the Internet for a calorie-burning calculator. Calculate how many calories you can burn during exercise. Record your findings and refer to them when you exercise.**

   Key Search Words:
   - **calorie-burning**
   - **fitness calculator**

2. **Search the Internet for information on exercise. Write down the proper form for your favorite exercise and find at least one new type of exercise to add to your routine.**

   Key Search Words:
   - **exercise form**
   - **exercise types**

# How To...

## Design a Workout

### State the Task

- Design an exercise workout. (*Note:* If you are taking any medication, check with your doctor before starting any routine.)

### Develop a Plan

1. Make a list of all the types of exercise that you could enjoy.
2. List the benefits of each exercise.

### Implement the Plan

1. Choose exercises for both your upper and lower body.
2. Begin your workout with a warm up and end with a cool down.
3. Choose the remainder of your exercises. Create a tracking chart similar to the example on this page.
4. In your notebook, make a list of what muscle group each of your exercises benefits.
5. Record your chest, waist, hip, thigh, calve, and arm measurements.
6. Mark off the exercise each time you do it.
7. Record your measurements at the end of each week.

**SAFETY FIRST**

Be sure to drink plenty of water while working out. Fluids must be replaced to prevent dehydration. Signs of dehydration can include dizziness, dry mouth, decreased urination, and even low blood pressure or shock.

### Evaluate the Result

1. How can regular exercise benefit your body?
2. How can regular exercise benefit your mind?

| Jamie's Workout | Sat | Sun | Mon | Tues | Wed | Thurs | Fri |
|---|---|---|---|---|---|---|---|
| **Warm up stretches** | | | | | | | |
| **Stair climber (15 min.)** | | | | | | | |
| **Treadmill (15 min.)** | | | | | | | |
| **Bicep curls** | | | | | | | |
| **Tricep curls** | | | | | | | |
| **Sit-ups** | | | | | | | |
| **Leg lifts** | | | | | | | |
| **Squats** | | | | | | | |
| **Cool down stretches** | | | | | | | |

# areer CHOICES

## Food Scientist

Uses scientific research to create new and improved foods. Performs tests on the physical, chemical, and microbiological composition of foods. Also determines blends of foods to create new products.

## Dance Therapist

Plans, organizes, and leads dance and body movement activities. Observes and evaluates patient's mental and physical abilities to determine dance and movement treatment.

## Weight-Loss Counselor

Assists people in devising and carrying out a weight-loss plan. Interviews person to obtain information on weight history, eating habits, and medical restrictions. Discusses eating habits that encourage good nutrition.

## Emergency Medical Technician

Administers first-aid treatment. Transports sick or injured persons to medical facility. Works as a member of an emergency medical team. Responds to instructions from the emergency medical dispatcher. Drives specially-equipped vehicle.

## Exercise Physiologist

Develops exercise programs. Promotes physical fitness. Records patient's heart activity while client undergoes stress test on treadmill, under physician's supervision. Checks general physical condition of client.

**AT** School

Select three of the careers listed. Research the education, training, and work experience required for each career. Compare the results to select a career to investigate further.

**IN THE** Workplace

Name five ways healthy employees benefit the workplace. Compare findings with your classmates.

**Weight-loss counselors can help people establish better eating and exercise patterns.** Investigate a health and fitness career to see if you are suited for it.

## Chapter Summary

- Health and fitness are important to your physical and mental well-being.
- Exercise benefits your self-esteem, gives you energy, helps you relax and sleep, and gives you more physical and mental stamina.
- Eating disorders can lead to depression, anxiety, and even death.
- Maintain a healthy weight by eating a balanced diet and exercising regularly.

## Words You Learned

1. What does fitness mean?
2. What is stamina?
3. Define obesity.
4. What are eating disorders?

5. Which eating disorder involves starving yourself?
6. Which eating disorder involves vomiting or the use of laxatives?
7. Which eating disorder means not being able to stop eating?
8. Explain why a fad diet doesn't work.

## Check Your Facts

1. Why is being obese unhealthy?
2. Why is being underweight unhealthy?
3. What do you have to balance to control your weight?
4. How are calories related to your diet and the amount of exercise you get?
5. What is a sensible approach to controlling your weight?

## Apply Your Learning

1. Choose one fruit or vegetable and find out its history. Convince a classmate to try the fruit or vegetable by telling him or her the history of that food.
2. Cut out an advertisement for junk food. Now make your own advertisement for a fruit or vegetable. Either cut out pictures, or draw your own. Write your ad to convince people to buy the fruit or vegetable.
3. Write a short essay on how exercise benefits the mind as well as the body.
4. **Fitness Picnic.** Take a group of friends to the park. Fly kites, play baseball, toss a football, run laps, do sit-ups and push-ups, or other simple exercises. Picnic on fresh fruits and vegetables, breads, and cheeses after you've had a good workout.

# Chapter 22

## Working in the Kitchen

### You Will Discover . . .

- the sources of food contamination.
- how to handle food safely.
- ways to keep the kitchen clean.
- the causes of common kitchen accidents.
- ways to prevent common kitchen accidents from occurring.

### Key Words

- contamination
- E. coli
- salmonella
- perishable
- flammable
- conduct

When Samantha gets home from school, she washes her hands in warm, soapy water and looks for a snack. She finds some leftover chicken in the refrigerator, but because it smells funny, she throws it out. Samantha knows that eating unsafe food can make you very sick. Do you practice food and kitchen safety?

## ➤ Keeping Food Safe

Keeping food safe can prevent **contamination**, or becoming infected with harmful bacteria. By following some simple procedures when handling and preparing food, you can reduce the risk of food contamination. In mild cases, people may experience headaches, stomach cramps, and fever. In more severe cases, however, medical attention may be necessary.

A few types of bacteria cause most food poisoning. **E. coli** is the most deadly form of food poisoning. E. coli bacteria are found in contaminated water, raw or rare ground beef, and unpasteurized milk. For this reason, you should only eat hamburger that has been fully cooked. Another common type of food poisoning is caused by salmonella (SAL-muh-NEHL-uh) bacteria. **Salmonella** are often found in raw or undercooked foods, such as meat, eggs, fish, and poultry. Salmonella grow quickly at room temperature and can be spread by hands and cooking utensils. Thoroughly cook all meat, poultry, fish, and eggs. Wash your hands, knife, and cutting board with soap and hot water whenever you cut raw meat, fish, or poultry.

**Fig. 22-1 Put away leftovers promptly.**

## Handling Food

Another way to reduce the risk of food poisoning is to handle perishable foods carefully. See Fig. 22-1. Foods that are **perishable** are likely to spoil quickly. Perishable foods include meat, poultry, fish, eggs, and dairy products. Hot foods such as hamburgers should be kept hot, and cold foods such as yogurt should be kept cold until they are eaten. Keep hot foods at 140°F (60°C) or above, and cold foods at 40°F (4°C) or below. Otherwise bacteria will grow.

Foods that have been cooked shouldn't stand at room temperature for more than two hours. For a packed lunch or picnic, use cold packs and a cooler to keep the cold foods cold.

## Storing Leftovers

To keep leftovers from spoiling, refrigerate or freeze them immediately after the meal. Put leftovers in a tightly covered shallow container, and store them in the refrigerator. Many leftovers can also be frozen for use at a later date. When freezing leftovers, pack them in an airtight container, and label them with the name of the food and the date. Freezing food keeps bacteria from growing until the food is thawed. Most foods can be stored in the freezer for several months.

## Cleaning the Kitchen

You should always clean up the kitchen as you cook. Wipe up spills immediately and clean off the countertops. As you finish using pots, pans, and cooking utensils, wash them in hot, soapy water. By keeping the kitchen clean, it will be a more healthful and pleasant place to work. See Fig. 22-2 on page 408.

### DID YOU know?

**Cleaning With Vinegar.** White vinegar is a great cleaning agent. Try these cleaning tips:

- Soak cloudy glasses in vinegar to remove hard water deposits.
- Clean the coffee maker by pouring vinegar through it.
- Pour a cup of vinegar in the dishwasher during the rinse cycle to remove water spots.
- Mix ¼ cup of vinegar with a quart of water to make a good window cleaner.

**Fig. 22-2**

# Ways to Prevent Food Contamination

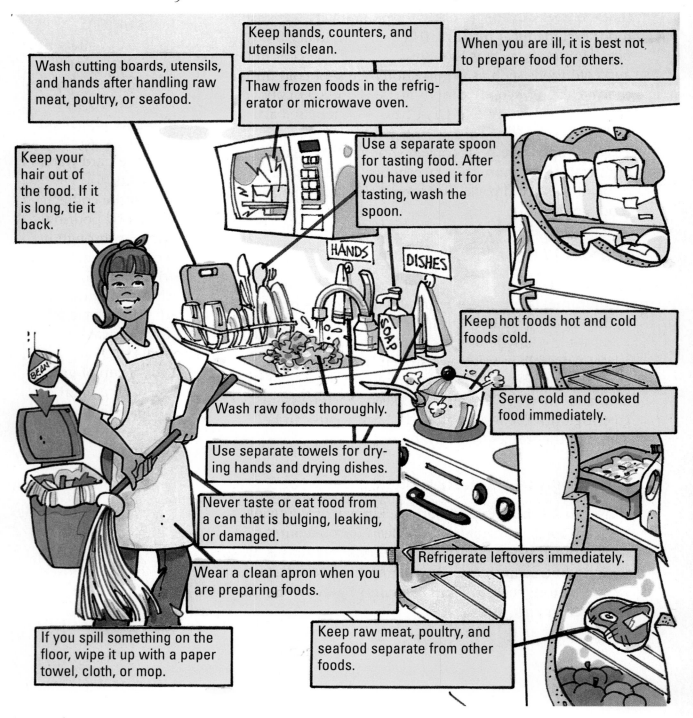

Wash cutting boards, utensils, and hands after handling raw meat, poultry, or seafood.

Keep hands, counters, and utensils clean.

When you are ill, it is best not to prepare food for others.

Thaw frozen foods in the refrigerator or microwave oven.

Keep your hair out of the food. If it is long, tie it back.

Use a separate spoon for tasting food. After you have used it for tasting, wash the spoon.

Keep hot foods hot and cold foods cold.

Wash raw foods thoroughly.

Serve cold and cooked food immediately.

Use separate towels for drying hands and drying dishes.

Never taste or eat food from a can that is bulging, leaking, or damaged.

Refrigerate leftovers immediately.

Wear a clean apron when you are preparing foods.

If you spill something on the floor, wipe it up with a paper towel, cloth, or mop.

Keep raw meat, poultry, and seafood separate from other foods.

# Internet ACTIVITIES

1. **Search the Internet for information on an illness caused by improperly cooked food. Find out how it is caused, the symptoms, and ways to prevent it.**

   **Key Search Words:**
   - **cooking safety**
   - **food poisoning**

2. **Search the Internet for information on proper table settings. On plain paper, illustrate different ideas and save them for reference.**

   **Key Search Words:**
   - **table settings**
   - **table etiquette**

## ➤ Preventing Accidents

The most common kitchen accidents include falls, burns, fires, cuts, and electric shocks. See Fig. 22-3. These types of accidents are usually preventable if you develop good, safe work habits.

### Falls

To prevent falls, follow these guidelines.

- Stand on a short stepladder or a sturdy step stool with a waist-high hand bar to get at high or hard-to-reach items.
- Turn pot and pan handles toward the center of the stove or counter so that the pots or pans won't get knocked over.
- Clean up spilled foods or liquids immediately.
- Keep cupboard doors and drawers closed when not in use.

**Fig. 22-3** Don't stand on a chair to reach items on high shelves. Use a step stool or ask for help.

## Burns

You can prevent most burns in the kitchen by following these safety precautions.

- Use dry potholders when cooking hot foods and liquids or removing them from the stove, oven, or microwave.
- When cooking, remove pan lids by tilting them away from you. This allows steam to escape safely at the back of the pot, away from your hands and face.
- Use medium or low temperatures for cooking greasy foods, such as French fries or fried chicken.

## Fires

Fires can happen too easily in the kitchen. Follow these safety precautions.

- Keep a fire extinguisher in the kitchen where you can reach it quickly and safely. Be sure that you know how to use it properly.
- Don't wear clothing with long, loose-fitting sleeves when cooking. The sleeves can easily catch fire.
- If your hair is long, tie it back.
- Keep all flammable objects, such as paper bags, potholders, kitchen towels, curtains, and plastic containers, away from the stove. **Flammable** means capable of burning easily.
- Avoid leaving the kitchen if you have food cooking. Fire can spread in seconds.
- If a grease fire starts, turn off the heat and smother the fire with a tight-fitting lid. Never use water. It will make a grease fire spread.

## Cuts

To prevent kitchen cuts, observe the following safety rules.

- Keep knives sharp. Sharp knives are safer than dull ones.
- Cut food away from your body. Use a cutting board for all cutting jobs—even if it's only a single apple.
- Wash knives and sharp objects separately from other utensils.

# How To...

## Chop, Slice, Dice & Mince

**State the Task**

- Chop, slice, dice, and mince foods. (*Note:* Be extra careful when using knives.)

**Develop a Plan**

1. Gather a cutting board, a chef's knife, a squash, a tomato, a carrot, and a stalk of celery.
2. Use the correct cutting method for each food.

**Implement the Plan**

1. Choose your vegetable, knife, and cutting board. (*Note*: Choose a knife longer than what you are cutting.)
2. **To chop:** To cut long vegetables, such as squash, hold the knife handle with one hand and the vegetable with your other hand. Cut your squash straight down and away from you into the desired size pieces.

3. **To slice:** Cut your tomato straight down and away from you into large, thin pieces.

4. **To dice:** Cut long vegetables, such as carrots, into strips, then into ¼ to ½ in. (6–12 mm) squares.

5. **To mince:** Cut your celery stalk into small strips. Turn the strips and dice the strips. Continue cutting into tiny pieces using the chopping position described in item 2.

**Evaluate the Result**

1. What did you find out about using knives safely?
2. What did you learn about cutting vegetables and herbs?

**Types of Knives.** Each knife has a specific purpose.

- **A paring knife is used for trimming and peeling fruits and vegetables.**
- **A chef's knife is used for chopping and mincing.**
- **A bread knife has a scalloped edge and is used to cut through breads without tearing them.**
- **A carving knife is used to slice meat.**
- **A cleaver is used to cut through thick meats and bone.**

- Store knives in a special compartment in the drawer or in a knife holder. Put them away immediately after cleaning them.
- Never pick up broken glass with bare hands. Sweep it into a dustpan immediately. See Fig. 22-4. Then wipe the floor with several thicknesses of damp paper towels, put the broken pieces into a bag, and place the bag in a trash can.

## Electric Shocks

Electrical appliances make kitchen tasks easier, but they can also cause electric shocks. To prevent shocks, take the following precautions. See Fig. 22-5.

- Avoid using any appliance with a frayed or worn cord.
- Dry your hands before using electrical equipment.
- Disconnect appliances by pulling out the plug, not by tugging on the cord.
- Keep portable appliances unplugged when not in use.
- Always unplug a toaster before trying to pry food from it. Forks, knives, or other metal utensils can **conduct**, or carry, electricity and cause an electrical shock.

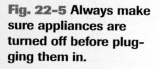

Fig. 22-4 Carefully sweep broken glass into a dust pan.

Fig. 22-5 Always make sure appliances are turned off before plugging them in.

# ➤ Small Equipment

Not all kitchen tools and cookware are essential. For example, you don't have to have a vegetable peeler to peel a carrot. You can also do the job with a paring knife. However, a kitchen equipped with the basic tools and cookware makes food preparation much easier.

Many types of utensils, or kitchen tools, and cookware are available. The most commonly used utensils include those for cooking, mixing, and slicing or cutting. A hand mixer is a small appliance. Commonly used small appliances include toasters, food processors, and blenders. See Fig. 22-6.

The best cookware to use depends on the type of food you are cooking and where you are cooking it. For instance, you could use a metal cake pan to bake cookie bars in a conventional oven, but not in a microwave oven.

Fig. 22-6 A food processor can be used to mix or cut a variety of ingredients or foods.

# A CLOSER LOOK

## ...at Kitchen Tools & Cookware

You can cook just about anything if you have the basic kitchen utensils, cookware, and appliances and know how to use them. Preparing food will be easier, more enjoyable, and safer when you select the right tools for the job.

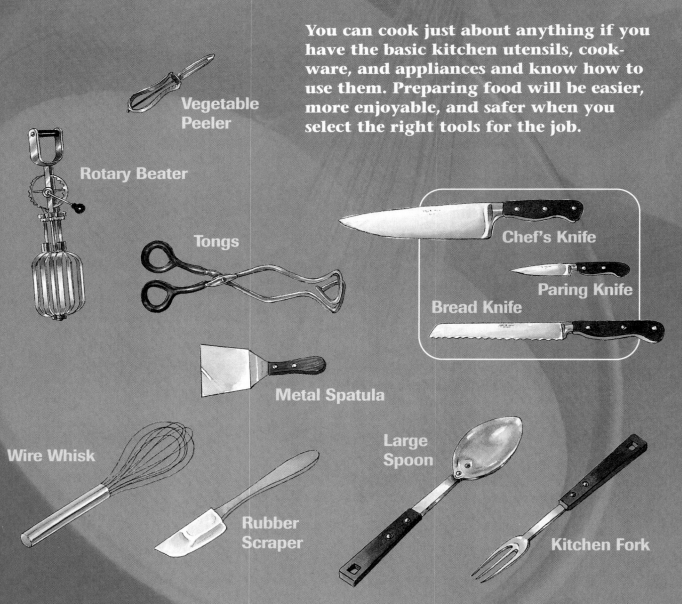

Vegetable Peeler

Rotary Beater

Tongs

Chef's Knife

Paring Knife

Bread Knife

Metal Spatula

Wire Whisk

Rubber Scraper

Large Spoon

Kitchen Fork

**Grater**

**Colander**

**Double Boiler**

**Saucepan**

**Sifter**

**Casseroles**

**Mixing Bowls**

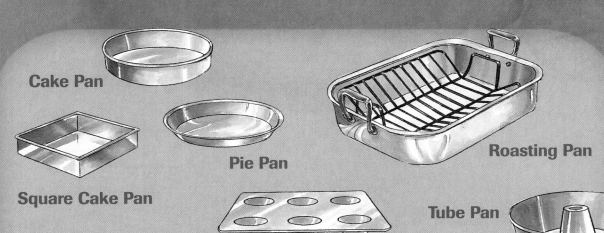

**Cake Pan**

**Square Cake Pan**

**Pie Pan**

**Roasting Pan**

**Muffin Pan**

**Tube Pan**

**Cookie Sheet**

**Loaf Pan**

## ➤ Large Equipment

Large kitchen equipment includes stoves, convection ovens, microwave ovens, refrigerators, and dishwashers. The cost of large kitchen equipment varies, depending on the extra features that are included. For example:

- Refrigerators may have the freezer on the side, on the top, or on the bottom. Some are self-defrosting and have extra freezer space, ice makers, or ice cube and water dispensers.
- Dishwashers vary in the number and depth of racks they contain. Quiet-running models tend to be more expensive.
- Stoves usually come with conventional ovens. Some stoves also include microwave ovens, while others include convection ovens.
- A convection oven uses a high-speed fan to circulate hot air throughout the oven, which speeds up the cooking. Conventional ovens may be self-cleaning or continuous cleaning. An automatic timer that can turn the oven on or off is another possible feature.
- Microwave ovens are fast, convenient, and easy to use. They come in a variety of sizes and have a range of power settings. See Fig. 22-7. You will learn more about microwave ovens in Chapter 25.

Fig. 22-7 You can use a microwave oven to prepare a snack or a meal. What foods do you microwave at home?

# Explore

## Napkin Folding

### Supplies
- Fabric napkins
- Napkin rings
- Water glass
- Dinner plate

### State the Task
- Learn several ways to fold napkins.

### Develop a Plan
1. Choose the mood of dining, such as casual, formal, or a theme, before choosing a napkin fold style.
2. Choose the napkin fold and follow the drawings to complete it.

### Implement the Plan
1. Choose a napkin. Fold it into several styles. Use one of the examples provided, or experiment with napkin folds found in other books or on-line.
2. Try the folded napkin by itself, on a dinner plate, sitting inside a water glass, or with a napkin ring around it. Decide which looks best for each folded style.
3. Make a list of which fold and type of presentation looked best together.

### Evaluate the Result
1. Which fabrics did not easily fold into which styles?
2. What did you learn about napkin folding?

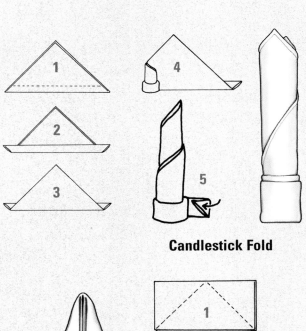

**Candlestick Fold**

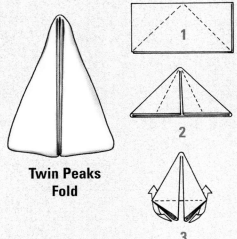

**Twin Peaks Fold**

# Career CHOICES

## Flavorist

Identifies the chemical compounds in food flavors. Conducts experiments to test different flavors. Blends and creates flavors.

## Kitchen Helper

Maintains kitchen work areas and restaurant equipment and utensils. Removes trash. Washes pots, pans, and trays. Cleans storeroom. Helps verify inventory.

## Food Server

Presents menu to guests. Suggests menu items and answers questions regarding foods. Brings beverage and food orders to guests. Checks with guests to see that they are satisfied. Clears the table and presents the check.

## Caterer

Provides food for parties, special dinners, and receptions. Meets with clients to discuss menus. Delivers and serves food. Cleans dining area when clients are done.

## Health Inspector

Visits foodservice locations to document health conditions. Evaluates areas for food safety hazards. Recommends safe food-handling practices to restaurant and cafeteria managers.

### AT School

Select three of the careers listed. Research the education, training, and work experience required for each career. Compare the results to select a career to investigate further.

### IN THE Workplace

Name five types of businesses that would likely have onsite foodservice facilities. Compare your answers with your classmates' answers.

**Many teens become food servers in full-service or fast-food restaurants. Compare job opportunities for food servers in your community.**

## Chapter Summary

- Handling, preparing, and storing food safely can prevent food contamination.
- Perishable foods must be kept at the proper temperature to avoid spoiling. Keep hot foods hot and cold foods cold.
- Most kitchen accidents can be prevented by developing safe work habits.

## Words You Learned

1. What can happen to a person as a result of food contamination?
2. Give an example of how you could be infected with E. coli.
3. Explain how you can avoid salmonella poisoning.

4. Give two examples of perishable foods.
5. Name some flammable items found in a kitchen.
6. What type of kitchen appliances can cause electrical shock?

## Check Your Facts

1. What causes food poisoning?
2. What should you do to keep leftovers from spoiling?
3. What are the four most common types of kitchen accidents?
4. Name four ways to prevent kitchen falls.
5. Give three examples of knives and their uses.

## Apply Your Learning

1. Write two food safety slogans you might find helpful. If possible, display them in the kitchen at home.
2. Imagine that your class is having a dinner party for parents. Your job is to make sure that the food served is safe to eat. Write down all the procedures you would follow to make the food safe.
3. Find out how to treat a minor burn, or cut. Write a paragraph explaining the proper first-aid procedure and list the supplies you would need.
4. **Kitchen Safety.** Work in teams to design a series of brochures about kitchen safety. Each brochure should include illustrations and written safety guidelines. Focus each brochure on a specific topic such as knife safety, using fire extinguishers, or food handling. Post your team's brochures in the classroom. Remember to share them with family members at home.

# Chapter 23

# Preparing to Cook

## You Will Discover . . .

- how to plan meals.
- why it is helpful to plan before you shop for food.
- how to store foods safely.
- how to follow different recipe formats.
- the meanings of recipe terms and abbreviations.

## Key Words

- appetizer
- meal patterns
- garnish
- texture

Whether you are throwing a birthday party for a friend or cooking a meal for your family, it is best to start by making a plan. Serving tasty, attractive, and nutritious meals requires more than just being a good cook. Planning meals, reading recipes, and shopping for food take management skills.

## ➤ Planning Meals

As you plan, think of meals that are simple and nutritious. Include a variety of foods, and consider your skills, time, and money. For good nutrition, plan meals that include foods from each food group. See Fig. 23-1.

- **The Meats, Beans, Fish, and Nuts Group.** Growing teens need 5 ounces every day. Foods from this group are usually served as the main dish in a meal.
- **The Grains Group.** You need 5 to 6 ounces every day. Some foods in this group, such as brown rice, whole-wheat bread, and oatmeal are whole grains. You should eat at least 3 ounces of whole grains.
- **The Vegetable Group.** Growing teens need 2 to 2½ cups every day. Raw vegetables can be eaten as a salad, a snack, or an **appetizer**—a dish served before the meal. Raw or cooked vegetables can also be served as a side dish.
- **The Fruit Group.** You need 1½ cups of fruit every day. These may include fresh, frozen, dried, and canned fruit as well as fruit juice. Fruit can be part of any meal.
- **The Milk and Other Calcium-Rich Foods Group.** As a growing teen, you need three cups every day. Foods from this group can accompany any meal.

Fig. 23-1 Plan meals by using a variety of nutritious foods.

## Your Meal Pattern

Most people follow **meal patterns**, or habits that determine when and what they eat each day. They usually select similar types of foods each day for breakfast, lunch, dinner, and snacks. See Fig. 23-2. For example, your meal pattern for one day might be as follows:

- **Breakfast:** cereal with fruit and nuts, juice, milk
- **Lunch:** sandwich, fruit or vegetable, dessert, milk
- **Dinner:** meat or poultry, vegetable, rice or pasta, milk
- **Snack:** fresh fruit

Meal planning is easy when you are aware of your meal patterns and choose nutritious foods. Simply choose a combination of foods from the five food groups that fit your meal pattern. To plan a lunch for the meal pattern above, you might choose a tuna salad sandwich, carrot sticks, oatmeal cookies, and milk.

Meal patterns should be flexible. Your schedule may change, you may be trying to gain or lose weight, or you may be invited to eat at a friend's home.

**Fig. 23-2 Knowing your meal patterns will help you plan meals.**

## Meal Appeal

Including a variety of foods in each meal makes eating more interesting. Eating many different foods also makes it easier to get all the nutrients you need. Meals planned with variety in mind look and taste better.

One way to add variety is to vary the way foods are prepared. Another way is to choose foods that provide different colors, sizes and shapes, textures, flavors, and temperatures.

- **Color.** Choosing foods of different colors will make the meal look more interesting. For instance, having a salad with tomatoes and carrots will add color to your meal. Adding a garnish is another way to provide more color. A **garnish** is a small amount of a food or seasoning to decorate the food. Parsley, lemon wedges, orange slices, and paprika are garnishes.

- **Size and shape.** Varying the sizes and shapes of foods will give you a much more appealing meal.
- **Texture.** Foods with different textures add variety to a meal. **Texture** means the way food feels when it is eaten. Raw vegetables are crisp and pudding is smooth. One way to vary the textures of foods is by preparing them in different ways. For example, think of the difference in texture between raw carrots and cooked carrots.
- **Flavor.** Combine flavors that complement each other. Steak and mushrooms and broccoli and cheese are some flavors that go well together.
- **Temperature.** Vary the temperatures of food in a meal. Plan some hot food items and some cold food items.

## ➤ Planning Ahead

As you plan your meals, take time to read through the recipes carefully and make sure that you have all of the resources you will need.

- **Skills.** You may want to avoid complicated recipes, if you are a beginning cook. Could you choose convenience foods for part of the meal? For instance, you might make a dessert from a mix rather than make it from scratch. See Fig. 23-3.
- **Equipment.** Some recipes will require a specific utensil. Make sure that you have all of the necessary tools and equipment.
- **Ingredients.** Make sure you have all the ingredients the recipe calls for before you start cooking.
- **Money.** Do the ingredients fit your food budget? Can you save money with coupons or use foods that are less expensive because they are in season?
- **Time.** When you know that you will be working within a time frame, such as having only one hour to cook dinner, choose foods that can be prepared within the time allowed.

Fig. 23-3 Using packaged mixes is a good way to lean the basics of cooking.

It is also important to make sure that all foods are ready to serve at the right time. Some dishes take longer than others to prepare, and some foods take longer than others to cook. For this reason, you must know what to do first and when to do it. See Fig. 23-4.

## Special Dietary Needs

You may need to take into account special diet considerations for a family member, friend, or even yourself. When cooking for guests, ask in advance if anyone has any special diet needs. For example, someone with high blood pressure would need to limit his or her salt and sodium intake. Many cookbooks are available with special diet recipes. You can also find recipes on the Internet.

**Fig. 23-4** Using a time schedule will help you make sure all the foods will be ready at the same time.

**First list the job that will take longest to do. Then list in order the other jobs to be done until you have listed them all.**

Some foods take longer to cook than others, so you must plan what to do first and when to do it.

**Besides cooking time, consider that some dishes take longer to prepare than others.**

Don't forget to allow time for setting the table, serving the food, and cleaning up.

**Plan a time schedule backward, from the end to the beginning. First decide at what time you will serve the meal. Then figure out how much time you will need to prepare each of the different foods.**

It is easier to follow a time schedule if the preparation jobs are listed in the order in which they are to be done.

Sample Time Schedule

4:30 Start preparing chicken.
4:45 Turn on oven.
5:00 Place chicken in oven.
5:15 Wash and chop broccoli.
5:30 Begin cooking rice.
5:40 Set table.
5:50 Steam broccoli in microwave.
5:55 Remove broccoli, rice, and chicken.
6:00 Serve the meal.
6:45 Wash dishes and clean up kitchen.

# Explore

## Food Shopping

### State the Task

- Plan for food shopping.

### Develop a Plan

1. Make a weekly meal plan.
2. Make a complete list of grocery items needed.
3. Make a list of stores where you might buy the groceries.

### Implement the Plan

1. Create a one-week meal plan for your household.
2. Review all of the recipes in the meal plan to see what ingredients you need to buy.
3. Make a shopping list. Identify items that are less important in case you exceed your budget. You can put these items back.
4. Discuss the budget with your parent or another adult.
5. Make a list of the stores where you will need to shop.
6. Shop for the food items you need. Use the information on product labels and unit pricing to help you select items.

### Evaluate the Result

1. Did you forget to list any items on your shopping list?
2. What did you learn about food shopping?

**Hints:** Before you head for the store, review your shopping list for the following:

- Don't forget to check your staple foods. Staples are foods that you are likely to use often. Examples of staples include milk, eggs, and salt.
- Clip coupons, organize them, and take them with you to the store.
- You can save money by adjusting your menus to take advantage of weekly specials. Check your local newspaper to find out what items are on sale.
- Take a calculator with you so you can keep track of what you are spending.
- Products that are packaged fresh, such as bread, milk, and meat, have a date on their labels. The date shown is the last day a food may be sold as fresh.
- Buy meat, poultry, and fish that is wrapped in fresh, undamaged packaging material.
- Buy fresh fruits and vegetables that are in season and do not have spots.
- Never buy dented or bulging cans. The food may be spoiled.
- Keep raw foods away from cooked and ready-to-eat foods.
- Pick up frozen and refrigerated foods last.

# Internet ACTIVITIES

1. **Search the Internet for tips that will help you save money on your groceries. Make a list of shopping tips and share it with your classmates.**

   **Key Search Words:**
   - **shopping tips**
   - **shopping savings**

2. **Search the Internet for tips on planning a special dinner. Make a list of tips and share it with your classmates.**

   **Key Search Words:**
   - **event planning**
   - **theme dinners**

## ➤ Smart Shopping

Learning how to find the best buys is an important part of being a smart shopper. Some brands are better buys than others. Store brands and generic brands are usually less expensive than national brands.

- **National brands.** Products that you see advertised on television or in newspapers or magazines are known as national brands. These products often cost more than others because the manufacturer spends a great deal of money on packaging and advertising. These costs are added to the price of the product.
- **Store brands.** Products that have the store's name or another name used only by that store on the label are called store brands. They usually cost less because there is little or no advertising cost. They often have the same ingredients and nutrients as national brands.
- **Generic brands.** Products with labels listing only the product name and nutritional information are generic brands. These often cost even less than store brand products.

Products will vary in price, quality, and taste. However, price is not an indicator of quality or taste. You will want to compare national brands, store brands, and generic brands to see which ones you prefer.

# A CLOSER LOOK

## ...at Food Labels

**Imagine going to the supermarket and discovering that none of the packaged foods have labels. You would be missing a lot of important information. In addition to identifying the contents of the package, food labels help you make wise food choices.**

**❶** Serving size is an important reference because calorie and nutrient content are based on this amount. Foods that are similar, such as breakfast cereals, will have similar serving sizes.

**❷** Knowing the number of calories from fat can help you meet the Dietary Guidelines. These guidelines state that 30 percent or less of your daily calories should come from fat.

**❸** Percent Daily Values are based on a diet of 2,000 calories a day. You can adjust the Percent Daily Values to your own diet and calorie intake.

**❹** Nutrient content is provided in grams or milligrams and by Percent Daily Values. This information is useful for comparing foods.

**❺** Information about certain nutrients is required on the food label. These nutrients are total fat, saturated fat, cholesterol, sodium, total carbohydrate, dietary fiber, sugars, protein, vitamins A and C, calcium, and iron.

**❻** A reference chart provides information for both 2,000- and 2,500-calorie diets. The chart shows the highest amount of total fat, saturated fat, cholesterol, and sodium that a person should consume. It also shows the ideal intake for total carbohydrate and dietary fiber.

**❼** Some labels show the number of calories supplied by one gram of fat, carbohydrates, and protein.

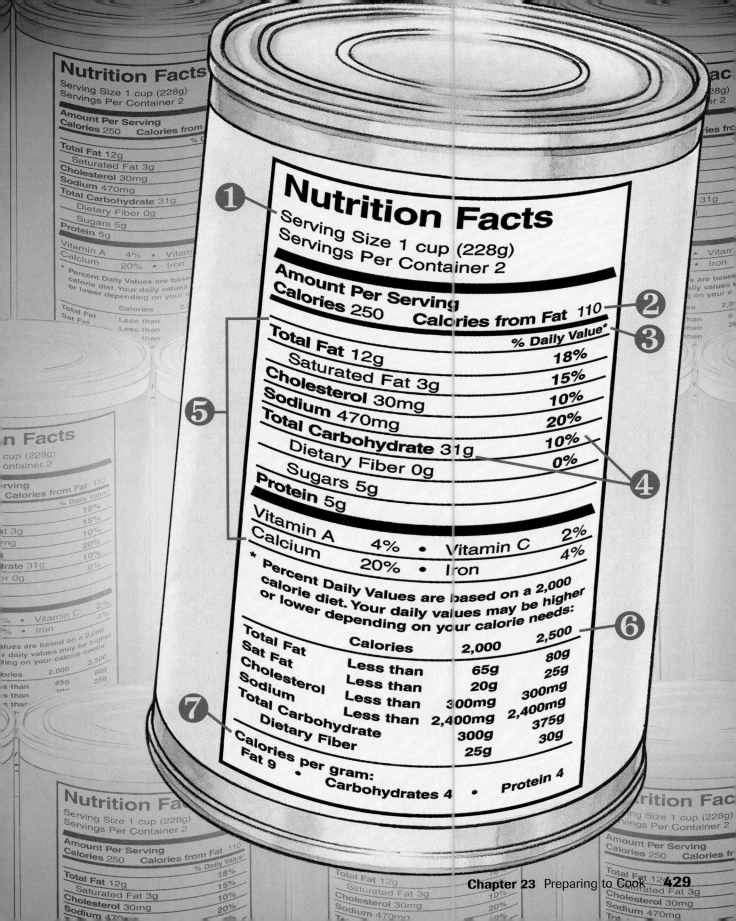

**Nutrition Facts**

Serving Size 1 cup (228g)
Servings Per Container 2

**Amount Per Serving**

Calories 250    Calories from Fat 110

|  | % Daily Value* |
|---|---|
| **Total Fat** 12g | 18% |
| Saturated Fat 3g | 15% |
| **Cholesterol** 30mg | 10% |
| **Sodium** 470mg | 20% |
| **Total Carbohydrate** 31g | 10% |
| Dietary Fiber 0g | 0% |
| Sugars 5g | |
| **Protein** 5g | |

| | | | |
|---|---|---|---|
| Vitamin A | 4% | Vitamin C | 2% |
| Calcium | 20% | Iron | 4% |

* Percent Daily Values are based on a 2,000 calorie diet. Your daily values may be higher or lower depending on your calorie needs:

| | Calories | 2,000 | 2,500 |
|---|---|---|---|
| Total Fat | Less than | 65g | 80g |
| Sat Fat | Less than | 20g | 25g |
| Cholesterol | Less than | 300mg | 300mg |
| Sodium | Less than | 2,400mg | 2,400mg |
| Total Carbohydrate | | 300g | 375g |
| Dietary Fiber | | 25g | 30g |

Calories per gram:
Fat 9   •   Carbohydrates 4   •   Protein 4

# How To...

## Store Food

### State the Task

- Learn how to properly store food.

---

**Food Storage List**

1. Apples
2. Strawberries
3. Brown sugar
4. Tuna casserole
5. Carrots
6. Crackers
7. Lettuce
8. Cheese
9. Baking potatoes
10. Canned soup
11. Deli turkey
12. Boxed spaghetti
13. Frozen corn
14. Catsup
15. Baked beans
16. Hamburger meat
17. Mayonnaise
18. Coleslaw
19. Bread
20. Eggs

---

### Develop a Plan

1. Recognize the differences between fresh and prepared foods.
2. Learn storage methods for fresh, frozen, hot, canned, and packaged foods.
3. Recognize different types of storage containers.

### Implement the Plan

1. Consider these storage methods: freezing, refrigerating, or storing in a cool, dry place.
2. Consider these storage containers: heavy foil, clear wrap, freezer wrap, or containers sold specifically for storage.
3. Consider how you can most easily access the items. For instance, you might want to cut up leftover lasagna into single serving sizes before freezing.
4. Make a chart listing how and where each item on the Food Storage List will be stored.

### Evaluate the Result

1. What method do you like best for storing leftovers?
2. What can you do to ensure that older items are used before new items?

# Food Storage

When you get home from the supermarket, you will need to store the food you bought. Heat, light, time, and moisture destroy nutrients. They can also affect the flavor and spoil foods. Storing foods properly helps them keep their freshness and flavor.

Many food items need special treatment to stay fresh. Items you can't use before the expiration date can be saved by freezing. Here are a few food storage tips:

- Keep butter and margarine covered in the refrigerator, as they absorb odors.
- Keep baking powder tightly covered, as it can lose its strength.
- Fruits and vegetables can be sliced and frozen before they spoil.
- Store onions and potatoes separately, as potatoes will spoil faster when stored near onions.
- Store a container of ice cream inside a heavy, brown bag to prevent freezer burn, the fuzzy ice that appears on the surface.
- Freeze leftover broth in ice cube trays. Pop out the broth cubes and store them in a freezer bag for later use.
- Cook fresh meat and freeze it for use at a later meal.

# Reading Food Labels

Food labels give you valuable nutrition information and shopping information. By law, food labels must provide the following:

- The name of the food.
- The name and address of the product's manufacturer.
- The nutritional content, including serving size, calories, and nutrient amounts per serving.
- A list of ingredients in order of amount. For example, a box of dry cereal might list oat flour first, then sugar, followed by other ingredients, to show that oat flour is the main ingredient, then sugar, and so on.
- The total weight. For example, which is a better value: a 1-lb. (500-gram) bag of tortilla chips for $1.99 or an 11-oz. (300-gram) bag for $1.49?

Unit pricing means showing the cost of the product per unit. Examples of units include ounces, pounds, grams, liters, and gallons. Look for the unit pricing label on the edge of the store shelf. It will give you the product name, the size, and the price per unit. You can easily decide which size is the best buy.

## Grade Labeling

Understanding and using grade labeling can also help you when you shop. Grade labeling is a measurement of food quality using standards set by the government. Many food items including eggs, poultry, and meat are graded. The highest grade is the highest in quality. For example, Grade AA eggs are of higher quality than Grade A eggs.

## ➤ Recipes

Almost all cooks use recipes. A recipe is a list of directions for preparing a specific food. If you know how to read and follow recipes, you will greatly increase your chances of success in the kitchen.

Some recipes are easier to follow than others. See Fig. 23-5. While you are learning to cook, look for easy-to-read recipes that:

- state the amount of each ingredient.
- provide step-by-step instructions on how to combine the ingredients.
- mention the sizes of pans that will be needed.
- specify the cooking time and temperature.
- estimate the yield, or the number of servings.

In whatever format a recipe appears, the procedure for following the recipe remains the same. Here are some general guidelines for using recipes.

- Read through the entire recipe. Make sure that you understand all the terms and abbreviations.
- Assemble all the ingredients and equipment before you start.
- Do any necessary preparation, such as preheating the oven or greasing a pan.

*Cheese Bake*

Yield: 6 servings, 3/4 cup each

10 slices bread
1 1/2 c. cut-up cheese
3 eggs

1 1/2 c. milk
1 tsp. prepared mustard
1 1/2 tsp. salt

1. Preheat oven to 350°F.
2. Cut bread into 1-inch squares.
3. Mix bread and cheese in a greased 9 x 13-inch baking pan. Set aside.
4. Beat eggs. Add milk, mustard, and salt. Mix well.
5. Pour egg mixture over bread and cheese in pan.
6. Bake for 25 minutes. Serve at once.

**Fig. 23-5 Recipes come in different formats. Which format do you prefer?**

**Narrative Format**

**Cheese Bake: Preheat oven to 350°F. Cut 10 slices of bread into 1-inch squares. Mix with 1 1/2 cups cut-up cheese in greased 9 x 13-inch baking pan. Set aside. Beat 3 eggs. Add to the eggs 1 1/2 cups milk, 1 teaspoon prepared mustard, and 1 1/2 teaspoons salt. Mix well and pour over bread and cheese in pan. Bake for 25 minutes. Serve immediately. Yield: 6 servings, 3/4 cup each.**

## Making Connections

**Math.** Recipes are written to yield a certain number of servings. You can make more or less servings by converting, or changing, the amount of each ingredient. This is called recipe conversion. To increase the number of servings, multiply all the ingredients by the same number. To decrease, divide all the ingredients by the same number.

### Get Involved!

Find a recipe that yields 4–6 servings. Convert the recipe so that it yields twice as many servings. Then convert the original recipe so that it will yield half as many servings.

## ➤ Recipe Terms

Recipes have their own special language. To be able to follow them, you need to know some common terms and abbreviations. Here are some commonly used cooking terms.

- **Preheat.** Heat the oven to the right temperature before putting in the food.
- **Bake.** Cook in the oven without a cover.
- **Boil.** Cook in liquid hot enough to bubble rapidly.
- **Braise.** Simmer gently in a small amount of liquid in a covered pan. The food may be browned first.
- **Broil.** Cook under direct heat.
- **Brown.** Cook in a small amount of fat over high heat to brown the surface.
- **Chill.** Put in the refrigerator until cold.
- **Cook.** Prepare food by dry heat or moist heat.
- **Cook by dry heat.** Cook food uncovered without adding any liquid.
- **Cook by moist heat.** Cook in a covered pan with liquid added.
- **Deep-fat fry.** Cook in hot fat deep enough to cover the food.
- **Fry.** Cook in hot fat.
- **Roast.** Cook in the oven in dry heat.
- **Sauté.** Fry in a small amount of fat until done.
- **Scald.** Heat milk until it steams and just begins to bubble around the edge of the pan.
- **Simmer.** Cook to just below the boiling point so the liquid barely bubbles.
- **Steam.** Cook over boiling water.
- **Stew.** Cook slowly in liquid.
- **Stir fry.** Cook quickly in a small amount of fat at high heat.

It is equally important to understand mixing terms. For example, do you know how to blend pudding? See Fig. 23-6.

# Abbreviations

Recipes often show measurements in shortened form to save space. To follow the recipe, it is essential to understand what the abbreviations mean. Can you imagine how your vegetable soup would taste if you added one tablespoon of salt instead of one teaspoon?

## Recipe Abbreviations

| | | | |
|---|---|---|---|
| **t. or tsp.** | teaspoon | **lb.** | pound |
| **T. or Tbsp.** | tablespoon | **°F** | degrees Fahrenheit |
| **c. (or C.)** | cup | **mL** | milliliter |
| **pt.** | pint | **L** | liter |
| **qt.** | quart | **g** | gram |
| **gal.** | gallon | **°C** | degrees Celsius |
| **oz.** | ounce | | |

**Fig. 23-6**

## Mixing Terms

**Whip.** Beat fast with an electric mixer, rotary beater, or wire whip to add enough air to make the mixture fluffy.

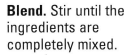

**Blend.** Stir until the ingredients are completely mixed.

**Cream.** Blend until smooth and fluffy.

**Stir.** Move the ingredients in a circular motion to mix or to prevent burning.

**Toss.** Tumble ingredients lightly with a spoon and fork.

**Combine.** Mix two or more ingredients together.

**Beat.** Mix or stir quickly, bringing the contents of the bowl to the top and down again.

# Career CHOICES

## Veterinarian

Diagnoses and treats diseases and injuries of dogs, cats, birds, and farm animals. Treats animals surgically or medically. Examines animal to determine nature of disease or injury.

## Agronomist

Conducts experiments or investigations on field-crops. Develops new methods of growing crops for more efficient production, higher yield, and improved quality.

## Agricultural Engineer

Applies engineering technology and knowledge of biological sciences to agricultural problems. Concerned with power and machinery, structures, soil and water conservation, and the processing of agricultural products.

## Cake Decorator

Designs cakes and pastries for sale. Forms decorations on specialty cakes, birthday cakes, and wedding cakes.

## Farmer

Raises both crops and livestock. Determines kinds and amounts of crops to be grown and livestock to be bred. Monitors market conditions, weather, and capacity of the farm.

**An agronomist is an expert on field crops. Farmers seek this expertise to solve their problems. What careers might you pursue that would turn you into an expert?**

**AT School**

Select three of the careers listed. Research the education, training, and work experience required for each career. Compare the results to select a career to investigate further.

**IN THE Workplace**

Give five examples of how technology has changed the food prepared and served in the workplace. Provide at least two sources to support your answer. Compare findings with your classmates.

## Chapter Summary

- Plan meals based on nutritious foods that fit your meal patterns.
- Plan before you shop and choose the best buys.
- Store foods in the freezer, refrigerator, or a cool, dry place.
- Recipes are written in different formats. Step-by-step is the easiest format to use.
- To follow a recipe, you must understand common terms and abbreviations.

## Words You Learned

1. Why might you serve an appetizer before dinner?
2. How can recognizing your meal patterns help you plan better?

3. Why would you add a garnish to a soup or sandwich?
4. Define the term texture.

## Check Your Facts

1. Name five ways to add variety to meals.
2. List five resources that you should consider before preparing a meal.
3. Name four types of information that are provided on a food label.
4. Explain the difference between boil and broil.
5. Explain the difference between whip and blend.
6. Give the meaning of the following abbreviations: Tbsp., tsp., ml, L.

## Apply Your Learning

1. What is the advantage of planning meals for a whole week?
2. Name three ways to save money when shopping for groceries.
3. When unpacking groceries, what foods should you store first?
4. Why do you need to learn how to read a recipe?
5. Why is a time schedule important when preparing meals?
6. **Recipe Round Up.** Create a class cookbook by having everyone contribute a favorite recipe. Make sure that all the recipes are in step-by-step format and use the correct abbreviations. Make copies of the cookbook for everyone in the class.

# Chapter 24

# Cooking Basics

## You Will Discover . . .

- how to prepare convenience foods.
- the best measuring tool for each task.
- techniques for measuring dry and liquid ingredients.
- how to cook fruits, vegetables, breads, milk products, meat, poultry, fish, legumes, and eggs.

## Key Words

- convenience foods
- scald
- curdles
- legumes
- quiche
- omelet

*J*ust about everyone knows how to cook something. Maybe you're a whiz at scrambled eggs or pancakes. Perhaps you are already in charge of preparing entire meals. Whatever level of experience you have in the kitchen, you can improve your cooking skills with a few tips and guidelines.

## Basic Ingredients

When cooking, the success of your dish depends in part on following step-by-step instructions. As you learn to cook, you will notice that some common ingredients are found in many recipes. These basic ingredients are flour, sugar, shortening or butter, milk, eggs, and spices. Each ingredient in a recipe is used for a specific purpose. Leaving one out could ruin the dish. See Fig. 24-1.

**Fig. 24-1 Follow the recipe carefully. Have you ever left out an ingredient? What did you do when it happened?**

## Using Convenience Foods

Sometimes you may want to use convenience foods when you cook. **Convenience foods** are already partly prepared to save you time. For instance, you might buy a bag of tossed salad instead of purchasing all the ingredients and cutting them up yourself. A common type of convenience food is a mix. Many people use cake and muffin mixes. See Fig. 24-2.

### Follow the Directions

When you use convenience foods, you should always follow the directions given on the package. Make sure that you have all the ingredients and utensils you will need and that you understand all the instructions.

When you are using a general-purpose baking mix, use only the recipes provided on the box. Don't try to substitute the mix for ingredients in another recipe.

**Fig. 24-2 Convenience foods must be made according to the package directions. Have you used a prepared mix to make pancakes or brownies?**

## Measuring Ingredients

By measuring accurately, using the proper measuring tools, and following directions, you will ensure that your recipes turn out the same every time you use them. See Fig. 24-3.

When you cook, you will probably use traditional units of measure, or customary measurements such as cups for volume and pounds for weight. Metric units used in cooking include milliliters for volume and grams for weight. See Fig. 24-4.

**Fig. 24-3** Measure accurately and use the proper measuring tools.

**Fig. 24-4** These are measurement equivalents. You can use any of the three types when cooking. Do you have recipes that ask for metric amounts?

| Customary | Customary Equivalent | | Approximate Metric Equivalent | |
|---|---|---|---|---|
| 1 teaspoon | ⅓ | tablespoon | 5 | milliliters |
| 1 tablespoon | 3 | teaspoons | 15 | milliliters |
| ½ cup | 8 | tablespoons | 125 | milliliters |
| 1 cup | 16 | tablespoons | 250 | milliliters |
| | 8 | fluid ounces | | |
| 2 cups | 1 | pint | 500 | milliliters |
| 4 cups | 1 | quart | 1000 | milliliters or 1 liter |
| 1 pound | 16 | ounces | 500 | grams |

When you want to be sure that your recipe will come out right, it is always best to measure the ingredients accurately. That means using the right tools and the right techniques. Then you can be sure of getting the right result. Cakes, cookies, and other baked goods require accurate measurements for good results. If ingredients are not measured accurately, the baked good may not rise or it may burn. With other foods such as soups, pizza, and casseroles you can more easily experiment. See Fig. 24-5.

## ➤ Cooking Fruit

Ben's grandmother likes to bake fruit for dessert. Her favorites are baked apples and baked pears. She used to bake them in a conventional oven, but now she prefers to use the microwave oven. There is no change in the color or flavor of the fresh fruit, and she knows that fewer nutrients are lost during microwave cooking as well.

Sabrina likes to cook fruit on the stove. She adds a little bit of water to her favorite fresh fruit and covers the pan with a lid. To reduce the amount of nutrients lost in cooking, she uses a heavy-bottomed pan and cooks the fruit at a low, even temperature. She refrigerates the fruit after it cools and adds it to plain yogurt for an afternoon snack.

Fruits taste and look best when they're cooked properly. During cooking, small amounts of some vitamins such as B vitamins and vitamin C are lost. Some dissolve in water and some are destroyed by heat and air. To minimize nutrient loss, use low heat and as little water as possible.

**Fig. 24-5 Cooking pizza with your friends gives you a chance to experiment with different ingredients.**

# Explore

## Measuring Basics

### State the Task

- Measure different ingredients.

### Develop a Plan

1. Gather measuring utensils.
2. Gather ingredients.
3. Measure ingredients.

### Implement the Plan

1. Gather your measuring utensils and ingredients.
2. Sift and measure 1 cup of flour.
3. Press shortening into a dry measuring cup, making sure there are no air pockets. Level it with a metal spatula. Remove shortening with a rubber scraper.

4. Place the liquid measuring cup on a flat surface. Pour oil up to the ½ cup line. Check it at eye level.
5. Pour ¼ t. baking soda into the measuring spoon. Level the top with a metal spatula.

### Evaluate the Result

1. Why must you measure ingredients exactly?
2. Write down three tips that you learned from this experience.

---

**Supplies**

- Flour sifter
- Dry measuring cups
- Liquid measuring cup
- Measuring spoons
- Metal spatula
- Rubber scraper
- Flour
- Shortening
- Oil
- Baking soda

---

Fig. 24-6 Choose the freshest fruit you can in order to get the best flavor. When are strawberries in season?

**DID YOU know?**

**Fruit Cubes.** Freeze grapes and berries and use them in place of ice cubes in juices and teas.

## Selecting Fruit

Besides tasting great, fruit provides important vitamins and minerals, carbohydrates, and fiber. It's easy to get the recommended number of daily servings because fruit goes well with any meal and is a great snack. Vanessa likes to eat dried fruit on her breakfast cereal. Luke enjoys an apple or orange with his lunch.

Some produce, like strawberries, is seasonal, or more readily available and less expensive at certain times of the year. See Fig. 24-6. When you buy produce in-season, you get the best possible quality and also save money. Produce that is available out-of-season is often more expensive. It may also be less nutritious because it is often artificially ripened or shipped a long distance.

If fresh fruits are not available, you might choose processed fruits. Processed means that a food is changed from its raw form before being sold. Fruits that are frozen, canned, or dried are considered processed. Fruit juices are also processed.

## ➤ Cooking Vegetables

Vegetables can retain their nutrients and keep their texture and flavor if they are cooked properly. Cook vegetables until they are tender and crisp, not soft. To prevent vitamin and mineral loss during cooking:

- add as little water as possible.
- use a lid to speed cooking time.
- avoid overcooking.

To determine whether vegetables are overcooked, look for color changes. Vegetables that are cooked properly have a somewhat brighter color than raw ones. For example, green beans are bright green when they are done and olive green when they have cooked too long.

Vegetables can be cooked and served as a side dish or added to other ingredients to make a casserole. See Fig. 24-7. The most common ways to cook vegetables are:

- **Simmering.** To simmer, cook vegetables in a small amount of liquid, just below the boiling point. Cover the pan with a tight-fitting lid.
- **Steaming.** To steam vegetables, place them inside a steamer over simmering water inside a covered pan. The vegetables should not touch the water.
- **Baking.** Vegetables, such as potatoes, are baked without removing their skins. Before placing them in the oven, be sure to pierce the skins several times to prevent them from bursting.
- **Frying.** Vegetables, such as potatoes and cauliflower, are cooked in fat. This cooking method is not as healthful as others, however.
- **Stir-frying.** Cook vegetables quickly over high heat while stirring them in a small amount of oil.
- **Microwave cooking.** Cut the vegetables in pieces and place them in an appropriate container. Chapter 25 covers microwave-cooking techniques.

**SAFETY FIRST**

**Carefully remove lids from pots and pans when cooking to avoid steam burns. Moisture can build up inside and create steam. When the steam hits the air to escape, it can cause severe burns.**

**Fig. 24-7 Vegetable casseroles taste great.** Find a recipe for a squash casserole and see how easy it is to prepare.

## Selecting Vegetables

Vegetables are a delicious part of a well-balanced diet. They are also valuable sources of carbohydrates, fiber, and many important vitamins and minerals. New varieties are developed each year. Like fruits, vegetables are most nutritious when they are fresh. Vegetables are seasonal, but most are available year-round. You can usually buy them frozen, canned, or dried, if you prefer.

Fresh vegetables need to be refrigerated until you are ready to use them. For best results, they should be used within a few days after you buy them. Before serving fresh vegetables, wash them carefully under cold running water. If you plan to eat them raw, you may want to peel the vegetables and blot them dry. To keep raw vegetables crisp, do not wash them too far in advance of serving time.

## Internet ACTIVITIES

1. **Search the Internet for cancer-fighting foods. Make a list of at least 20 foods and share it with your classmates.**

   **Key Search Words:**
   - **cancer-fighting foods**
   - **antioxidants**

2. **Search the Internet for cooking sites. Find a new recipe for each food group. Exchange recipes with your classmates.**

   **Key Search Words:**
   - **recipes**
   - **cooking**

# How To...

## Cook a Casserole

### State the Task

- Prepare a casserole.

### Develop a Plan

1. Gather your ingredients.
2. Read the steps in the recipe.
3. Bake the *Macaroni & Cheese With Vegetables* casserole.

### Implement the Plan

1. Peel and chop the onion. Set it aside.
2. Clean and chop the broccoli. Set it aside.
3. Cook the macaroni in boiling, salted water until tender. Follow the directions on the box.
4. Drain the macaroni and set it aside.
5. Melt the butter in a saucepan.
6. Stir in the flour, salt, and pepper.
7. Add in the milk.
8. Cook and stir until bubbly. Be careful not to let the mixture burn.
9. Add in the onion, broccoli, and cheese.
10. Mix the cheese sauce with the vegetables and macaroni.
11. Pour the entire mixture in an oven-safe casserole dish.
12. Bake at 350°F (177°C) for 35 to 40 minutes.

**Supplies**

- 1½ c. elbow macaroni
- 8 oz. package of shredded cheddar cheese
- 1 c. chopped broccoli
- ¼ c. chopped onion
- 2 c. milk
- 2 T. butter
- 2 T. flour
- ½ t. salt
- ⅛ t. pepper
- Saucepan
- 1½ qt. casserole dish

### Evaluate the Result

1. How did your casserole turn out?
2. What food groups are represented in your casserole?
3. What else could you serve with your casserole to get all five of the food groups included in the meal?

## ➤ Baking Breads

People serve breads at most meals. Breads are made from whole wheat, rye, white, or corn flour. Other ingredients are added to give each type of bread a particular flavor, texture, and appearance. The two main types of breads are quick breads and yeast breads.

### Quick Breads

When preparing quick breads, it is important to mix the batter just long enough to blend the ingredients. Too much mixing makes quick breads flat and heavy. Air bubbles, which form during baking, make quick breads light and fluffy. Baking powder and baking soda cause the air bubbles to form, making the bread rise quickly as it bakes. See Fig. 24-8.

### Yeast Breads

Yeast breads are also made with flour, but it is yeast that makes the bread rise. They take longer to prepare than quick breads. Most sandwich breads, French and Italian breads, and hamburger buns are yeast breads.

Fig. 24-8 **Quick breads are easy to make and they taste great.** Try making some banana bread or carrot-raisin muffins.

A dough made with yeast must rise twice. First, you must let it rise in a warm place outside the oven for an hour or more. Then you punch it down, shape it, and let it rise in the pan before baking. You can buy frozen yeast dough, if you want to take a short cut. Then all you have to do is let the dough warm to room temperature and rise until it is ready to be baked.

An even easier way to make breads is with a bread machine. Simply put your ingredients in the bread machine, turn it on, and the machine mixes the dough, lets it rise, and bakes it at the proper temperature.

# Making Sandwiches

One of the most popular ways to eat bread is as part of a sandwich. See Fig. 24-9. Although there are many kinds of sandwiches, all good sandwiches include:

- bread that is fresh.
- mustard, mayonnaise, honey, or butter to keep the bread moist.
- a filling, such as tuna salad, spread to the corners of the bread, or slices of meat or cheese.
- ingredients that add extra flavor and texture, such as lettuce and tomatoes.

Sandwiches don't have to be cold. For variety, you can make a tuna melt by putting tuna and cheese on a bagel or bread and melting the cheese in the oven or broiler. Peanut butter with banana slices on oatmeal bread provides foods from three of the five food groups.

Fig. 24-9 You have probably made cold sandwiches. How are hot sandwiches made?

# Cooking Grains

Some foods made from grains must be cooked before you eat them. These include some breakfast cereals, rice, and pasta. Because they all contain starch, some of the cooking techniques are similar.

## Cereals

When you think of cereal, do you think about the kind you pour out of the box and eat cold with milk? Many people also enjoy eating cooked cereals, such as oatmeal, grits, and cream of wheat.

Like other grains that are cooked, cereals expand to two or three times their original volume. They can be cooked with water or milk on top of the stove or in a microwave oven.

**Fig. 24-10**

# Cooking Pasta

**2** Measure water and salt into a large pot. You will need 2 quarts (2 L) water and an optional 1 teaspoon (5 mL) salt for every 8 ounces (224 g) pasta. Add one teaspoon (5 mL) cooking oil to the water. This helps to keep the water from boiling over. It also helps keep the pasta from sticking together.

**1** Choose a large enough pot. Pasta doubles in size when it is cooked.

**3** Bring the water to a boil.

**4** Add the pasta slowly to the water. The water should continue to boil. If it stops, the pasta might stick together.

**5** Stir the pasta from time to time. This also helps keep it from sticking. Cook the pasta only until it's tender. The package directions tell you how long.

**6** Pour the pasta into a colander to drain. Don't rinse the pasta with water.

## Rice

One type of grain that must be cooked is rice. Rice should be simmered in water, not boiled. When cooked properly, rice is light and fluffy, not heavy or gummy. When you cook rice, follow these tips:

- Don't rinse rice; rinsing removes nutrients.
- Use a little oil in the cooking water to help the grains separate and to prevent foaming.
- Don't remove the lid while the rice is cooking.
- Because all of the water is absorbed during cooking, rice does not need to be drained.
- Fluff the rice with a fork before serving.

Before you cook rice, read the directions on the package. Different kinds of rice require different amounts of water and lengths of cooking time.

There are many ways to serve rice. For example, rice can be rolled in a flour tortilla with cooked chicken and beans. It is also an important ingredient in some soups and in rice pudding.

## Pasta

Spaghetti and macaroni are types of pasta. Pasta is made from flour and water. It is formed into shapes, such as noodles, spirals, and shells. Fig. 24-10 shows you how to cook pasta.

## ➤ Cooking With Milk Products

Have you ever cooked foods with ingredients that included milk, buttermilk, or cream? For example, you might use milk or cream to make soups, sauces, puddings, and custards. Milk and buttermilk are often used in cakes, pies, breads, and muffins.

Thick, creamy sauces add flavor to many dishes. For example, a basic white sauce made with milk can be served over vegetables or noodles. For extra flavor, add cheese or herbs to the sauce. See Fig. 24-11 on page 452.

Fig. 24-11 Sauces, soups, puddings, and custards are made from milk. What foods taste best with a sauce added?

## Milk

When cooking with milk products, it is important to be especially careful. Milk burns, or scorches, easily if the temperature is too high or if it is cooked too long. To cook milk you need to **scald** it, or bring it slowly to a temperature just below the boiling point. Never let milk boil. Heat only until little bubbles begin to appear around the edge of the pan.

Milk may curdle if you do not handle it properly. When milk **curdles**, it separates into little particles or curds. Adding tomatoes or fruit juices to milk may cause curdling, as they contain acid. To avoid this, add ingredients very slowly and stir the milk constantly.

## Yogurt

Yogurt contains most of the same nutrients as milk. Because yogurt is easier to digest than milk, many people who cannot drink milk can still eat yogurt. Yogurt can be used instead of sour cream or mayonnaise in some recipes. It comes in a wide variety of flavors. For dessert, serve yogurt over fruit and granola. Frozen yogurt is a special treat.

## Cheese

Can you imagine what some of your favorite foods would taste like without cheese? Pizza and lasagna just wouldn't be the same. Cheese is an important ingredient in many recipes. See Fig. 24-12. For the best results, though, it must be cooked carefully. Cooking cheese too long or at high temperatures may cause it to burn or become rubbery or stringy. When cooking with cheese, follow these tips:

- Use low to medium heat.
- Grate or shred hard cheeses, such as cheddar, before adding them to other ingredients. The cheese will blend faster and more evenly.
- Add cheese at the end of the cooking time so that the cheese won't become overcooked.

Besides cooking with cheese, you can also enjoy cheese by itself or along with a variety of foods. For example, try sprinkling grated cheese on soups, chili, baked potatoes, or burritos. For an easy snack, eat cheese with crackers, crusty bread, or fresh fruit. Firm cheeses that can be sliced, such as cheddar and Swiss cheese, taste best at room temperature. Take them out of the refrigerator about an hour before they will be eaten.

**Fig. 24-12 Macaroni and cheese is a favorite dish to people in all age groups.** Compare cooking this dish from scratch to using a packaged mix. Which tastes better?

## ➤ Cooking Meat, Poultry & Fish

Protein-rich foods such as meat, poultry, and fish are popular main dishes. They are not only cut and sold in a variety of ways but can also be prepared in countless ways. When cooking meat, poultry, or fish, the two basic methods you will use are moist heat and dry heat. The method you choose depends on the recipe you are following and the tenderness of the meat or poultry. See Fig. 24-13 on page 455.

## Moist Heat

Have you ever eaten pot roast or beef stew? If so, then you have tasted meat cooked with moist heat. It involves cooking food slowly in a covered container, usually with water, broth, or a sauce.

Moist-heat cooking methods are good to use with tougher cuts of meat and poultry. When you cook these cuts slowly in liquid, they become more tender and flavorful. Use moist heat to cook:

- Stew meat
- Pot roast
- Round steak
- Chuck roast
- Corned beef
- Spareribs
- Pork blade steak
- Stewing chicken

## Dry Heat

Do you enjoy eating roast turkey, broiled steak, or baked fish? Each of these foods is cooked with dry heat. Dry-heat cooking is best to use when cooking tender cuts of meat and poultry. Most fish is also cooked with dry heat. Use dry heat to cook:

- Beef rib roast
- Sirloin steak
- Ground beef, pork, turkey
- Pork chops
- Ham
- Pork sausage
- Leg of lamb
- Frying chicken

Hamburger, pork, and poultry must be cooked thoroughly to destroy harmful bacteria. Otherwise, they are not safe to eat. Other meats can be cooked to different levels of doneness. Rare meat is pink on the inside. Well-done meat is thoroughly cooked inside and out. Medium is between rare and well done.

**Fig. 24-13**

# Methods of Cooking Meats

**Roasting and Baking.** Place the meat, poultry, or fish on a rack in a shallow pan, uncovered, in the oven.

**Braising.** To braise food, such as a pot roast, brown the meat. Then put the food in a covered pan with a small amount of liquid. Cook it slowly until tender.

**Stewing.** Cut meat into small pieces. Cover with liquid and cook slowly according to recipe directions.

**Frying.** Meat, poultry, or fish can be fried in oil, butter, or margarine. Thin slices of meat, poultry, or fish can be stir-fried, which means that they are cooked quickly in a small amount of fat at a high temperature.

**Microwave Cooking.** Meat, poultry, and fish can be cooked in a microwave oven. They won't brown much, however.

**Deep-fat Frying.** Chicken and fish are sometimes fried in a lot of oil. The oil must be hot, but not too hot. Chicken and fish are usually coated with a batter before deep-fat frying.

**Broiling.** Place the meat, fish, or poultry on a broiler pan under the oven broiler. High heat from the broiler cooks food from the top. Turn the food over so that it cooks on both sides.

## ➤ Meat Substitutes

Other high-protein foods can be used as the main dish instead of meat, poultry, or fish. Beans and eggs are two good substitutes. Not only are they high in protein, vitamins, and minerals but they are also low in cost. In fact, they are two of the most versatile and nutritious foods you can cook.

### Cooking Legumes

**Legumes**, or dry beans and peas, come in a variety of tastes and textures. Have you tasted red kidney beans, black beans, white beans, lentils, lima beans, split peas, and black-eyed peas? These and other legumes offer healthful alternatives to meat, poultry, and fish dishes. See Fig. 24-14.

When you buy dry beans, they will be hard. To soften them, soak them in water as directed. Then the beans can be prepared in many ways. For example, you can make baked beans or roll them in tortillas with rice and cheese to make burritos. To save time, you can buy canned or frozen legumes.

**Fig. 24-14 Legumes are a great source of fiber and they taste great too.**

## Cooking Eggs

What is your favorite way to cook eggs? No matter how you like them, there are two basic rules to follow: (1) Keep the temperature low so that the eggs don't get tough. (2) Cook eggs thoroughly so that the whites and yolks are firm. Harmful bacteria in raw or under-cooked eggs can make you sick.

- **Hard-cooked eggs.** When you hard-cook eggs in the shell, cover the eggs with cold water and bring the water to a boil. Cover the pan and remove it from the burner. Let the eggs stand in the hot water for 15 minutes. That allows both the whites and yolks to harden. Then run cold water over the eggs immediately to stop the cooking process.

- **Fried eggs.** Fried eggs are usually cooked in butter, margarine, or oil. To fry an egg, crack the shell gently, and slip the white and the yolk into a greased pan.

- **Scrambled eggs.** To make scrambled eggs, beat the whites and yolks together. Then pour the eggs into a hot frying pan that has been sprayed with a nonstick spray. Cook eggs slowly over low heat, stirring them gently and frequently so that they cook evenly. In Chapter 25 you will learn how to make scrambled eggs in a microwave oven.

- **Quiches and omelets.** Eggs can also be used in quiches and omelets. A **quiche** is a main-dish pie filled with eggs, cheese, and other ingredients such as ham, spinach, and mushrooms. An **omelet** is a well-beaten egg that is first cooked in a frying pan without stirring. Then it is topped with other ingredients, such as mushrooms, peppers, and cheese, and folded over.

## ➤ Herbs & Spices

Herbs and spices are the special ingredients that separate average cooks from great cooks. Learning which herbs and spices to use, and how much, is based on experience. Pages 458 and 459 will introduce you to a few herbs and spices to begin your cooking experience.

# A CLOSER LOOK

## ...at Herbs & Spices

Herbs and spices add color and aroma to foods. They are the special ingredients that make some recipes better than others. There are many varieties of herbs and spices.

**Basil**
This popular herb has a mild flavor. It is often used in soups and salads.

**Chives**
This herb has a mild onion flavor. It's often used as a garnish and to add flavor to soups and dips.

**Cilantro**
This herb has a unique flavor and odor. It is often used in salsas and dips.

**Parsley**
Often used as a garnish, this herb is also found in green sauces, such as pesto. It has a soothing effect on your taste buds.

**Dill Weed**
This herb has a delicate flavor. It is often used in dips and fish dishes.

### Cinnamon
This spice comes from the bark of the laurel tree. Ground cinnamon is used a lot in cakes and cookies.

### Cumin
Commonly found ground or as a whole seed, this spice is somewhat hot. It is often used in marinades and sauces.

### Nutmeg
This spice comes from the fruit of the nutmeg tree. It has a nutty, mild flavor. It is used often in pies and puddings.

### Saffron
This yellow spice comes from the crocus plant. It is used to lend its yellow color and flavor to foods.

### Garlic
This strong spice is a dried root from the lily family. It grows in a bulb that is then minced or chopped.

# Career CHOICES

## Menu Planner

Works closely with executive chef to select menu items to be offered. Participates in cost control, ordering of supplies, and some food preparation.

## Food Tester

Performs tests to determine physical or chemical properties of food or beverage products. Ensures compliance with quality and safety standards.

## Food Technologist

Conducts new product research for the development of foods. Involved in the quality control, packaging, processing, and use of foods.

## Meat Cutter

Cuts and trims meat to size for display or as ordered by customer. Cleans and cuts fish. Packages meat and fish for display and sale.

## Pastry Chef

Prepares a wide variety of pastries and desserts. Supervises pastry cooks. Plans work schedules. Orders supplies.

**AT School**

Select three of the careers listed. Research the education, training, and work experience required for each career. Compare the results to select a career to investigate further.

**IN THE Workplace**

Plan three nutritious brown-bag lunches that you could take to work. Compare your examples with those of your classmates.

**Pastry chefs create works of art that you can eat!** Research two food-related careers that would require you to use creativity. Would you be interested in pursuing one of these careers?

## Chapter Summary

- When using convenience foods, follow the package directions, just as you would follow a recipe.
- There are several basic measuring tools: measuring spoons, dry measuring cups, and liquid measuring cups.
- It is important to measure accurately.
- Fruits and vegetables can be served raw, cooked, or as part of other dishes.
- Rice and pasta are high-energy grain products that must be cooked.
- Cooking with milk products is a good way to include dairy foods in your diet.
- Meat, poultry, and fish are cooked with moist heat or dry heat.

## Words You Learned

1. What are convenience foods?
2. What causes milk to scald?
3. What causes milk to curdle?
4. What are legumes?
5. What is a main-dish pie?
6. What is fried before it is topped with ingredients and folded over?

## Check Your Facts

1. What happens if ingredients are not measured accurately?
2. Name three ingredients that could be measured in a liquid measuring cup.
3. Give an example of a seasonal fruit.
4. How can you prevent vegetables from losing vitamins and minerals during cooking?
5. Give three tips for cooking with cheese.

**Apply Your Learning**

1. Think about the ways to ensure variety in meals—texture, color, size and shape, flavor, and temperature. Which of these do you think is most important to vary for an appealing meal? Explain your answer.
2. Create your own omelet recipe. Be creative and try to think of unusual combinations. Share your recipe with your classmates.
3. **Snack Basket.** Create several low-fat or healthful snacks. Arrange them in a basket or another container. Add the recipe for your favorite snack. Give the snack basket to a friend or family member.

# Chapter 25

# Microwave Basics

## You Will Discover . . .

- how a microwave oven works.
- how to use a microwave oven.
- ways to prepare foods for microwave cooking.
- safety tips for using a microwave oven.

## Key Words

- magnetron
- arcing
- variables
- superheating

*M*any people use microwave ovens for jobs that, in the past, could be done only by stoves and conventional ovens. In fact, microwave ovens have features that make them more versatile than many other kitchen appliances. The microwave is fast and easy to use, and saves time for today's busy families.

# ➤ Understanding Microwaves

Although microwave ovens vary in size, power, and features, they all operate the same way. They produce microwaves, or energy waves that heat food. This process results in heat that cooks the food much quicker than a conventional oven. Here's how a microwave works:

• A wall outlet provides electricity to the microwave oven through the power cord.
• Electricity moves through the inside wiring and reaches the magnetron. The **magnetron** is the key part inside the oven that moves the microwaves around the oven. As the microwaves vibrate the molecules of water, fat, and sugar inside the food, it creates heat and cooks the food.

Because microwaves are moving all over the inside of the oven, the food is cooked inside and out. Microwaves even bounce off the food. However, the microwaves stay inside the oven when the door is closed. See Fig. 25-1.

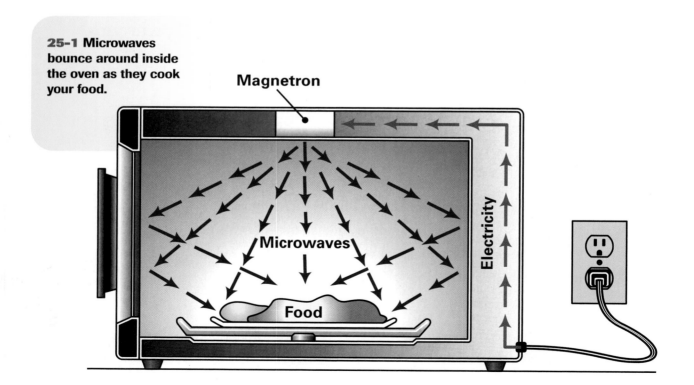

**25-1 Microwaves bounce around inside the oven as they cook your food.**

Magnetron

Microwaves

Food

Electricity

Microwaves are similar to radio and television waves. They consist of two types of energy: electric and magnetic. The two energies combine to form a wave that travels outward in an up-and-down rippling motion. A microwave travels at the same speed as light, more than 186,000 miles per second, or 700 million miles per hour. See Fig. 25-2.

## A Simple Beginning

Percy L. Spencer was the creator of the microwave oven. He was an electronics genius that discovered microwave energy in 1946. As Spencer stopped briefly in front of a magnetron tube that was sitting in a radar set, he felt the chocolate bar in his pocket begin to melt. This got Spencer's attention so he tried an experiment. He placed unpopped popcorn near the magnetron and watched as it began to pop. From an accidental discovery, Spencer went on to create the microwave oven. Today the microwave oven is a necessary appliance in many homes.

**DID YOU know?**

**Microwaves.** The first microwave oven was called the "Radarange." It weighed 750 pounds and stood over 5 feet tall. Microwave ovens cost between $2,000 and $3,000 in 1947.

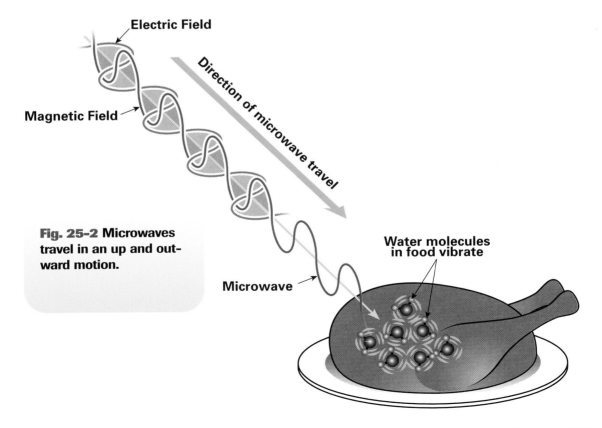

**Electric Field**

**Magnetic Field**

Direction of microwave travel

**Fig. 25-2 Microwaves travel in an up and outward motion.**

**Water molecules in food vibrate**

**Microwave**

## Oven Operation

Microwave ovens are a fast and convenient way to cook. Foods cook up to 75 percent faster than in a conventional oven. You can reheat leftover food, cook food, or defrost frozen food.

Because microwave ovens cook food so quickly, they use less electricity than other methods of cooking. The nutrients in food are better preserved because of the quick cooking time and because little or no water needs to be added to foods such as vegetables. See Fig. 25-3.

The amount of power that an appliance uses is measured in watts. Most household microwave ovens use a maximum of 500 to 1,000 watts. The higher the wattage, the faster most foods will cook. If you are unsure of the wattage, you can look it up in the instruction manual or on the label attached to the microwave oven.

Although you cannot control the wattage, you can control the amount of power with which you cook. Many control panels are numbered from 1 to 10. The "1" means 10 percent of the available power and the "10" means 100 percent. Some control panels list common foods with specific power settings and cooking times. Other control panels simply have settings for low, medium, and high.

**Fig. 25-3 When cooking foods such as vegetables in the microwave, little or no water needs to be added.**

## Microwave Cookware

"Microwave safe" containers will not get too hot, melt, crack, or shatter from the heat produced in the oven. Round containers allow more even heating and cooking than square or rectangular ones.

Metal containers should never be used in a microwave oven, and aluminum foil should not be used as a cover. The microwaves that heat the food cannot pass through metal. Metal can also cause **arcing** (AHR-keen), or electrical sparks that can damage a microwave oven and start a fire. Brown paper bags and other products made from recycled paper should also be avoided because they can catch fire.

Fig. 25-4 Always pierce a potato before placing it in the microwave. This allows steam to escape as the food cooks.

## Preparing to Cook

Microwave ovens cook food differently from conventional ovens. You need to follow specific guidelines when preparing food for microwave cooking. See Fig. 25-4.

1. Choose a container that will fit into the microwave oven without touching the sides or the top. To keep liquids from boiling over, use a deeper container that has extra space in it.
2. Arrange the food so that it can cook evenly. Cut foods into pieces of the same size so that they will cook at the same rate. Place the thickest pieces toward the outside of the container, where they will receive the most energy.
3. Use a fork or knife to pierce foods that are encased in a skin, such as whole potatoes and hot dogs. This will ensure that the steam does not build up and cause them to burst.
4. Cover foods so that they hold in their moisture and do not spatter. You can use paper towels, waxed paper, plastic wrap, or covers that come with microwavable containers. Cover the food loosely, or make a vent by turning back a corner to let steam escape.

**SAFETY FIRST**

Cook food immediately after defrosting it. Waiting to cook food until a later time may allow harmful bacteria to grow.

- - - - - - - - - - - -

# A CLOSER LOOK

## ...at Microwave Cookware

Not just any container is appropriate for use in a microwave oven. Before you start to cook, check that the container is labeled safe for use in a microwave oven.

### Plastic
Not all plastics are created equally. Only use plastic that is specifically labeled for microwave use. This means it is safe and will not melt.

### Paper
Paper plates and paper towels can be used safely in the microwave to warm up leftovers. They are also handy covers to keep foods from spattering.

## Glass

Glass containers are popular for cooking casseroles and vegetables in the microwave. They come in a variety of sizes and shapes. Handle glass carefully as it can break.

## Corningware®

Corningware® is a line of cookware appropriate for microwave cooking, conventional baking, and stovetop cooking. It is versatile and long lasting. Note that like glass, it can break if dropped or mishandled.

## Stoneware®

Stoneware® is a heavy-duty type of specialty cookware. It is especially good for heating up soups and stews in the microwave. Stoneware can break or chip if it is dropped or mishandled.

## ➤ The Cooking Process

You will often need to use certain techniques when cooking foods in a microwave oven. Here are some examples:

- **Stirring.** To help some foods, such as soups and stews, to cook evenly, stir them after they are partially cooked. Because the outside cooks first, stir from the outer edge of the container toward the center. See Fig. 25-5.
- **Rearranging.** Some foods, such as baking potatoes, might have to be rearranged or turned over after a few minutes. Move pieces that have been on the outer edges of the container into the center so that they can cook evenly.
- **Rotating.** Some foods need to be rotated a quarter-turn or a half-turn in the oven. This allows the microwaves to enter the food on all sides. The package directions or the recipe you are following will usually specify how often to rotate the food. (*Note:* Most microwave ovens have a turntable that automatically rotates whenever the oven is in use.)
- **Standing time.** Microwave recipes tell you to let the food stand after the power shuts off. This standing time is required to let the temperatures equalize. In fact, standing time is almost as important as cooking time for the food to turn out just right.
- **Turning.** Turn thick foods over part way through the cooking process to allow even heating.
- **Covering.** Cover foods with a lid or microwave-safe wrap to hold in moisture and ensure even heating.
- **Piercing.** Foods with a skin, such as potatoes, will need to be pierced to allow heat to escape.

**Fig. 25-5** Some foods must be stirred halfway through the cooking process. Be sure to stir well so the food will cook evenly.

# Explore

## Microwaving Eggs

### Supplies

- Eggs
- Milk
- Microwave-safe container
- Fork or wire whisk
- Measuring spoons

### State the Task

- To produce fluffy scrambled eggs in the microwave.

### Develop a Plan

1. Gather the necessary supplies.
2. Discuss the steps that should be taken to prepare the eggs.
3. Discuss the length of time to microwave the eggs.

### Implement the Plan

1. Break an egg into a microwave-safe container.
2. Add a tablespoon of milk.
3. Stir the egg mixture briskly with a fork or wire whisk.
4. Set the bowl in the microwave.
5. Close the door on the microwave and set the time for half of the total cooking time.
6. Turn on the oven.
7. Stir the egg when the time indicator sounds.
8. Close the oven door and set the time for the remaining half of the total cooking time.
9. Remove the container when the indicator sounds and close the oven door.
10. Taste your scrambled eggs.

### Evaluate the Result

1. Did the eggs cook completely? Were they over- or under-cooked?
2. Are there any changes you would make to this microwave scrambled egg recipe? Explain your answer.

**Microwave Cooking Times.**
**Consider the difference in cooking times among several types of foods.**

- **Leftover casserole, one serving (2 minutes)**
- **6 muffins (4 to 6 minutes or until all the wet spots disappear)**
- **Medium baked potato (6 minutes)**
- **2.5 pound meatloaf (20 minutes)**

## Cooking Variables

When you use a microwave oven, you need to follow different procedures to cook different types or sizes of food. That is because of variables in microwave cooking. **Variables** are conditions that determine how long a food needs to be cooked and at what power level. Variables include the following:

- **Density.** The denser the food, the longer it takes to cook. The heavier a food feels for its size, the denser it is. For example, a slice of meat is denser than a slice of bread of the same size.
- **Volume of food.** The amount, or number of servings, determines how much power and time are needed. Generally, the smaller the amount of food, the faster it cooks.
- **Shape of food.** Round foods, such as pancakes, cook more evenly than foods that have corners, such as lasagna. This is because the corners can overcook.
- **Temperature of food.** If food is at room temperature, it will heat faster than food taken directly from the refrigerator or freezer. Remember to use a potholder when removing the food container from the microwave oven. See Fig. 25-6.

**Fig. 25-6** Remove food containers carefully as they may be too hot to handle. It is best to use a potholder when removing microwaved foods from the oven.

## Internet ACTIVITIES

1. **Search the Internet for information on radio waves and how microwaves evolved from them. Write an essay on how microwaves have changed people's lives.**

   **Key Search Words:**
   • **radio waves**
   • **microwave inventor**

2. **Search the Internet for your favorite recipe cooked in a conventional oven. Discuss what steps were needed to convert it from conventional to microwave. Try the microwave recipe to see how well it works.**

   **Key Search Words:**
   • **recipes**
   • **microwave cooking**

## ➤ Microwave Oven Safety

Cooking in a microwave oven can be safe and easy as long as you take a few basic precautions.

- To avoid fires and other accidents, use "microwave safe" dishes.
- Remove covers slowly after food is cooked. Tilt the cover so that steam escapes away from you.
- Do not microwave foods in containers that are completely sealed. When pressure from steam builds, the container can burst. See Fig. 25-7.
- Do not use an extension cord with a microwave oven or plug it into the same electrical outlet as other large electrical appliances.
- If the oven door does not close tightly or if you hear unusual sounds coming from the oven, tell an adult.

Fig. 25-7 Food containers used in the microwave oven should not be completely sealed.

- If there are sparks inside the oven or if there is a fire, turn off the oven or unplug it immediately and get help.
- **Superheating** can occur when a liquid is heated in a container that doesn't allow bubble formation, or boiling. When a liquid overheats, but does not boil, the liquid can explode when it comes into contact with atmospheric pressure. For example, when a spoon breaks the surface, the hot liquid can explode. The result could be severe burns if the superheated liquid comes into contact with your skin. To make sure liquids do not superheat, warm them a little at a time, adding 30 seconds as needed until the liquid is hot. If your microwave oven has a beverage setting, you should use it. See Fig. 25-8.

**Fig. 25-8** Heating water in a microwave can lead to superheating. Use the beverage setting to avoid this risk.

# How To...

## Convert Conventional Oven Recipes

### State the Task

- Convert a recipe typically cooked in a conventional oven so that it can be cooked in a microwave oven.

### Develop a Plan

1. Choose a recipe that contains some liquid ingredients such as water, milk, or juice. (*Note:* Save recipes that call for crisping or browning for a conventional oven.)
2. Reduce the liquid in the recipe by one-quarter. (*Note:* Less evaporation occurs in the microwaving process.)
3. Reduce the amount of seasoning. (*Note:* Add more seasoning later, if desired.)
4. Choose a cooking dish similar in size to the one you would use for conventional cooking. Make sure that it is microwave-safe. (*Note:* Choose a deeper dish for cakes and soups because the food volume will increase temporarily during the microwave cooking process.)

### Implement the Plan

1. Mix the ingredients.
2. Reduce the amount of cooking time by a quarter to a half. (*Note:* Recipes containing fat, sugar, and liquid will cook faster.)
3. Cook the food.
4. Unless you are making bread or cake, stir the contents of the dish to make sure it heated throughout.
5. Test for doneness as you would test a dish from a conventional oven.

### Evaluate the Result

1. Did the dish turn out as it would have in a conventional oven? Why or why not?
2. What safety precautions did you take when preparing your microwave recipe?

# Career CHOICES

## Electrical Assembler

Routes, assembles, and installs electrical components according to specifications. Reads work orders and blueprints. Conducts tests. Replaces parts.

## Appliance Repairer

Repairs electrical appliances. Examines appliance for mechanical defects. Disassembles appliances. Replaces defective wiring and parts.

## Freezer Room Worker

Moves racks of packages filled with food into freezing room. Records identifying data, such as brand name, package size, and time of entry into the freezing room. Checks packages after specified time to test solidity of freeze.

## Design Engineer

Designs and develops electronic components and systems. Applies principles of electronics, design, and engineering. Creates concept designs for new electronic products.

## Electronics Technician

Tests, troubleshoots, and repairs electronic parts. Changes electronic parts, equipment, and systems. Applies principles of electronics and physics. Reads schematics and diagrams circuits.

### AT School

Select three of the careers listed. Research the education, training, and work experience required for each career. Compare the results to select a career to investigate further.

### IN THE Workplace

List five products developed in the last 20 years that have significantly affected the workplace. Share lists with your classmates.

**Microwave ovens were introduced in 1947, but it took several decades for them to become a favorite appliance.** Can you see yourself inventing the new food technology of the future?

## Chapter Summary

- Microwave ovens cook food quickly.
- When using a microwave oven, you need to use microwave-safe cookware, follow specific guidelines for preparing food, and use special cooking techniques.
- Variables to consider when using a microwave oven include the density, volume, shape, and temperature of food.

## Words You Learned

1. How does a magnetron help heat food?
2. How can arcing be avoided?
3. What are variables in microwave cooking?
4. Define superheating.

## Check Your Facts

1. Why is it important to use microwave-safe containers when cooking food in a microwave oven?
2. Why would you use a microwave oven to defrost food?
3. Name three types of microwave-safe cookware.
4. Why is standing time necessary after food is cooked in a microwave oven?
5. Name six safety precautions to take when using a microwave oven.

## Apply Your Learning

1. Why do foods cook faster in a microwave oven?
2. What are the disadvantages to cooking food in a microwave oven?
3. Why would an egg crack if it were cooked in its shell in a microwave oven?
4. What is the greatest safety risk involved with microwave ovens?
5. **Pop Up.** Make a bag of plain microwave popcorn. String it to create a decorative garland. Use a needle and standard thread, doubled for extra strength. Add dried cranberries, mini-marshmallows, or bright ribbons for color.

# Glossary

## A

**AIDS**—Acquired Immune Deficiency Syndrome. (Ch. 3)

**abstinence** (AB-stuh-nuhnts)—Refusing to participate in unsafe behaviors or activities. (Ch. 3)

**accented neutral color scheme**—The use of neutral colors plus another color as an accent. A combination of black and red is an example of an accented neutral color scheme. (Ch. 15)

**accessories**—Interesting items added to make a living space or an item of clothing more personal. (Ch. 13, 15)

**acne**—A skin problem caused by your oil glands working too hard. The extra oil on your skin clogs your pores. (Ch. 1)

**active listening**—Restating what the speaker says to make sure the message is understood. (Ch. 4)

**acquaintance** (uh-QUOHNT-ence)—A person you greet or meet fairly often but with whom you do not have a close relationship. (Ch. 3)

**addiction**—A physical or mental need for a drug or other substance. (Ch. 3)

**adolescence** (AD-uhl-EHS-ens)—A period of great growth and change between childhood and adulthood. (Ch. 1)

**adrenaline** (uh-DREH-nuh-luhn)—A substance released by your adrenal glands, which will increase your heart, pulse, and respiration rates. Usually occurs when faced with a threatening situation. (Ch. 3)

**advertisement**—A message that persuades consumers to buy a product or service. (Ch. 11)

**alteration**—A change made to clothing to make it fit. (Ch. 17)

**alternatives**—Choices. (Ch. 6)

**amino** (UH-mee-noh) **acids**—The building blocks that make up proteins. (Ch. 20)

**analogous color scheme**—Made up of hues found next to each other on the color wheel. Red-violet, violet, and blue-violet form an analogous color scheme. (Ch. 15)

**anorexia nervosa** (an-uh-REK-see-yuh ner-VOH-suh)—An eating disorder which involves an extreme urge to lose weight by starving oneself. (Ch. 21)

**apathetic** (AP-uh-THEH-tik)—A lack of interest. (Ch. 5)

**appetite**—The desire to eat. (Ch. 20)

**appetizer**—A dish served before the main meal. (Ch. 23)

**applied casing**—A separate strip of fabric or bias tape stitched to the garment, often at the waistline. (Ch. 18)

**aptitudes**—Natural abilities or talents. (Ch. 7)

**arcing** (AHR-keen)—Electrical sparks caused by using metal in a microwave that can start a fire. (Ch. 25)

**assertive**—Standing up for yourself in firm but positive ways. (Ch. 3)

**attention span**—The length of time a person can concentrate on any one thing. (Ch. 9)

**attitude**—The way you feel about something. (Ch. 6)

**autocratic leaders**—Leaders who dictate. (Ch. 5)

## B

**B-complex vitamins**—Give you energy by helping your body use calories from carbohydrates, fats, and proteins. (Ch. 20)

**babysitting**—Being totally responsible for the safety and well-being of the children in your care. (Ch. 10)

**backstitch**—Made by carrying the thread back half the length of the preceding stitch. (Ch. 18)

**bake**—Cook in the oven without a cover. (Ch. 23)

**balance**—Provide equal visual weight. (Ch. 13)

**basil**—An herb that has a mild flavor. It is often used in soups and salads. (Ch. 24)

**basting stitch**—A temporary stitch used to hold fabrics together. (Ch. 18)

**beat**—Mix or stir quickly, bringing the contents of the bowl to the top and down again. (Ch. 23)

**beginning stage**—The first stage of the family life cycle in which couples are newly married without children. (Ch. 2)

**bias**—The diagonal of a fabric. (Ch. 18)

**binge eating**—An eating disorder which involves not being able to resist food. (Ch. 21)

**biodegradable**—Broken down and absorbed by the environment. (Ch. 14)

**blanket stitch**—A stitch that can be used as a decorative edge finish. (Ch. 18)

**blend**—Stir until the ingredients are completely mixed. (Ch. 23)

**blended family**—A family that is formed when two people marry and at least one has children from a previous marriage. (Ch. 2)

**body language**—Gestures and body movements. (Ch. 4)

**boil**—Cook in hot liquid that bubbles rapidly. (Ch. 23)

**braise**—Simmer gently in a small amount of liquid in a covered pan. (Ch. 23)

**brand name**—A trademark used by a manufacturer to identify its products. (Ch. 16)

**bread knife**—Has a scalloped edge and is used to cut through breads without tearing them. (Ch. 22)

**broil**—Cook under direct heat. (Ch. 23)

**brown**—Cook in a small amount of fat over high heat to brown the surface. (Ch. 23)

**budget**—A plan for using your money. (Ch. 11)

**bulimia nervosa** (byoo-LIM-ee-yuh ner-VOH-suh)—An eating disorder which involves extreme overeating followed by vomiting or by using laxatives to get rid of the eaten food. (Ch. 21)

**bully**—A person who physically or verbally abuses someone and intends to cause injury or discomfort. (Ch. 3)

## C

**CPR**—Cardiopulmonary resuscitation is a life-saving technique. (Ch. 10)

**calcium**—Helps build bones and teeth and ensures normal growth. (Ch. 20)

**calorie**—A unit used to measure the energy used by the body and the energy that food supplies to the body. (Ch. 20)

**carbohydrates**—Starches and sugars that give the body most of its energy. (Ch. 20)

**care label**—Describes fiber content and how to care for a garment. (Ch. 16)

**career objective**—States what you would like to achieve in the workplace. (Ch. 8)

**carving knife**—Used to slice meat. (Ch. 22)

**casings**—Fabric tunnels that are made to enclose elastic or drawstrings. (Ch. 18)

**chain stitch**—A serging stitch that uses two threads to baste fabric. (Ch. 18)

**chain stores**—Stores that bear the same name and carry the same merchandise. (Ch. 11)

**check**—A written order directing a bank to pay the person or business named on the check. (Ch. 11)

**chef's knife**—Used for chopping and mincing. (Ch. 22)

**child abuse**—Physical, emotional, or sexual injury to children. (Ch. 9)

**child neglect**—Failure to meet a child's physical and emotional needs. (Ch. 9)

**childproof**—A safe environment for children. (Ch. 10)

**chill**—Put in the refrigerator until cold. (Ch. 23)

**chives**—An herb that has a mild onion flavor. (Ch. 24)

**cholesterol** (kuh-LES-tuh-rahl)—A waxy substance that is part of every cell of your body. (Ch. 20)

**cilantro**—An herb that has a unique flavor and odor. (Ch. 24)

**cinnamon**—A spice that comes from the bark of the laurel tree. (Ch. 24)

**citizen**—A member of a community such as a city, state, or country. (Ch. 5)

**citizenship**—The way you handle your responsibilities as a citizen. (Ch. 5)

**classic styles**—Styles that remain in fashion for a long time. (Ch. 15)

**cleaning plan**—A list of daily, weekly, and occasional household jobs and the family member responsible for each job. (Ch. 13)

**cleaver**—Used to cut through thick meats and bone. (Ch. 22)

**clothing label**—Contains the name of the manufacturer, country of origin, fiber content, and instructions for care. (Ch. 11)

**color fast**—Fabric that keeps its original color through many washings. (Ch. 16)

**color wheel**—Shows how colors are related to one another. (Ch. 13, 15)

**combine**—Mix two or more ingredients together. (Ch. 23)

**communication**—A process of sending and receiving messages about ideas, feelings, and information. (Ch. 4)

**community resources**—Includes schools, hospitals, police and fire departments, museums, youth programs, parks, and recreational facilities. (Ch. 12)

**complementary colors**—The colors that are opposite each other on the color wheel, such as orange and blue. (Ch. 15)

**complementary color scheme**—Gives contrast by using colors opposite each other on the color wheel. Orange and blue used together form a complementary color scheme. (Ch. 15)

**complete proteins**—Foods that contain all the essential amino acids. (Ch. 20)

**comprehension**—Understanding what you read. (Ch. 8)

**compromise** (KAHM-pruh-myz)—An agreement in which each person gives up something in order to reach a solution that satisfies everyone. (Ch. 4)

**conduct**—Carry electricity. (Ch. 22)

**conduction**—The transfer of heat through the exchange of energy. (Ch. 25)

**cones**—Large cylinders that are used to hold thread on a serger. (Ch. 18)

**conflict**—Any disagreement, struggle, or fight. (Ch. 4)

**conflict resolution**—Working out your differences in a way that satisfies both you and the other person. (Ch. 4)

**consequences** (CAHN-suh-kwen-sez)—The results of your choice. (Ch. 6)

**conservation**—The saving of resources. (Ch. 14)

**consideration**—To think about other people and their feelings. (Ch. 2)

**constructive criticism**—An evaluation of you that helps you grow and improve yourself. (Ch. 1)

**consumer**—A person who buys goods and services. (Ch. 11)

**contamination**—Becoming infected with harmful bacteria. (Ch. 22)

**convenience foods**—Foods that are already partly prepared to save you time. A cake mix is a common convenience food. (Ch. 24)

**conversation**—The sharing of ideas, thoughts, and feelings. (Ch. 4)

**cook**—Prepare food by dry heat or moist heat. (Ch. 23)

**cool colors**—Colors that give a sense of calm, such as blue, green, and violet. (Ch. 15)

**cooperation**—To pitch in and do your share of work. (Ch. 2)

**cooperative play**—Playing together with one or two other children and sharing toys. (Ch. 9)

**Corningware®**—Cookware that is appropriate for microwave cooking, conventional baking, and stovetop cooking. (Ch. 25)

**cost per wearing**—The amount of money spent each time you wear an article of clothing. (Ch. 16)

**cream**—Blend until smooth and fluffy. (Ch. 23)

**credit**—A method of payment which enables you to buy merchandise now and pay later. (Ch. 11)

**culture**—Ways of thinking, acting, dressing, and speaking shared by a group of people. (Ch. 1)

**cumin**—A spice commonly found ground or as a whole seed. It is somewhat hot. (Ch. 24)

**curdles**—When milk separates into little particles or curds. (Ch. 24)

## D

**darts**—Tapered, V-shaped seams used to give shape to clothing. (Ch. 17)

**decisions**—Choices. (Ch. 6)

**decompose**—Break down. (Ch. 14)

**deep-fat fry**—Cook in hot fat that is deep enough to cover the food. (Ch. 23)

**default decisions**—Letting someone else, or the circumstances, make a choice for you. (Ch. 6)

**democratic leaders**—Leaders who involves everyone in the decision-making process. (Ch. 5)

**department stores**—Carry a wide range of merchandise such as clothing, shoes, household items, and electronic equipment. (Ch. 11)

**dermatologist**—A doctor who treats skin disorders. (Ch. 1)

**design**—The art of combining elements in a pleasing way. (Ch. 13)

**de-stress**—To relax. (Ch. 12)

**developmental tasks**—Achievements, such as walking and talking, that can be expected at various ages and stages of growth. (Ch. 9)

**digestion**—The process of breaking down food into a form the body can use. (Ch. 20)

**dill weed**—An herb that has a delicate flavor. (Ch. 24)

**discipline**—The task of teaching a child which behavior is acceptable and which is not. (Ch. 9)

**discount stores**—Carry a selection of items at low prices. (Ch. 11)

**dry heat cooking**—Cooking food uncovered without adding any liquid. (Ch. 23)

## E

**E. coli**—The most deadly form of food poisoning. E. coli bacteria are found in contaminated water, raw or rare ground beef, and unpasteurized milk. (Ch. 22)

**ease**—The amount of fullness added in a garment for movement and comfort. (Ch. 16, 18)

**eating disorders**—Extreme eating behaviors that can lead to depression, anxiety, and even death. (Ch. 21)

**electronic shopping**—Consumers can view pictures and descriptions of merchandise on the Internet from many different stores and manufacturers. (Ch. 11)

**elements of design**—Space, shape, line, texture, and color. (Ch. 13)

**emotional decisions**—Choosing the alternative that feels right, without thinking it through. (Ch. 6)

**emotional needs**—Needs that are basic to your well-being, such as feeling safe and secure. (Ch. 1, 9)

**empathy** (EHM-pah-THEE)—The ability to put yourself in another person's place. (Ch. 2)

**emphasis**—Interest. (Ch. 13)

**empty-calorie foods**—Foods that are high in calories but low in nutrients, such as potato chips, candy, and soft drinks. (Ch. 20)

**energy-efficient**—Made to use less energy. (Ch. 14)

**entrepreneur** (AHN-truh-pruh-noor)—A person who starts and runs his or her own business. (Ch. 7)

**exchange**—A trade of one item for another. (Ch. 11)

**exercise**—Physical activity that helps control weight and gives you a healthy glow. (Ch. 21)

**expectations**—A person's ideas of what should be or should happen. (Ch. 3)

**expenses**—The monies you spend to buy goods and services. (Ch. 11)

**extended family**—A family that has one or two parents and children as well as other relatives, such as grandparents or aunts and uncles. (Ch. 2)

## F

**FCCLA**—Family, Career and Community Leaders of America. (Ch. 7)

**factory outlets**—Carry only one manufacturer's products. (Ch. 11)

**fad diet**—A type of diet that promises quick weight loss through unusual means. (Ch. 21)

**fads**—Fashions that are very popular for a short time. (Ch. 15)

**family life cycle**—Four stages which include the beginning stage, parenting stage, launching stage, and senior stage. (Ch. 2)

**fashions**—Styles of clothing that are popular at a particular time. (Ch. 15)

**fats**—Store energy and help regulate body temperature. Help your skin stay smooth and your nervous system work properly. (Ch. 20)

**faux** (FOH)—French for "fake." (Ch. 19)

**feedback**—The response given to a message sent. (Ch. 4)

**fiber**—Plant material that your body cannot digest. It provides bulk, which helps move food through your digestive system. It also helps your body eliminate waste. (Ch. 20)

**fibers**—Tiny strands that are used to make most fabrics. (Ch. 16)

**first impression**—An instant opinion that people form about you the first time they meet you. (Ch. 1)

**fitness**—The ability to handle daily events in a healthy way. (Ch. 21)

**flammable**—Capable of burning easily. (Ch. 22)

**flatlock stitch**—A serging stitch that works well for flat, stretch seams and for decorative stitches. (Ch. 18)

**flexibility**—The ability to adjust easily to new conditions. (Ch. 8)

**floor plan**—A drawing of a room and how its furniture is arranged. (Ch. 13)

**fluoride**—A mineral that helps make teeth strong. (Ch. 20)

**fold-down casing**—Fabric tunnels made to enclose elastic or drawstrings. (Ch. 18)

**food labels**—Must contain the name of the product, the name and address of the manufacturer, weight of the contents, and a nutrition label on all processed foods. Also gives information on how to prepare the food. (Ch. 11)

**friend**—Someone you like and who likes you. It is someone you can talk to who shares similar interests and goals. (Ch. 3)

**fry**—Cook in hot fat. (Ch. 23)

## G

**garlic**—A strong spice that is a dried root from the lily family. It grows in a bulb that is minced or chopped. (Ch. 24)

**garnish**—A small amount of a food or seasoning that can be used to decorate food. (Ch. 23)

**generic brands**—Products with labels listing only the product name and nutritional information. These often cost even less than store brands. (Ch. 23)

**goal**—Something you want to achieve. (Ch. 6)

**goods**—Products made for sale. (Ch. 11)

**gossip**—Talking about other people and their personal lives. (Ch. 4)

**grade labeling**—A measurement of food quality using standards set by the government. (Ch. 23)

**grain**—The direction threads run in a fabric. (Ch. 16)

**guidance**—Direction. (Ch. 9)

**guide sheet**—A set of step-by-step instructions for sewing a pattern. (Ch. 18)

**gusset**—A triangle- or diamond-shaped piece of fabric cut on the bias. (Ch. 19)

## H

**hem stitch**—A stitch that is made by taking a tiny stitch in the garment, then bringing the needle diagonally through the hem edge. (Ch. 18)

**hemming**—A common alteration used to adjust length. (Ch. 18)

**heredity** (huh-red-ih-TEE)—The passing on of traits from parents to their children. (Ch. 1)

**hues**—Names of colors. The three basic hues are red, yellow, and blue. (Ch. 15)

**hunger**—The physical need to eat. (Ch. 20)

## I

**image ads**—Connect a product or service to a lifestyle that consumers would like to have. (Ch. 11)

**impulse buying**—Making a sudden decision to buy. (Ch. 11)

**impulse decisions**—Taking the first alternative available when making a choice. (Ch. 6)

**incineration**—Disposing of waste by burning. (Ch. 14)

**income**—The amount of money you earn or receive regularly. (Ch. 11)

**incomplete proteins**—Foods that come from plants, but that lack one or more of the essential amino acids. (Ch. 20)

**independent**—Being able to perform tasks by yourself. (Ch. 9)

**independent play**—Playing alone. (Ch. 9)

**information ads**—Describe the features of a product or service and give facts about its price and quality. (Ch. 11)

**inhalants**—Sniffing or huffing chemicals which in turn can cause severe damage to your heart. (Ch. 3)

**initiative** (IHN-ish-uh-tiv)—Taking action without being asked. (Ch. 1)

**intellectual needs**—Needs such as a stimulating environment and opportunities to explore. (Ch. 9)

**intensity**—The brightness or dullness of a color. (Ch. 15)

**intruder**—Someone who uses force to get into a home. (Ch. 10)

**iodine**—A mineral that helps the thyroid gland work properly. (Ch. 20)

**iron**—Helps carry oxygen to your brain, your muscles, and all of your body's cells. (Ch. 20)

## J

**jealousy**—An emotion that occurs when you don't want to share something or someone with another person. It also results when someone else has something that you want. (Ch. 3)

**job interview**—A meeting between an employer and a job applicant to discuss his or her qualifications. (Ch. 8)

## L

**landfills**—Huge pits where waste is buried between layers of earth. (Ch. 14)

**launching stage**—The third stage of the family life cycle in which teens become independent and leave home. (Ch. 2)

**launder**—Clean. (Ch. 16)

**layaway plan**—A scheduled payment plan in which you put a small amount of money down and make regular payments until you have paid for the item. (Ch. 11)

**layouts**—Diagrams showing how pattern pieces should be placed on fabric. (Ch. 18)

**leader**—A person with the ability to guide and motivate others. (Ch. 5)

**leadership**—Direction, or guidance, that helps a group accomplish its goals. (Ch. 5)

**legumes**—Dry beans and peas that come in a variety of tastes and textures. (Ch. 24)

**lines**—Form the outer shape, or outline, of a garment. (Ch. 15)

**listening**—Trying to understand the message that is being communicated. (Ch. 4)

**long-term goals**—Goals that may take months or even years to reach. (Ch. 6)

**loopers**—Rounded parts that hold the thread inside a serger. (Ch. 18)

## M

**magnesium**—A mineral that helps muscles contract. (Ch. 20)

**magnetron**—The key part inside a microwave oven that moves the microwaves around the oven. (Ch. 25)

**management**—Using what you have to accomplish something. (Ch. 12)

**markings**—Guides located on pattern pieces. (Ch. 18)

**material resources**—Possessions, objects, and money. (Ch. 12)

**meal pattern**—A habit that determines when and what you eat each day. (Ch. 23)

**membership warehouses**—Stores that sell merchandise at discounted prices. (Ch. 11)

**microwave oven**—Cooks food much quicker than a conventional oven. (Ch. 25)

**microwave safe containers**—Containers that will not get too hot, melt, crack, or shatter from the heat produced in a microwave oven. (Ch. 25)

**microwaves**—Energy waves that heat food in a microwave oven. (Ch. 25)

**minerals**—Elements needed in small amounts for sturdy bones and teeth, healthy blood, and regular elimination of body wastes. (Ch. 20)

**moist heat cooking**—Cooking food in a covered pan with liquid added. (Ch. 23)

**monochromatic color scheme**—Use of one hue and the tints and shades of that hue. (Ch. 15)

## N

**nap**—A one-way texture, such as corduroy fabric. (Ch. 17)

**national brands**—Well-known products that often cost more than others because the manufacturer spends a great deal of money on packaging and advertising. (Ch. 23)

**natural fibers**—Fibers that absorb perspiration and generally feel cooler. Cotton, linen, silk, and wool are examples. (Ch. 16)

**natural resources**—Materials that are supplied by nature such as air, water, soil, and the energy derived from coal, oil, and gas. (Ch. 14)

**natural sugars**—Found in fruits and milk. (Ch. 20)

**needle**—Sewing tool used for hand sewing. (Ch. 17)

**negotiation** (ni-GOH-shee-AY-shuhn)—The process of talking about a conflict and deciding how to reach a compromise. (Ch. 4)

**netiquette**—The accepted rules of conduct for Internet users. (Ch. 12)

**networking**—Making use of personal connections to achieve goals. (Ch. 7)

**neutral colors**—Black, white, beige, and gray. (Ch. 15)

**niacin**—B-complex vitamin that promotes a healthy nervous system. (Ch. 20)

**nonrenewable**—Resources that will no longer be available if they are used up or permanently damaged. (Ch. 14)

**nonverbal communication**—Messages that are sent without using words. (Ch. 4)

**notions**—Items you need to complete a sewing project, such as thread, fasteners, or elastic. (Ch. 17)

**nuclear family**—A family that includes two parents and one or more children. (Ch. 2)

**nutmeg**—A spice that comes from the fruit of the nutmeg tree. It has a nutty, mild flavor. (Ch. 24)

**nutrients** (NOO-tree-uhnts)—Substances that are important for the body's growth and care. There are six kinds of nutrients: proteins, carbohydrates, fats, vitamins, minerals, and water. (Ch. 20)

**nutrition**—The study of nutrients and how the body uses them. (Ch. 20)

## O

**obesity**—A condition in which a person's weight is 20 percent or more above his or her healthy weight. (Ch. 21)

**omelet**—A well-beaten egg that is first cooked in a frying pan without stirring. Then it is topped with other ingredients, such as mushrooms, peppers, or cheese and folded over. (Ch. 24)

**osteoporosis**—A condition in which bones gradually lose their mineral content and become weak and brittle. (Ch. 20)

**outlet**—A means of release. (Ch. 19)

**overedge stitch**—A serging stitch that uses two threads to secure the edges of fabric and prevent raveling. (Ch. 18)

**overlock stitch**—A serging stitch that combines three threads and is most often used on stretch seams and fabrics of moderate to heavy weight. (Ch. 18)

## P

**parenthood**—The function of being a parent. (Ch. 9)

**parenting stage**—The second stage of the family life cycle in which children are born and parents care for their needs. (Ch. 2)

**paring knife**—Used for trimming and peeling fruits and vegetables. (Ch. 22)

**parsley**—An herb that is often used as a garnish. (Ch. 24)

**pattern**—A plan for making a garment or project. (Ch. 17)

**pattern sizes (female)**—Based on four measurements: bust, waist, hip, and back waist length. Examples include: Girls', Juniors', Misses', Petites', and Talls'. (Ch. 17)

**pattern sizes (male)**—Based on five measurements: chest, waist, hip or seat, neck, and sleeve length. Examples include Boys', Teen Boys', and Men's. (Ch. 17)

**peer groups**—Groups of people the same age. (Ch. 3)

**peer mediation**—Process by which peers help other students find a solution to a conflict before it becomes more serious. (Ch. 4)

**peer pressure**—The influence you feel to go along with the behavior of your peers. (Ch. 3)

**peers**—People the same age as you. (Ch. 3)

**perceptions**—How you select, organize, and interpret information. (Ch. 4)

**perishable**—Foods that are likely to spoil quickly. (Ch. 22)

**personal resources**—Time, energy, knowledge, skills, and people. (Ch. 12)

**personality**—Shows in the way you look, the way you communicate, and the way you act. It is the part of you that you reveal to other people. (Ch. 1)

**phosphorous**—A mineral that helps calcium and vitamin D keep bones and teeth strong and healthy. (Ch. 20)

**physical needs**—Items that are basic to your survival and well-being, such as food, clothing, and shelter. (Ch. 1, 9)

**pincushion**—A convenient holder for pins and needles. (Ch. 17)

**pinking shears**—Scissors that have a zigzag edge. (Ch. 17)

**planned decisions**—Weighing all the facts before making a choice. (Ch. 6)

**pollution**—Changing air, water, and land from clean and safe to dirty and unsafe. (Ch. 14)

**potassium**—A mineral that helps regulate body fluids and muscles. (Ch. 20)

**preheat**—To heat the oven to the right temperature before putting in the food. (Ch. 23)

**prejudice** (PRE-juh-dis)—An opinion about people that is formed without facts or knowledge about them. (Ch. 4)

**pre-treat**—Apply a stain remover before laundering. (Ch. 16)

**primary caregiver**—Responsible for providing a safe, loving, and stimulating environment for children. (Ch. 9)

**primary colors**—Red, yellow, and blue. (Ch. 15)

**principles of design**—Rules that govern how the elements of design are organized. (Ch. 13)

**prioritize**—To rank in order of importance. (Ch. 1, 12)

**processed**—Food that is changed from its raw form before being sold. (Ch. 24)

**procrastinate** (PRO-cra-stuh-nayt)—To put things off. (Ch. 12)

**promotion**—A move into a job with more responsibility. (Ch. 8)

**proportion**—The relationship of each design element to the whole and to the other elements. (Ch. 13)

**proteins**—Nutrients that are needed to build, repair, and maintain body cells and tissues. (Ch. 20)

## Q

**quiche**—A main-dish pie that is filled with eggs, cheese, and other ingredients such as ham, spinach, and mushrooms. (Ch. 24)

## R

**recipe**—A list of directions for preparing a specific food. (Ch. 23)

**recycling**—Turning waste items into products that can be used. (Ch. 14)

**redirect**—Turning children's attention to something else. (Ch. 10)

**redress**—Action taken to correct a wrong. (Ch. 11)

**references**—People who can tell an employer about your character and quality of work. (Ch. 8)

**refund**—The return of your money in exchange for the item. (Ch. 11)

**refusal skills**—Help you deal with negative peer pressure. (Ch. 3)

**reliability**—Being dependable and doing what you say you will do. (Ch. 2)

**resistance decisions**—Choosing the alternative that will result in the least amount of conflict. (Ch. 6)

**resource**—A source of information or expertise that you can use to help you meet your goals. (Ch. 12)

**responsibly**—Being reliable. (Ch. 2)

**résumé**—A summary of qualifications, work experience, education, and interests. (Ch. 8)

**rhythm**—Pattern. (Ch. 13)

**riboflavin**—B-complex vitamin that helps keep your eyes and skin healthy. (Ch. 20)

**roast**—Cook in the oven in dry heat. (Ch. 23)

**role models**—People who help you see what is expected of you in certain situations. Role models can be parents, older siblings, relatives, teachers, coaches, or religious leaders. (Ch. 1)

**rolled hem stitch**—A serging stitch that creates narrow hems and seams and is also used for decorative stitching on knit or woven lightweight fabrics. (Ch. 18)

## S

**SQ3R**—A reading comprehension technique that involves surveying, questioning, reading, reciting, and reviewing the material. (Ch. 8)

**STDs**—Sexually transmitted diseases. (Ch. 3)

**safety stitch**—A serging stitch that uses four threads to create a stable seam on woven lightweight fabrics. The extra threads help to limit how much the fabric will stretch. (Ch. 18)

**saffron**—A yellow spice that comes from the crocus plant. (Ch. 24)

**salmonella** (SAL-muh-NEHL-uh)—A type of food poisoning. It is often found in raw or undercooked foods, such as meat, eggs, fish, and poultry. (Ch. 22)

**sandwich**—Two pieces of bread surrounding a filling, such as meat or cheese. (Ch. 24)

**saturated fats**—Fats found in food from animal sources such as meats, egg yolks, cheese, and butter. (Ch. 20)

**sauté**—Fry in a small amount of fat until done. (Ch. 23)

**savings plan**—Helps you put money aside for unexpected needs and for future use. (Ch. 11)

**scald**—Heat milk by bringing it slowly to a temperature just below the boiling point. (Ch. 23, 24)

**scale**—Using size-appropriate items in a room. (Ch. 13)

**scissors**—Sewing tool used for trimming, clipping, and cutting threads. (Ch. 17)

**seam ripper**—Pen-shaped sewing tool that has a small, hook-like blade at one end for removing stitches. (Ch. 17)

**seasonal clothes**—Clothes that are worn only for a few months each year. (Ch. 16)

**secondary colors**—Orange, green, and violet. (Ch. 15)

**self-actualization**—To realize your full potential. (Ch. 1)

**self-concept**—A mental picture of yourself. (Ch. 1)

**self-control**—Taking time to think before you act, setting limits, and using your knowledge of right and wrong to guide your actions. (Ch. 1)

**self-esteem**—The ability to respect yourself. (Ch. 1)

**selvage**—The tightly woven edge of fabric that has no visible loose threads. (Ch. 18)

**senior stage**—The fourth stage of the family life cycle in which parents adjust to being a couple again and enjoy more leisure activities or change careers. (Ch. 2)

**senses**—Sight, hearing, taste, touch, and smell. (Ch. 9)

**sequence**—Order. (Ch. 9)

**serger**—A high-speed machine that sews, trims, and finishes a seam in one step. It can handle slippery silks and stretchy knit fabrics. (Ch. 18)

**services**—Work performed for others. (Ch. 11)

**sewing gauge**—A 6-inch (16-cm) ruler with an adjustable pointer used to measure short spaces, such as hems and seam widths. (Ch. 17)

**sew-through button**—A button with two or four holes through it. (Ch. 18)

**shade**—A dark value of a hue. (Ch. 15)

**shank button**—A button with a stem on the back. (Ch. 18)

**shape**—The outline or form of solid objects. (Ch. 13)

**shears**—Large scissors that often have a raised handle for easier cutting. (Ch. 17)

**shoplifting**—Taking items from a store without paying for them. (Ch. 11)

**shopping plan**—A strategy for spending the money you have available. (Ch. 16)

**short-term goals**—Goals that can be reached in a few days or weeks. (Ch. 6)

**siblings**—Brothers and sisters. (Ch. 2)

**simmer**—Cook to just below the boiling point so the liquid barely bubbles. (Ch. 23)

**single-parent family**—A family that includes one parent and one or more children. (Ch. 2)

**skills**—An ability that comes from training or practice. (Ch. 12)

**slipstitch**—A stitch that provides an almost invisible finish. (Ch. 18)

**social needs**—Needs such as being held, cuddled, and comforted. (Ch. 9)

**sodium**—A mineral that helps regulate body fluids and muscles work properly. (Ch. 20)

**specialty stores**—Carry only a specific type of merchandise. (Ch. 11)

**stamina**—The ability to focus on a single activity for a long time. (Ch. 21)

**staples**—Foods that you are likely to use often. (Ch. 23)

**starches**—Excellent energy sources found in grains, such as oats, rice, and wheat. (Ch. 20)

**status**—Level of importance. (Ch. 15)

**status symbols**—Signs of popularity and importance. (Ch. 11)

**staystitching**—A row of stitching made on or very near the seamline within the seam allowance. Prevents stretching and helps in turning under edges. (Ch. 18)

**steam**—Cook over boiling water. (Ch. 23)

**steroids** (STARE-oyds)—Prescription drugs used for specific medical conditions. Not to be used as bodybuilding supplements. (Ch. 21)

**stew**—Cook slowly in liquid. (Ch. 23)

**stir**—Move the ingredients in a circular motion to mix or to prevent burning. (Ch. 23)

**stir fry**—Cook quickly in a small amount of fat at high heat. (Ch. 23)

**Stoneware®**—A heavy-duty type of specialty cookware. It is especially good for heating up soups and stews. (Ch. 25)

**store brands**—Products that have the store's name or another name used only by that store on the label. These products usually cost less and they often have the same ingredients as national brands. (Ch. 23)

**stress**—The body's reaction to changes around it. (Ch. 12)

**study skills**—Includes good reading skills, note-taking skills, test-taking skills, listening skills, and time-management skills. (Ch. 12)

**style**—The design of a garment. (Ch. 15)

**sugar**—A type of carbohydrate that is found in many foods. It provides calories. (Ch. 20)

**superheating**—Heating a liquid in a container that doesn't allow bubble formation, or boiling. This causes the liquid to overheat, and it can explode when it comes into contact with atmospheric pressure. (Ch. 25)

**synthetic fibers**—Fibers made partially or entirely from chemicals. Examples include polyester and nylon. (Ch. 16)

## T

**tail chain**—A length of thread shaped like a chain. It keeps the fabric from raveling and eliminates the need to tie off the threads of the serged seam. (Ch. 18)

**talent**—Natural ability. (Ch. 12)

**tape measure**—A flexible tape that is used to take body measurements. (Ch. 17)

**team**—A group of people working together toward a common goal. (Ch. 8)

**teamwork**—Working together toward a common goal. (Ch. 5, 8)

**telemarketing**—Calling a person's house to discuss a product or service. (Ch. 11)

**terminate**—Leave a job. (Ch. 8)

**texture**—The way something feels or looks as if it would feel. (Ch. 13, 15, 23)

**thiamine**—B-complex vitamin that promotes a healthy nervous system. Found in meat, dry beans, and some grain products. (Ch. 20)

**thimble**—Small sewing tool that protects your finger while you're hand sewing. It makes it easier to push the needle through the fabric. (Ch. 17)

**thrift shops**—Stores that sell merchandise at discounted prices. (Ch. 11)

**tint**—A light value of a hue. (Ch. 15)

**toss**—Tumble ingredients lightly with a spoon and fork. (Ch. 23)

**trade-off**—Something that you give up in order to get something more important. (Ch. 6)

**traditions**—Customs and beliefs handed down from one generation to another. (Ch. 2)

**traffic pattern**—The path people take to move around within a room as well as enter and exit the room. (Ch. 13)

## U

**understanding**—Respecting other people's viewpoints and feelings. (Ch. 2)

**unit pricing**—The cost of a product per unit. (Ch. 23)

**unity**—Combining similar elements to accent their similarities. (Ch. 13)

**unsaturated fats**—Fats found mainly in vegetable oils, such as olive, corn, or canola. (Ch. 20)

**utensils**—Kitchen tools. (Ch. 21)

## V

**values**—Your ideas about right and wrong and about what is important in life. (Ch. 1)

**variables**—Conditions such as density, volume, shape, and temperature of food. (Ch. 25)

**verbal communication**—Messages sent using spoken or written words. (Ch. 4)

**viewpoint**—How you see a problem or situation. (Ch. 4)

**vitamin A**—Enables your eyes to adjust to the dark. It also helps keep your skin healthy and helps your body resist infection. (Ch. 20)

**vitamin C**—Keeps your gums healthy and helps your body fight infection. (Ch. 20)

**vitamin D**—Helps your body use minerals, such as calcium and phosphorus. It is essential for normal bone and tooth development. (Ch. 20)

**vitamin E**—Keeps red blood cells healthy. Found in vegetable oils, yellow vegetables, grains, nuts, and green leafy vegetables. (Ch. 20)

**vitamin K**—Helps blood clot. (Ch. 20)

**vitamins**—Substances needed in small quantities to help regulate body functions. (Ch. 20)

**volunteer**—A person who donates time and energy, without pay, to help others. (Ch. 5)

## W, X, Y, Z

**wants**—Things that you would like to have, but are not necessary for survival. (Ch. 1)

**warm colors**—Bright and cheerful colors such as red, yellow, and orange. (Ch. 15)

**warranty**—The manufacturer's written promise to repair or replace a product if it does not work as claimed. (Ch. 11)

**water**—Helps regulate your body functions and carries nutrients to body cells. It aids in digestion, removes wastes, and helps control your body temperature. (Ch. 20)

**wellness**—Reaching for your best level of health. (Ch. 20)

**whip**—Beat fast with an electric mixer, rotary beater, or wire whip to add enough air to make the mixture fluffy. (Ch. 23)

**work ethic**—A personal commitment to doing your very best. (Ch. 8)

**work record**—A written record of how well an employee performs on the job. (Ch. 8)

**zinc**—A mineral that helps speed the healing of wounds. (Ch. 20)

# Index

**F**

## K

## L

## M

## O

## P

## S

**Cover and Interior Design:**
Squarecrow Creative Group

**Closer Look Backgrounds:**
Getty/PhotoDisc Royalty Free

Allsport/Getty, Cover
Arnold & Brown, 192, 265
BRK Brands, Inc., 250
Shirley Bortoli, 315, 332, 340, 346
Bill Burlingham, 187
Anthony Cericola, 319, 374, 375, 399, 441
Ken Clubb, 69, 182-183, 226, 240-241, 278, 279, 283, 289, 298, 301, 428-429
Comstock, Comstock Production Department, 124-125, 127

Comstock Images, 215
Corbis, 53, 360
    Paul Barton, 42-43, 53, 122-123
    C/B Productions, 60-61
    Gary Chowanetz/Elizabeth Whiting & Associates, 243
    Ralph Clevenger, 78-79
    Dennis Degnan, 20-21
    Neville Elder, 76
    Rick Gomez, 18-19, 272-273
    Charles Gupton, 105
    Michael Heron, 68
    Richard Hutchings, 27
    Bob Krist, 234-235
    Rob Lewine, Cover
    LWA-Dan Tardis, 110, 352-353
    Tom & DeeAnn McCarthy, 51, 166
    Bill Morsch, 256
    Mug Shots, 94-95, 119, Cover
    Jose Luis Pelaez, Inc., 232
    Michael Pole, 172
    Steve Prezant, 72
    Roger Ressmeyer, 92. 120

    Chuck Savage, 203, 230
    Ariel Skelley, 52
    Tom Stewart, 108-109, 140-141, 395
    David Stoecklein, 158-159
    William Whitehurst, 3, 132
Bob Daemmrich Photography, 170, 284
David R. Frazier, Frazier Photolibrary, Inc., 106, 270
Tim Fuller, 163, 171, 212, 214, 220, 413, 441, 466,
Ann Garvin, 10, 11, 12, 211, 268, 299, 307, 309, 328-329, 354, 357, 372, 376, 380-381, 387, 406, 409, 412, 416, 422, 423, 424, 442, 444, 445, 447, 448, 452, 459, 456, 467, 470, 472, 473, 475
Getty
    Brian Bailey, 4, 65
    Benelux Press, 67
    Peter Cade, 258
    Daly & Newton, 53
    Digital Vision, 119, 263
    Howard Grey, 116
    Walter Hodges, 52

The Publisher wishes to thank the following businesses, schools, and individuals for their assistance in obtaining photographs and illustrations for this textbook: Susie Jauch; Maria Diaz; Art MacDillo's/ Gary Skillestad; Jeff Stoecker; Marshall Greenberg; Metamora Township High School, Metamora, IL; Bergner's Department Store, Peoria, IL; JoAnn Fabrics & Crafts, Peoria, IL; and Churchill Junior High School, Galesburg, IL.